How to Manage Your Money

HOW TO MANAGE YOUR MONEY
A Woman's Guide to Investing

ELIZABETH M. FOWLER

Little, Brown and Company
Boston | Toronto

COPYRIGHT © 1973 by Elizabeth M. Fowler

ALL RIGHTS RESERVED. NO PART OF THIS BOOK MAY BE REPRODUCED IN ANY FORM OR BY ANY ELECTRONIC OR MECHANICAL MEANS INCLUDING INFORMATION STORAGE AND RETRIEVAL SYSTEMS WITHOUT PERMISSION IN WRITING FROM THE PUBLISHER, EXCEPT BY A REVIEWER WHO MAY QUOTE BRIEF PASSAGES IN A REVIEW.

FIRST EDITION

T 05/73

Library of Congress Cataloging in Publication Data

Fowler, Elizabeth M
  How to manage your money.

  Bibliography: p.
  1. Investments. 2. Stock-exchange. I. Title.
HG4921.F64   332.6'78   72-12731
ISBN 0-316-28958-2

Published simultaneously in Canada by Little, Brown & Company (Canada) Limited

PRINTED IN THE UNITED STATES OF AMERICA

Half for

FRANCES THOMPSON BUEL,

who gave me an idea for a novel

Half for my favorite women investors

CATHERINE APPLETON
BARBARA EASLEY
ALICE ABELL FRANKLIN
CYNTHIA FRASER
POLLY GOODMAN
HELEN HOLMES
NANCY MACGRATH
MARGARET MENARD PRICE
MIMI STARRETT

Contents

	Preface	ix
1.	Happiness Is . . .	3
2.	Elsie and Dan	15
3.	Dismal Thinking Pays Off	29
4.	Getting to Know You	45
5.	To Auction, to Auction, to Buy a Fat Stock	56
6.	Figures, Straight and Not Curvy	68
7.	The Man in Your Investment Life	84
8.	Analysts without Couches	104
9.	The Mysterious Mr. Dow	119
10.	The Feeling Isn't Mutual	130
11.	Togetherness Can Be an Answer	141
12.	The Stuff of Dreams	155
13.	How to Be a Bear without a Growl	173
14.	Desirable Bottoms, Dangerous Tops	189
15.	The Care and Feeding of Securities	199
16.	Your Demanding Uncle	217
17.	Investments with Unusual Personalities	232
18.	The Magic of 72 and Other Helps	253
19.	Planning Your Portfolio	271
20.	Don't Be a Hetty Green	292
	Bibliography	306

Preface

At a cocktail party recently an attractive thirty-five-year-old mother of three children sat herself down beside two longtime friends: a male editor for the *Wall Street Journal* and a female financial writer for the *New York Times,* more specifically the author of this book.

"Next fall I'm going back to work as a teacher. I'll make about $5,500 the first year, and after taxes and my expenses I can invest $1,200 a year. What shall I put it in? Bill and I will have two children in college at the same time for a period of six years."

"Mutual funds," said the *Wall Street Journal* man. "Growth-type funds."

"No, good growth stocks," I replied. "The loading charge for most funds is too high, and I think an intelligent woman like you can do better on your own."

This book is for women interested in investments — women who don't know much about the various facets of the stock market, as well as women who know something but want to increase their working knowledge.

The book's basic premise is that an intelligent woman who can raise children and run a successful home, perhaps even do paid or volunteer work, can also learn to operate profitably in the investment world, if she is willing to master the fundamentals and keep applying them. Investing can add a new talent to her life, paying dividends both in cash and in satisfaction.

How to Manage Your Money

1 | Happiness Is . . .

Happiness for a woman is not money exactly, but money helps. Most women thrive on the sense of security that money expectations can give. As one wit put it, women can acquire money three ways — make it, marry it or inherit it.

The ideal, of course, would be to combine all three.

A woman who at some time during her life earns her own money knows a feeling of security and achievement, along with a sense of independence, and she has gained some understanding of how business operates. Marrying money is fine as long as it does not make a woman too dependent on a husband and too willing to relax and forget that in an insecure world the safety of home and money can vanish. Much the same can be said about inheriting money. It shouldn't be allowed to stultify a woman's thinking.

Whether you make your own money, whether you marry a successful man, or whether you inherit money, you should know how to take care of it and how to make your capital grow. The care and feeding of your money is almost as important as nourishing body and mind.

Why invest in securities? More than 32,000,000 Americans (at least half of them women) have found common stocks a sound method of investing, offering growth possibilities against inflation.

Even if you don't own a share of stock now, you probably still are an investor indirectly because insurance companies in which you have life, fire and casualty coverage invest their billions of dollars in securities; so do banks. The company for which you or your husband works invests pension fund money in stocks.

Like a torn slip hanging below a dress, inflation has created a ragged edge of self-doubt and worry in the minds of most women. What can be done about the constant raveling of the dollar's value year by year in terms of higher prices? Especially, what can be done now in 1973 and in the foreseeable future, as the rate of inflation increases so noticeably and inexorably? Since the government appears unable to do more than slow the inflationary pace, how can women keep up?

When a woman realizes that her family's standard of living is in danger she can react quite violently. Remember the noisy picketing by women's groups in front of supermarkets in 1966? The retailers piously claimed that they were not the cause of rising prices. As usual in such a fracas everyone tried to shift the blame. But women can rightfully claim that one supermarket charges a penny or two more for Hellmann's mayonnaise than other stores in the neighborhood, while another adds a penny or two on Minute Maid frozen orange juice prices. Still another hikes Jones sausage five cents a pound above a competing store. This makes it difficult and maddening for the cost-conscious shopper.

Her knowledge of quality often tells her that she must be on the outlook continually against getting gypped, by the supermarket, by the plumber, by the auto dealer, by the television repair shop. While women can protest at the store level against individual tradesmen or stores and show their resentment by patronizing others, they feel helpless when they consider how little attention the consumer as a person receives from the government, from politicians, even from husbands too busy to worry about the little daily, ever-rising costs of living.

Why invest? It's a firm self-protective step into an uncertain future. It gives a woman a feeling that she is taking at least some action. Let's consider the reasons for investing in a less metaphorical way.

WHY INVEST? IT'S A MEANS OF COMBATING INFLATION. The housewife living on a food budget probably feels the impact of inflation much more quickly than her husband. She begins to wonder if she has lost her grip when her $45–$50 weekly food money for a family of four no longer stretches to cover two roasts in a week. Yet it would have done so a few years ago. Now she needs $50 or more. She feels the pinch, too, when she buys children's clothes and shoes. She reads about the ever-rising cost of education at schools and colleges.

Inflation, then, is simply a rise in the cost of living in terms of dollars. They just don't buy as much.

Sometimes, if salaries and other income rise fast enough the impact of higher prices is not felt so keenly. But the trouble is that when a husband receives a $1,000 yearly raise, he and his wife kiss and say "hurrah," sharing at first the mutual glow that a raise can bring. Then comes a rude awakening. What really happens to the money after the first happy thoughts about how to spend the extra $1,000?

Table 1 shows it in dollar terms for a husband, wife, and two children when the husband's salary jumps from $12,000 to $13,000; and for another such family when the husband's pay rises from $19,000 to $20,000.

Out of a "$1,000" raise the increase in the family's standard of living in the first instance amounts to a mere $181 a year, and nothing in the case of the family in the higher income tax bracket. In fact, it has not even kept pace with the rise in the cost of living.

A wife aware of the importance of financial planning will be less shocked by these figures and hence not so disappointed, especially if she has an investment plan she knows will help their dollars increase in number to help combat inflation's toll.

The difficulty becomes more serious in the case of older people living on retirement income. True, they have some tax advantages that younger persons do not but their pension money and social security payments seldom rise as fast as inflation. The single career woman is in much the same box, and she needs a lift out of it with investment income that rises enough to help her keep climbing financially. In fact, it is hard to think of how a working woman these days can face inflation imperturbably without investing.

Income	$13,000	$20,000
Additional Federal income tax on $1,000: about B	220	268
State, city, income tax, estimated	75	100
5% increase in living costs due to inflation applied to all net income for one year, after taxes	524	792
Total deductions from $1,000 raise	819	1,160
Take-home money due to raise after considering inflation's impact	plus $ 181	minus $ 160

Table 1

But I do know a few. There's a wealthy widow living in a hotel in New York who every three months receives a personal visit from a young bank officer of one of the largest banks in New York City. Like a glorified office boy he delivers to her by hand a check for $250,000. Her income comes completely from tax-exempt mutual funds in a trust set up by her husband. She doesn't worry about money. I know, too, of a few women professors so deeply engrossed in their research that they can be impervious to inflation — and even to what they eat.

The fact that the ranks of investors are growing fast is a sign not only of prosperity but of a widespread realization of the need to fight inflation. Even more dramatic is the number of women returning to work — an army that constitutes more than 30,000,000 persons, of which half are married and have families or are household heads.

For years liberal economists have claimed that a 1.5 percent increase in the cost of living was a fair price to pay to keep the economy busy enough to insure virtually full employment. Naturally in a population of more than 215,000,000 persons there will always be several million without jobs because they are looking for work after resigning or being fired, because they are seasonal workers like construction men or berry pickers, because they are mentally or physically incompetent, or because they are in the armed forces or elsewhere.

Even five years ago, many economists scoffed at the possibility that we might ever have a galloping inflation that could really hurt consumers. Yet 1969 was the year of the gallop, and the fast pace has continued throughout 1971.

The pace did proceed at the acceptable 1.5 percent for quite a few years: an admirably steady and uncontroversial rate. Then it began to increase quite sharply, partly because of factors like the expense of the Vietnam war, the nation's balance of payment difficulties (more money flowing out of this country than coming into it from foreign nations), the heavier federal spending on programs to ameliorate ghetto conditions and for the underprivileged; and partly because of the propensity of dollar-happy Americans to lavish money on consumer goods and services.

Thus the rate of inflation increased at a worrisome speed in two years — from about 4 percent in 1968 to about 6 percent in 1969 and more slowly since then. Another way of putting it is that your living dollar has lost about 25 percent or one quarter of its value since 1967 when the government began its latest consumer price index.

More than ever perhaps, inflation has become a very real, down-to-earth reason to invest money in progressive, or growth-type companies, which can keep ahead of inflation by developing new products or services, increasing prices, creating new needs among customers, serving new markets, perhaps penetrating old ones more deeply. Out of increased sales they can sometimes earn large profits for their stockholders. This money can be passed out in the form of higher cash dividends. Sometimes, however, the companies retain most of their profits for further growth and since their potentials are bright the price of their stocks still rises.

The classic example of this is IBM — a company that by tradition has retained profits but paid small cash or stock dividends to shareholders. Over the years the price of the stock has soared, reflecting its fast sales growth in an industry essential to modern technology — computers. A schoolteacher who bought 10 shares of IBM at an adjusted price of only $10 a share in 1950* was not buying for income but because she believed the company would grow fast in its field. Today, allowing for stock dividends, each $10 share is worth about $380, an almost unbelievable increase. Thus an investment of $1,000 now is worth $38,000.

Many companies today have been caught in a rush to merge or diversify as a quick road to "growth." Hence, you will often read that Company A has offered two shares of its stock for each share of Company B's stock in a merger proposal.

There's nothing new about mergers. Some are carried off quite politely and respectably. Others create much furor and charges and countercharges, often leading to legal actions. Years ago the late John D. Rockefeller, Senior, had the habit of forcing other companies to sell out their oil businesses to his giant Standard Oil in return (sometimes) for Standard Oil shares. If they did not sell pleasantly they might find their company run out of business by price undercutting. Being much larger and more powerful, Standard Oil could afford to lower its prices to ruinous levels in a specific area, in order to drive the other fellow into bankruptcy. Many oilmen did accept stock offers and several became millionaires through holding Standard Oil shares.

In those days there were few ground rules that applied to businessmen like Rockefeller, whereas today the government's antitrust provisions would prevent many such actions such as price undercutting and forced mergers. Mergers persist today

---

*Adjusted means the price has been refigured to reflect payment of stock dividends or splits.

partly because they apparently help some companies grow stronger financially, and they often can be favorable to stockholders.

WHY INVEST? IT'S FASHIONABLE. Among sophisticated — and not so sophisticated — groups the stock market has become a conversational gambit. Brokers constantly are amazed by the variety of persons who invest.

One day recently I sat on a PATH train, a subway-type operation that runs between New York and New Jersey, in front of two roughly dressed workmen carrying lanterns. Their topic of conversation: What was the stock market going to do?

"Do you have any good cheap growth stocks now?" one of the men inquired.

Immediately his friend began to talk about a stock named Research-Cottrell,* describing how well he had done in it, but adding a friendly warning. "Ask your broker. It's a little too high right now."

At that point the train squealed to a halt, and the conductor pressed a button to open the doors upon the dark tunnel that goes under the Hudson River. In the middle of that nowhere the two workmen clambered off with their lanterns lit, flinging a thanks to the conductor who had opened the door. They were track workers.

Or there is the case of the young suburban matron who has the habit every time she goes to a cocktail party of buttonholing her husband's male friends, and casually but forcefully inquiring what they have been doing in the stock market recently. Her questions are probing but phrased to be complimentary to male egos. By acting much dumber than she really is she collects tidbits of information. Then she tosses the ideas at her broker for his reaction. In that way she has accumulated not only some useful knowledge about investing but occasionally some good opinions that have led her to buy some very successful stocks.

WHY INVEST? IT'S NO LONGER ESOTERIC. These days Americans have more leisure as well as more dollars than ever before, which means they have more hours to read about the stock market

---

*Maker of air pollution-control equipment.

and go to brokers' offices and watch the action on the quotation boards. This is especially true of housewives without careers and of older, retired persons.

Furthermore, tastes have changed. Perhaps the woman who would once have cherished a driving ambition for a mink coat has obtained the coat; or perhaps her sense of values has altered. Cadillacs, to many persons, have lost their appeal as a status symbol, and so have trips to Europe for families who have been there several times. People may not be getting more intellectual, but there certainly is a more noticeable importance attached to intelligence among women — intelligence as to personal finance, as to investments, as to raising children, as to knowing what's going on politically and economically, as to social consciousness.

To attract new shareholders, companies have been making real efforts to appeal to investors, partly as an indirect but effective method of interesting more consumers in their products. The auto companies, for example, load their stockholders with brochures about new models of their brand of cars. The Borden Company asks shareholders to buy its cheeses and other products. Phillips Petroleum sends its shareholders credit cards unasked, urging them to buy gas and have their cars repaired at its string of service stations here and in Canada. Companies have found that a large, happy family of stockholders can help provide a better credit rating. In fact, many companies when they try to raise money through a new stock or bond issue give their stockholders a chance to buy the securities first, often at a more-favorable-than-market price. This is called a preemptive right.* Often a company is required by its own bylaws to offer shareholders such an opportunity.

One noted company that has long given stockholders a first chance at its new securities is American Telephone and Telegraph Company. Out of about two dozen issues offered in the last twenty years, AT&T has permitted stockholders to buy shares before offering any leftover securities to the general pub-

---

* For a more detailed discussion of preemptive rights, see pages 202, 259–262.

lic. It's often good business for stockholders, since they get a bargain price.

WHY INVEST? IT'S SAFER THAN IN FORMER YEARS. Not many years ago, but long enough so that it seems as unbelievable as any fairy tale, it was hard to get access to financial information about companies. For example, a typical earnings report published by the New York, New Haven and Hartford Railroad Company in 1910 gave little information. In that period the New Haven was considered an investment for little old ladies and widows with children to support. Brokers talked with glowing pomposity about it, even though they could obtain little financial information about it, beyond the bare bones of yearly earnings figures. After all, they reasoned, everyone needs the railroad in New England. It carried coal to heat homes; it transported proper and improper Bostonians to and from the hinterlands, even to another city called New York. In the summer it carried thousands to their homes or hotels at the seashore.

What happened? Along with the mismanagement of the railroad, a gentleman in Detroit named Henry Ford helped spoil the railroad's outlook by developing a car for mass transportation which even before World War I was becoming a slight competitor. To carry cars, roads were built. Furthermore, electricity and gas began to replace coal as a source of heat for homes and industry. Trucks competed with the New Haven, which was called a short-haul carrier because its lines only ran about three hundred miles or so. Result: bankruptcy, not once but several times for the New Haven. For anyone with imagination (or vision) it was far from being a "widow's safe stock."

Yet no one reading the uninformative early reports of the New Haven or other companies would have guessed that progress and change were afoot to stub the corporate toes of many famous old corporate entities.*

Nowadays such a dearth of information about stocks listed

*In 1866 the New York Stock Exchange asked the Delaware Lackawanna and Western Railroad for a financial report, and its treasurer responded that the railroad makes "no reports and publishes no statements, and has not done anything of the kind for the last five years."

in the New York Stock Exchange or other exchanges is impossible. The government (via its regulatory agency, the Securities and Exchange Commission) and the exchanges themselves have strict rules. Companies must report at length upon their sales and earnings if they are listed on an exchange, not only for each fiscal year as a whole but also, in most cases, on a quarterly basis.* These reports must be signed by responsible accounting firms that have checked the figures and made tests of inventories, accounts receivable, and so on.

Brokerage firms, too, have large staffs of analysts constantly trying to outdo each other and find out more and pertinent information about companies. They relate what they find about an individual company to economic factors in the industry as a whole, since (for instance) in a bad year for auto sales, most auto stocks will go down in price. A few years ago the paper industry foresaw a huge increase in demand for paper and its products. All those busy typists in your husband's office; all that Kleenex your children use. Paper companies spent millions on expansion — too many millions, temporarily, because demand did not catch up with their aspirations for a while. Earnings were hurt for most all companies in the industry, with the result that their shares dropped sharply in price. Some analysts had predicted the decline and urged investors to sell out with profits before the turn came.

Investors still cannot find out all they want, or even need to know, for wise investment decisions, but certainly the trend towards more and more disclosure and deeper analysis favors the shareholder.

The depression is hardly mentioned anymore, although some middle-aged and old people remember it sorrowfully, with a pang of hurt. After all, millions of people suffered because of it; thousands lost their fortunes, even their homes; thousands

---

*Some companies, such as department stores like Macy's and Sears, Roebuck, use a fiscal year for reporting, rather than a calendar year. The reason is obvious: it takes them a month or so to compile their figures after the year-end rush of Christmas shopping. Other types of companies also have seasonal upswings in activity, such as the meat-packers, whose fiscal years usually end in the fall.

were never to recover financially. Still, once a depression has passed (as all business cycles do) the tragedy is written more in people's minds than in their checkbooks.

Many of the great depression's worst losers were investors, who sold at bargain prices because they were afraid or desperate for cash. Many others lost because they had bought heavily on margin, which means borrowed money, and they had to sell out when they could not raise more cash. Buying on margin has since lost some glamour and is hedged by restrictions, but it means essentially purchase of securities partly on cash, partly on credit arranged by a brokerage firm, which charges interest for so doing.

Times were different during the great depression (see Chapter 3 on business cycles). The government that President Hoover turned over to President Roosevelt had espoused a laissez-faire policy, meaning little interference with business or economic forces and equally little help for citizens in distress. Slowly under the New Deal of the thirties the role of government increased, and it has been growing more paternal all the time since then.

Today economists have drummed into the minds of the American people that we are on the upbeat and cannot have depressions. Recessions, yes, they can come with turns in the business cycle; but not deep declines. The reason is built-in economic cushions such as the Federal Reserve system, which pumps money in and out through purchases or sales of government securities very much the way an engineer controls the water level of a reservoir by using the overflow chutes of a dam. Social security payments, pensions, price floors under some agricultural commodities, government subsidies for some businesses like shipping, insurance funds to pay off depositors if a bank fails; these are some of the other stabilizers. In other words, big government has become Big Brother, watching us.

WHY INVEST? IT CAN PROVIDE INCOME. Naturally everyone wants to take action against inflation and see capital grow. But sometimes the need is immediate — steady high income for elderly people, for middle-aged couples with children going to

14 | HAPPINESS IS . . .

college, for growing families with heavy medical bills. Stocks offering high yields in the form of cash dividends are needed at such times. Stock investment provides the flexibility to meet changing needs.

Here are two stocks well known to most Americans, the first definitely a "growth stock," the second a stock for high income and relative security:

	PRICE RANGE 1971–72	LATEST PER SHARE DIVIDEND	YIELD
Eastman Kodak	72–100	1.32	1.3–1.8%
CPC*	27–39	1.70	4.5–5%

Investments can be tailored to the individual's requirements more readily than a woman these days can find a tailor to make her a suit.

WHY INVEST? IT'S EASILY UNDERSTANDABLE. There are other forms of investment which have prospered in recent years — buying land and houses, collecting antiques, purchasing works of art like Picassos or Renoirs. But such investing requires more specialized, more technical knowledge than the stock market demands, and may involve more time and study. Furthermore, such investments are not as portable as stocks and bonds. The stock market is as close to you as a phone call to a broker; price quotations may be no farther away than your daily newspaper.

While other reasons for investing in stocks can be advanced, there is still a final one worth considering — it's fun.

*CPC is a food company once called Corn Products Refining. Housewives know well its Hellmann's mayonnaise.

2 | Elsie and Dan

If you remember these two names — Elsie and Dan — and the stories that go with them, you can never forget the basic differences between bonds and stocks.

Elsie's story happened so long ago that it can begin like a fairy tale: once upon a time in the sixteen twenties there was a little girl named Elsken Jorisdochter (meaning Elsie the daughter of George). She owned a bond. Today the New York Stock Exchange has in its archives Elsie's bond, the gift of a Dutch-born broker. Each year it still pays interest — a record of three hundred fifty years of cash payments.

In this insecure world Elsie's perpetual bond is quite unusual in itself, but her ownership of it has some notable features, too. Women in Elsie's century did not own property often unless they happened to be queens or nobility who inherited titles and income-producing real estate. But Elsie, who lived so long ago that people did not even have surnames generally, had a prosperous as well as apparently indulgent father known only as George, who bought her the bond.

The family lived in the lowlands near the city of Utrecht, now part of the Netherlands. The winter of 1623 there was a raging storm on the North Sea, which burst the dikes and flooded the low-lying farms. Since most people in the area depended on farming for their livelihood they quickly banded together to repair the dikes. Living so perilously close to the sea, these

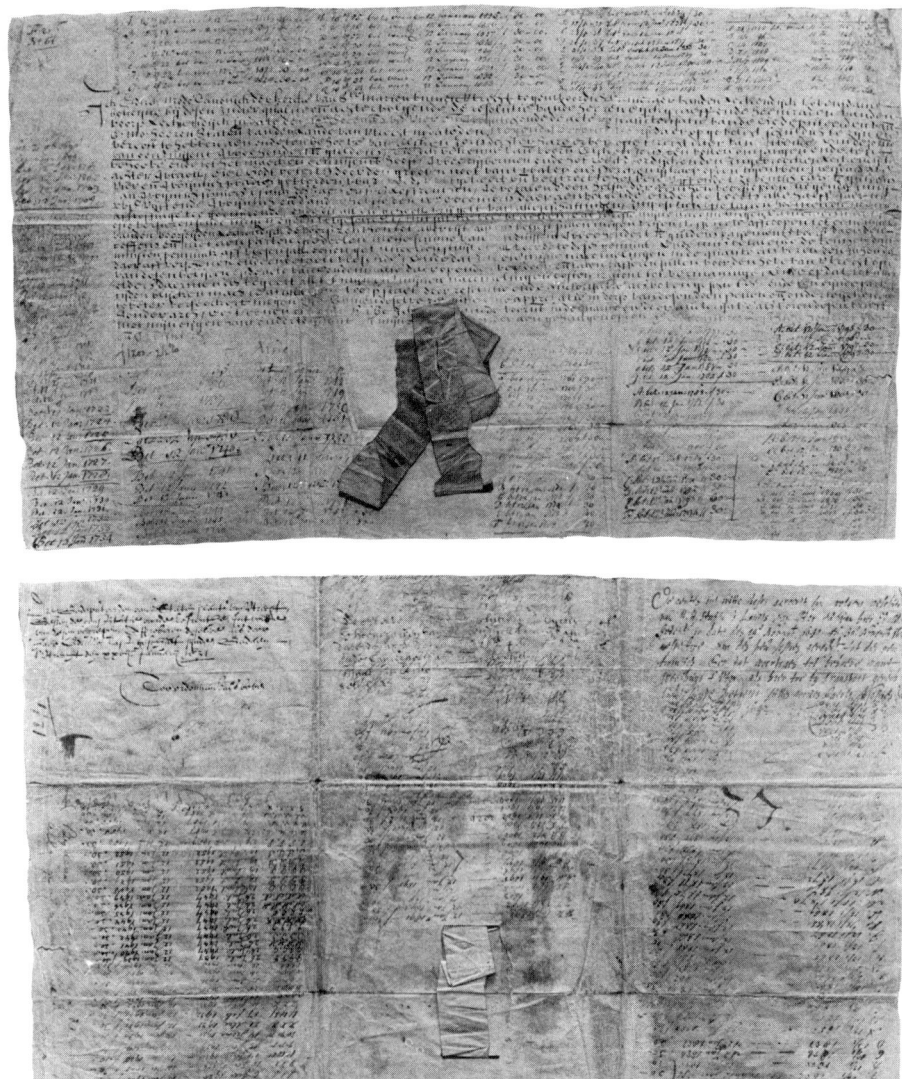

Elsie's Bond

Hollanders realized the importance of their dike system to hold back the salt water and the need of canals to irrigate the land. Thus, perhaps more than most nationalities, the Dutch of that period believed strongly in community action.

A bond issue was sold locally to finance the rebuilding of the dike, and each of the handwritten bonds bore on the indenture* the signature of the Catholic canon of St. Mary's Church in Utrecht, indicating not only the significance of the church in local affairs but also a shrewd acknowledgment that a bond issue needed the trapping of prestige and legality. Perhaps the canon was regarded as the most honest person available.

When George bought the bond he apparently had it registered in the name of daughter Elsie; another unusual feature, because most bonds in Europe then and even today are of the unregistered variety, known as bearer bonds, with no person's name on them.† It cost 1,200 gold florins, ‡ and originally paid 6¼ percent.

Still, the most interesting aspect of Elsie's bond is that though national boundaries have changed, governments have fallen, depressions have impoverished Europe periodically, and many wars have beset the area since the early sixteen hundreds, the bond has paid interest continually. During one period of financial stringency the bond's interest rate was lowered a little with the agreement of the bondholder, possibly one of Elsie's descendants. Most bonds issued these days are not perpetual like Elsie's, but bonds do tend to be issued for a relatively long period of years, such as twenty-five or thirty.

---

*The indenture of a bond is the written material, which might be called the contract, describing the rights of the bondholder and the duties of the bond issuers such as paying interest, redemption at maturity or before, etc.

†If you buy a bond, be sure to have it registered in your name because it is safer. Then the issuer of the bond will mail the interest on it directly to you. The trend nowadays in the U.S. is towards registered bonds.

Bearer bonds can be stolen easily or handed over to another person. In Europe, where many people like to keep their finances secret because of onerous taxes or unstable governments, the bearer bonds enable them to preserve a certain amount of anonymity. Such bonds have coupons attached which must be "clipped" or torn off, and mailed or presented in person to the issuer (or a bank handling the payments) for payment of interest.

‡This amount in 1623 was equal in purchasing power to about $350 today.

Elsie's bond has grown fragile over more than three centuries, and nowadays instead of mailing it to Amsterdam for the interest payment to be recorded on the bond, the New York Stock Exchange instead mails another document on which the proper endorsement is made. The check for the interest is donated to the Amsterdam Stock Exchange's employee fund.*

Bonds to most investors indicate security, and generally that is a feature they offer in most cases. Elsie's bond is a historic example. But the security of a bond is no better than the stability of the issuer. Consider the case of the impressive bonds issued by the once prestigious government of imperial Russia, one of the largest nations in the world. The year some bonds were issued was 1916, when Russia was in the throes of the First World War.

Today an imperial Russian bond is not worth much more than the crisp, impressive-looking paper on which its promises are printed. Gone are Czar Nicholas and his wife Alexandra, and his once glittering court, swamped by the tidal wave of the Russian Revolution. As might be expected, the Communist government repudiated the imperial bonds, although now and then at times when the U.S. government and the Russian government make amiable talk through their ambassadors, speculators who apparently will buy almost anything with the hope of a few dollars' profit trade the bonds. Once they were listed on the American Stock Exchange but today they are quoted over-the-counter, meaning not on an exchange.

Some of the imperial Russian bonds were turned in several years ago for a few dollars paid out of a fund made available by the U.S. government through seizure of some Russian assets in this country.

In the nineteen twenties there were many examples of bonds issued by South American nations through some major New York banks and brokerage firms which also due to upheavals of government, usually dictatorships, failed to pay bondholders.

*The Amsterdam Stock Exchange is the oldest existing stock exchange in the world.

Some were totally repudiated; some were redeemed for a few cents on the dollar.

During the depression in this country in the nineteen thirties some corporate bonds, especially those issued by railroads, were swept away during bankruptcy. Some were redeemed for a few cents on the dollar at face value, or bondholders received stock.

The basic point about bonds is that like an IOU they are a promise to pay. The owner of a bond is thus a creditor of the organization that issues the bond. A creditor has to rely for safety on the stability and trustworthiness of his debtor. Bonds can be as safe as Elsie's or as unsound as the imperial Russian issues.

Naturally there are many types of bonds.

Elsie's bond might be described in modern terminology as a "municipal" since it was issued by a community and backed by its credit. Cities, towns, countries, states, boards of education, bridge authorities, road commissions, all issue "municipals." Perhaps the next time you vote you will be asked to give a "yes" or "no" to a proposed municipal bond issue. The purpose might be to raise money for a new school, sewer system, road, city-owned electric light company, for an incinerator project or for dormitories at state colleges.

One interesting aspect of municipal bonds (which is discussed at greater length in Chapter 16) is that the interest on them has been exempt from federal income taxes for many years. This enviable characteristic is now under attack in Congress by persons who charge that the tax-exempt feature means that many wealthy people can avoid taxation on their income by owning municipal bonds. But it would probably require a constitutional amendment to do away with this tax-exemption.

One of the major issuers of bonds is the U.S. government. Its bonds vary widely in maturity dates, interest, and ownership requirements. Some, for example, cannot be owned by individuals; some are not eligible for ownership by banks. Partly to distinguish them from "municipals," the U.S. issues are called "governments," and they are *not* exempt from federal income taxation payable by individuals.

Corporations also issue bonds. For generations bonds have been especially popular with public utility companies which by tradition and by law try to keep a reasonable balance between bonds, preferred stock and common stock in their capitalization. The interest on all corporate bonds is subject to federal income tax.

One important variety of corporate bond that should have a place in the individual's investment thinking is called a convertible bond. Like the car of the same description, it offers a kind of two-in-one ride for your money. Convertible bonds are often issued by companies that want to attract investors' interest. The convertible feature acts like a "sweetener" — a kind of dashing quality that a convertible or other sports car offers a young man. During a stated period the owner of the bond can convert it into common shares of the company. Thus when he buys the bond he has the security of a fixed income investment, with the added lure of participating in the company's earnings growth through the common.

As a bondholder he is a creditor as mentioned before, and thus if the company runs into any trouble the bondholder has a claim on the company's assets ahead of stockholders. If the company fares well, the price of the stock probably will rise. At some point the bondholder might decide it was profitable and safe to convert his bond into a stated number of shares. At that point he becomes a stockholder, or an owner of the company. As a stockholder he receives dividends as declared by company directors, in contrast to interest at a stated rate on his bond.

Some, but not many bonds, are listed on the New York Stock Exchange or the American Stock Exchange. If you turn to a newspaper like the *Wall Street Journal* or the *New York Times*, which carry many quotations on securities, you can read the names of bonds listed on the exchanges as well as some sold over-the-counter, a more informal method of trading. As a matter of fact, most bonds are sold over-the-counter.

Bonds generally come in $1,000 denominations — at least for the average investor. For institutions and wealthy individuals, bonds can be obtained in much larger denominations such as $10,000 or $100,000 certificates. A few bonds are offered in $500 certificates.

In quoting the price of a bond, your broker might say it sells at 96, or you can read in the newspaper such a quotation, meaning that the $1,000 face value bond could be bought for $960. Or perhaps the bond sells at a premium, or higher than face value, such as a price of $110, meaning it would cost you $1,100 to buy the $1,000 bond. In other words bonds are quoted in terms of a hundred dollars.

Many bonds, especially these days, sell below 100, even though issued by prestigious companies like General Motors, American Telephone, E. I. Du Pont. At first thought, that probably seems puzzling, in view of the quality of the issuing company.

Remember that bonds unlike stocks pay a fixed return clearly stated on the certificate such as 3½ percent, 5 percent, etc. A $1,000 bond at 3½ would pay interest totaling $35; a 5 percent would pay $50 each year.

When a prestigious company like American Telephone issues a bond, it sells it to the public at the going interest rate for a high quality bond. Naturally, it wants to sell at the lowest current rate of interest for such a security. Thus, for example, American Telephone sold some 2¾ percent bonds in 1947.

But when money is "tight," meaning the cost of money is high, interest rates are high. In 1967 American Telephone issued more bonds, but this time it had to sell them with a 6 percent interest.

What happens, then, to the price of the 2¾ percent bond when current interest rates are much higher, as in 1969 when they rose to 7, 8 and 9 percent? The 2¾ percenter falls in price, despite the fine credit rating of the issuer. It has to fall in price because no investor in his right mind would buy a $1,000 bond at 2¾ percent when he could find other more recent issues of the same company paying much higher percent interest. This table tells the story:

NAME OF BOND ISSUE	1947 PRICE	1972 PRICE
AT&T $2^3/_4$ maturing in 1982	about 100	about 69

New investors often find it hard to understand that bond prices basically reflect changes in interest rates. Naturally, a change in the financial status of the issuer can influence a bond's price, along with stock market trends or the supply and demand for a particular bond. But the interest rate situation is the major factor.

Still another technical influence on a bond's price is the closeness of the maturity date. The maturity date is the time when the company must, according to the indenture, redeem the bonds by paying the bondholder the face value of $1,000 in cash. The price tends to move towards that level near the maturity date. If the bond is called for redemption sooner than its maturity date, the indenture usually specifies that a premium over face value must be paid to the bondholder.

For many years after World War II most investors, especially those interested in growth, scorned bonds. Typically, good bonds mean a fixed return, relative safety of principal — a truly conservative investment not for the eager speculator.

Lately, with the unusually high increase in interest rates, bonds have been attracting speculators, along with investors interested in high, safe yields. The reason is simple: many bonds offer capital appreciation if held to maturity, or if interest rates fall. Take for example a J. C. Penney 4½ percent bond selling at about 75, which now yields about 6 percent. The person buying such a bond not only gets a good return on his money but if he holds it the bond will be redeemed at maturity for $1,000, and he will receive $250 in capital gains. That's a return of about 33 percent on capital plus the good yield. A speculation? Hardly. A growth situation? Certainly.

To summarize, don't let anyone tell you glibly that a bond never offers a chance for capital gain. "Never" is a word to avoid in the fast-moving world of investments. However, the truism still holds that common stocks generally offer a better way than bonds for capital appreciation.

Don't let anyone tell you that bonds are always "safer" than stocks, either. Like stocks they have to be judged on their merits and their role in a person's investment planning. The imperial Russian government bonds turned out to be a poorer investment than a supply of caviar. An AT&T bond bought around par $1,000 and paying 3½ percent won't help a widow keep up with inflation, but the same bond bought at a good discount could pay a generous return.

Don't overlook the possibilities offered by convertible bonds in growing companies, because many of them have proved to be worthwhile investments because of the conversion feature.

In between bonds and common stocks is an area occupied by another species of investment which typically carries a fixed rate of return and yet is called a stock. Its name, somewhat of a misnomer I think, is preferred or preference stock, because it has a claim on earnings ahead of common stock.*

In the corporate hierarchy bonds have the prior claim on a company's income. In fact, interest is paid by a company on its bonds before it reports net income and hence ahead of figuring its income taxes. In other words, bond interest is a deductible payment before calculating federal income taxes — an important feature of their safety in contrast to stocks. Dividends are paid on preferred and common stock, in that order, after net income is figured. It can be said that net income comes out of earnings after taxes. Sometimes companies pay dividends even when they

---

*There are also convertible preferred stocks which, like convertible bonds, can be switched into so many shares of common stock.

have no earnings in a particular year, in which case the dividends are paid technically out of an item called surplus, which is nothing more than an accumulation of past earnings not paid out to stockholders but which may have been invested elsewhere (see Chapter 6).

In technical jargon, accountants often say that dividends are paid out of this item called surplus, in which they place each year's earnings — a bookkeeping technique. Don't let this technical point confuse you. The important thing to remember is that interest comes out before income taxes are calculated; and dividends after taxes. This is much the way you report on your federal income tax form — interest on your debts is deductible as an expense.

Just to make it clear Table 2 shows the effect on a company with and without interest to pay bondholders each year. Company A and Company B both have net operating earnings of $1,000,000. Company A must pay $100,000 interest on bonds, while Company B must pay $100,000 in dividends on preferred stock. What is left in each case for the common shareholders, if both companies are in the same 50 percent tax bracket?

Table 2 helps explain why sometimes companies find it more advantageous to sell bonds than stocks when they need to raise additional funds.

How then is stock different from bonds? Stock is *evidence* by means of a certificate of ownership of a company; a bond is a promise to pay a debt. Every corporation has to have stock, at least one or a few shares, as evidence of ownership. Often you will hear comments like this, "Oh, it's a hundred percent-owned family corporation," meaning that a family group owns the few shares outstanding. It might be described, too, as a closed corporation, meaning there is none available for sale to the public. Other companies are described as "closely held," meaning their shares are owned by a few people.

Suppose that you and I decide to enter the baby food business — a fine growing field because the population increases continually. We might start out as an informal partnership, doing the cooking and canning in our own kitchens. If we thought we could be successful we might take a forward step and consult a lawyer about setting up a corporation for tax reasons and also with the idea that we might need capital someday and therefore might want to sell some stock. The lawyer draws up the necessary incorporation papers in the state where we live, and thus we have a charter and stock. Let's say we start out with 100 shares divided equally among us. The fact that we are shareholders doesn't indicate how much money we have put into our enterprise or even whether we are making any money. It does indicate we are a corporation subject to state laws with stock outstanding in our two hands.

	Company A	*Company B*
Operating earnings	$1,000,000	$1,000,000
Bond interest	100,000	....
Taxable income	900,000	1,000,000
Taxes owed in 50% bracket	450,000	500,000
Net income	450,000	500,000
Preferred dividend	....	100,000
Net available for common	450,000	400,000
Net per share on 1,000,000 shares	45 cents	40 cents

Table 2

Over a period of years our business grows and we must expand, meaning hiring more help than our children and husbands can provide, renting a building, and buying some equipment such as large stoves, canning apparatus, a labeling machine, and trucks to deliver our products to supermarkets.

At this point our lawyer or the banker who has lent us money might suggest that we need permanent capital and therefore should sell either bonds or stock or both. We might consult a broker and he might point out that we are too new a company to sell bonds but he will help us sell our stock. He then suggests we split our 100 shares into 100,000 shares and offer 50,000 publicly at a low price, say $5 a share.

We are the same people we were before — with the same enthusiasm, the same amount of money — but now we have offered publicly 50,000 shares and the remainder — 50,000 shares — are owned by us. We have more cash.

The money is spent for a building, equipment, labels, and the purchase of inventories such as meat, raw fruits and vegetables. Some goes into the bank for an emergency and for working capital. We're in business in a big way now and we suddenly have new responsibilities to our stockholders, who will be looking over our shoulders and wanting us to make money as much as we want to do the same. We also pay ourselves a salary.

This is where we come to the story of Dan. A famous company known to almost every American mother by name began in a simple fashion like that I have just described. Dan Gerber, the founder, often fretted at how long it took his wife to feed one of their babies. He worked on the idea of prepared baby foods to make life easier not only for mothers but impatient husbands, too. Also, prepared foods could be more hygienic. He was not the first to think of it, but one of the most successful. Today Gerber Products Company has $350,000,000 in sales yearly.

ReaLemon juice, Minute Maid orange juice, Pepperidge Farm bread, Polaroid cameras, Toni permanent waves, and many other products resulted from some simple ideas and literally grew out of home kitchens or small laboratories or workrooms.

As a part owner of a company, a common stockholder has a right which bond owners generally do not. Stockholders can vote on issues presented to them at annual or special meetings. They are entitled to receive dividends if the directors vote such payments. They can elect the directors.

As mentioned before preferred stock ranks ahead of common in case earnings are not large enough to pay all stockholders dividends or if the company goes into bankruptcy or must be sold out.

Since preferred stock carries a stated dividend, say $5 preferred or 4 percent preferred, it acts in the market much like a bond, rising and falling in price in line with interest rates. If the company is doing badly or has a year of bad earnings, the price of the preferred stock may be weak along with the price of the common. But generally interest rates play a bigger role in the price of preferred stocks.

The point to remember is that common stock prices are more volatile generally than bonds or preferreds in the same company. Common shares reflect a variety of factors. The supply and demand for the particular stock. Some are well known and prestigious; some are new companies or companies barely known to the public. Almost everyone, for example, has heard of the Coca-Cola Company, which has $1.7 billion sales each year, but not many persons know the Halliburton Company, which has sales of $1.3 billion a year. It makes equipment for the oil and gas industries.

Other factors which influence common stock prices are general trends in the stock market, economic and political crises or changes, the company's outlook for growth and how it compares with other companies in the same industry. These myriad influences on common stocks are what makes investment at once difficult, challenging, and puzzling. It puts the investor in the position of diagnosing the health of any investment he is about to make.

Summary – Basics to Remember on Stocks

A bondholder is a creditor of a company. She is paid interest on her bond usually twice a year at a stated rate. If bond interest is not paid, the bondholder can start legal action to force the company into reorganization or bankruptcy.

A stockholder is an owner of part of a company, entitled to payments in cash called dividends if the directors vote them.

Sometimes dividends are paid in shares of stock. Usually dividends arrive quarterly. If the company has a record of stable earnings, it usually has a regular dividend rate which may be raised when earnings move up. In addition, certain companies pay "extra" or "special" dividends, often at year-end when directors find that the company has done well that year. But directors do not have to vote in favor of dividends; they can choose to retain the cash for corporate uses, a procedure used widely by growth-type companies such as International Business Machines. If the stockholder does not receive dividends, he has little recourse except to sell his shares.

As owners of the company, stockholders have a power that bondholders generally lack: they can vote for directors, they can change company bylaws, they can vote for other management proposals at annual meetings.

Preferred stockholders are entitled to a stated dividend, usually payable if earned, and always payable ahead of any common dividend. If preferred shares are described as "cumulative" then a company unable to pay a dividend one year must make up such a payment in later years when it does have the earnings, and it must do this before it makes payments to the common shareholder. Generally, like bondholders, preferred shareowners have no vote for directors and other company proposals, unless under company bylaws they receive a vote following a period of nonpayment of dividends.

3 | Dismal Thinking Pays Off*

In all of recorded history there have been business cycles. If you think back to the Old Testament, you remember it talks of the seven years of plenty and seven famine years.

In those early days the cause of a downswing in an economic cycle might be as simple as a crop failure, resulting from a drought or a plague of insects like locusts. Bread or other basic foodstuffs would become so scarce that families couldn't feed themselves. Commerce might slow to a halt because there was no surplus food to barter with other nations. Then painfully, slowly, the cycle would change with the harvest of a good crop and the granaries would fill again.

Often in history wars have brought a depression, or at least an unfortunate downswing in the business cycle, in their wake. The land was devastated; trained workers might have been killed or taken from their home areas; government treasuries would be empty, leading to repressive tax actions; trade was interrupted. The result: economic chaos.

For the sophisticated investor, awareness of events of the past is important for present response and planning against the future. Here is a roll call of major depressions or recessions in United States history, with some of the important reasons in each case.

*Many years ago economics became known as "the dismal science," partly because in those days the philosophers and sociologists and mathematicians, who became the early "economists," found the world an unhappy place and the outlook quite hopeless.

Anticipation of them, sometimes possible, could have helped investors.

1837. In 1836, the Treasury Department issued its famous Specie Circular requiring that payments in specie — good old hard cash in the form of coins, gold, etc. — be accepted for all public lands. Previously, notes issued by individual banks were accepted. (Remember, in those days almost any bank could print its own money!) Speculation in land sales dropped sharply. Banks contracted their loans; there was a crop failure in Europe, and a boom in southern cotton speculation ended. The results — a depression.

1857. Another "panic" or depression came in this year; among the causes were overspeculation in the railroads that were being built into the wilderness areas of the West, and tariff problems.

1873. Jay Cooke, the most prestigious financier of the nineteenth century, who almost singlehandedly financed bond sales for the North during the Civil War, stumbled on some railroad speculations. The failure of his firm sparked a downfall in the economy. At the time Europe was in the midst of a depression.

1884. This year brought a brief depression, involving the banking system and the circulation of silver dollars.

1893. In this year a more serious depression started, lasting for about seven years. British investors, who had provided large amounts of capital for expanding railroads and industrial companies, began to unload their securities, catching many speculators unaware. The situation could have become much more serious but fortunately this country had a good harvest that year, at a time when European nations had crop shortages.

1904. The "rich man's panic" occupied headline space in this year, mostly brought about by the attempts of leading financiers to corner markets on some leading railroads and industrial companies. Thus, the "panic" involved mostly overspeculation and paper profits turned into losses.

1907. By this year the nation's banking system had increased to 26,000 banks, with most of them chartered by the states, which were noticeably lax as far as making banks toe the line. Following a steady decline in stock market prices, the Knickerbocker Trust Company, a prestigious old New York City bank, suspended operations, leading to other bank failures or temporary suspensions. J. P. Morgan tried to help with large loans — $25,000,000 to New York banks.

1920–1921. A not-too-severe post World War I depression occurred, partly because of overexpansion in agriculture during the war.

1929. The great depression, a terrible, memory-searing one.

Since the 1929 depression, the nation has experienced some relatively mild recessions: in 1948–1949; in 1953–1954; in 1957–1958; 1961–1962; quite a sharp stock market decline in 1966, and the 1969–1971 recession.

In this century, and perhaps in world history, the worst economic crisis came in 1929, a vivid memory of many persons still alive. It was terrifying partly because its impact spread so widely through the world and partly because governments seemed to grope in economic darkness to find answers. Answers, even partial ones, came too late for many people.

Some roots of the depression could be traced to World War I: the devastation throughout most of Europe and the reparations that were required but that could be ill afforded by Germany. In the U.S. farmers posed a problem, one which was little understood in the early twenties. Many farmers had borrowed heavily from local banks during the war and bought marginal land for cultivation to meet the nation's heavy demands for food to export. After the war an impoverished Europe could not afford to buy the food, so the surpluses grew along with the farmers' burdensome debts. Meanwhile many nations built tariff walls high, to protect themselves from foreign goods and to spur domestic industry — an action taken also by the United States as well as leading European countries. But such retaliatory tariffs can be self-defeating, and in this instance they certainly slowed economic progress.

In this country millions of people cared or understood little about such problems plaguing the world. They had become used to securities, some finding their investment ideas whetted by the enthusiastic government bond-selling drives during the First World War. In the nineteen twenties many investors began to show interest in common stocks, in contrast to their earlier emphasis on bonds and preferred shares paying fixed returns and high yields. They wanted a part of the action in new companies that offered potential — car companies, food chains, electric light companies, and such.

Although based on a somewhat shaky economic foundation, as it turned out, a feeling of prosperity pervaded this country during the twenties, especially late in the decade.

Observers knew little about or paid no attention to the deepening plight of the farmers weighed down by heavy debt to the small rural banks, whose lending power in turn was dependent on the bigger city banks.

Americans invested heavily in some doubtful foreign government bonds, underwritten by many prestigious New York banks, such as the Chase Bank and the National City Bank. Such securities paid high rates of interest but entailed risk because of the potential turmoil in dictator-dominated nations in South America and Europe.

Investors also bought shares in good, growing industries. Yet it was a period when many utility empires were being created through a process called pyramiding — a holding company would buy control of an operating company which then might buy control of many other power companies, resulting in a top-heavy structure easily controlled by a few people in the management. Outside stockholders and bondholders anted most of the cash, thinking they were buying into a solid, growing venture, not unlike investors in conglomerates today.

But at that time there was no Securities and Exchange Commission to set the ground rules, as there is today. The stock exchanges required little of their listed companies in the way of financial reporting. Banks and brokerage firms, even highly respected ones, actively underwrote securities without much investigation. Thus many investors operated virtually in the dark, buying or selling on the prestige of the company or underwriter, on noticeable price trends, or on rumors.

Even though it was difficult for brokers to analyze companies, they can be criticized in retrospect for being so interested in selling stocks indiscriminately that they did little research. In a typical brokerage firm the job of analysis might be entrusted to one man on a part-time basis.

And lack of knowledge did not deter most investors of the period. Their buying pushed prices higher and higher, culminating in 1929 in a spree of unbridled enthusiasm that the stock exchanges like to forget nowadays. They also like to forget that a president of the New York Stock Exchange named Richard Whitney went to jail for some dishonest transactions — a dramatic fall from a lofty position of prestige, power and wealth because of speculation.

A runaway market has to slow down eventually, and in October 1929 it came a cropper. The tumble had to come because the world in the nineteen twenties was running on borrowed time — on overextended credit to farmers and to stock market and land speculators, on stifled world trade, on securities issued by promoters without regard to underlying values, on an unequal distribution of money in that millions of people were poor and a relatively small fraction of the population was rich. One more reason was little comprehension of basic economics by the public and government officials.

How did the stock market crash and the ensuing depression start? With a series of small events. An Austrian company could not pay bond interest, and a British investment banking firm went bankrupt, partly as a result. A respected economist named Roger Babson, like a Cassandra, kept giving speeches sounding dire warnings of a crash. A Massachusetts public utility commission refused to permit an electric company to issue more bonds, claiming the corporate structure was shaky. The *New York Times* financial editor warned from time to time about overspeculation.

34 | DISMAL THINKING PAYS OFF

There were other small, isolated events like telltales in the wind.

Stocks during the year 1929 showed volatile price changes, responding nervously to small news events. Mostly prices trended downwards.

It could be likened to the modest beginning of an avalanche. After a few stones loosened, there came boulders, followed by the plunge. The official date for the biggest drop in history for stock prices was October 29, 1929.

Table 3 shows some of the price drops in leading stocks during the crash in 1929, after it became apparent that even the leading international bankers like J. P. Morgan, the financier, and James Mitchell, chairman of the National City Bank, could do nothing to stem the plunge. Some of the names of the companies caught

	1929 Highs	Previous Day's High	High-Low Range for October 29, 1929
American Telephone	310 1/4	263	230 −204
Allied Chemical	354 3/4	275	218 −204 3/4
Eastman Kodak	264 3/4	220 5/8	186 −162
General Motors	91 3/4	53 1/4	45 1/2−33 1/2
U.S. Steel	261 3/4	202 1/2	192 −166 1/2

Table 3

in the downfall were as well known then as they are today, such as U.S. Steel Corporation, which even made a dramatic and unusual gesture to attempt — in vain — to bolster stockholders' confidence. It announced a short-term increase in its dividend rate before the final big break.

The date, of course, was Black Tuesday, October 29, 1929.

As bad as the depression was, some good evidently came out of it. Economists doubt that the United States can ever in this century have another really bad depression. We can and do have sharp business upswings and downturns reflected by sharp price changes in stocks, but nothing quite as grim as 1929.

Why? In the nineteen thirties, for the first time in history, the U.S. government under the leadership of President Roosevelt adopted a philosophy of taking an active role in mitigating economic declines. The government amassed huge deficits by spending money on public works to create jobs; it gave other assistance to the unemployed.

It provided complicated crop support programs; it espoused low interest rates to encourage borrowing and the launching of new business. It organized the Securities and Exchange Commission to act as a watchdog of Wall Street and to protect investors. It re-formed and strengthened the banking system, so that the small rural banks that financed farmers could not again be thrust into bankruptcy as so many were in the early nineteen thirties. It insisted that the big city banks divorce themselves from underwriting affiliates, leaving that to investment banking and brokerage firms. It launched social security to give most people retirement income.

Finally, late in that decade this country's economy got a boost from another source — an unpleasant one — the Second World War. With the help of low interest rates, bond sales and some rationing, the government managed to finance participation in this war more efficiently than in past wars.

At the end of World War II, many onlookers thought that once more we would have a depression or at least a recession because war industries were no longer needed. As before, many farmers had overexpanded; and thousands of returning veterans needed jobs.

However, the economic setting was different. World War II had changed people, mentally and financially. Taxation had helped redistribute the wealth more fairly. Many persons had managed to save substantial sums of money from their wartime work — money to invest in businesses and other opportunities or to spend on homes, cars, luxuries. Men returning from the armed forces found they could borrow easily to start new companies. Others returned to college under the GI Bill of Rights. They could buy homes at favorable mortgage rates, and a building boom was soon underway. The population had increased, which meant more babies to plan for. Scientists, no longer tied to defense projects, researched and developed new products, and new industries grew to meet ever-increasing consumer needs. Some of them are:

Baby food. Gerber's, for instance, has fared well in sales since World War II.

Cars. Watch the Fords go by in terms of sales increases and in relation to population.

Housing. The building figures for new homes show the upward trend.

Luxuries. The growing number of television sets, motorboats and tape recorders tell a story.

Department store sales. Housewives do much of the buying, and the trend indicates the health of the nation.

Business technology. Since IBM ranks as the nation's most important company in the computer and office equipment business, its sales growth reflects the growth in this area.

Supermarkets. The chain stores where most women shop for food have a small profit but large sales volume.

Airlines. The passenger trains that spanned the country thirty years ago have been largely eliminated as Americans have taken to the air, and the zoom in airlines' revenues indicates the trip.

Publishing. An exciting new post World War II development has been the stress on education. We have a new elite — the intelligentsia. Before the Second World War only relatively prosperous families could afford to send their children to college. Now a college education is a necessity and available to many more millions. Sales growth charts for textbook publishers show the way.

The United States still does have business cycles and ups and downs in the stock market, but in this fast-changing, bustling world it probably cannot again have a serious depression because of much growth momentum, a wider dissemination of knowledge of economic principles, and our ability to use some of the stabilizers that have been built into the economic system. What are some of them?

A government willing to spend money in an effort to buy its way out of a recession is one stabilizer. The manipulation of interest rates to encourage or discourage lending is another. Large amounts of social security and medicare payments constantly moving through people's hands, plus corporate pension money, have provided cushions. Growing use of life insurance to help widows with children and the elderly has been a factor. Crop support programs and aid to small businesses in the form of loans, expert advice, mortgage financing, and other programs has helped.

No one would venture to say that we won't have substantial swings in stock prices, reflecting investor psychology. The big decline of 1969–1970 is an all-too-immediate example. However, such swings can offer investors opportunities if they know how to take advantage of economic knowledge.

In 1962 there was a sharp drop in stock prices. That price decline in stocks came at a time when business profits remained high. However, it had been preceded by a period of rampant speculation when people were sold on the growth-stock idea. They were willing to pay high prices, fifty times and even a hundred times earnings per share, for the chance to buy stocks in companies whose profits they believed would grow.

Perhaps you recall that during this period when stocks were so overpriced, President Kennedy sharply rebuked the steel industry and insisted the steelmakers roll back a price increase because he thought it would be inflationary. Stock prices had been drifting down a little in the months prior to this fight between the President and the steel companies. At the end of May the sharp break came, set off apparently by the dispute. But no balloon like this bursts unless it has become overinflated.

Once again in another recent year — 1966 — there was a sharp decline. But the economic conditions had changed somewhat from 1962. There was tight money, meaning high interest rates, and people had begun to worry about the increasing pace of inflation. Heavy expenses for the Vietnam war caused talk of higher taxes. Business expansion and profits appeared to be slowing down. State and other taxes rose inexorably, especially property taxes.

In 1967 and 1968 the economy righted itself and regained ebullience; but in 1969 and 1970 inflation took an even firmer grip on the economy, with the result that taxes rose (through the imposition of the surcharge) and interest rates moved to record high levels. Bitterness between blacks and whites had shaken people's confidence, along with college riots. Unemployment rose steadily. At last, in 1971, the Nixon administration took the drastic step of a wage and price freeze — followed by a year-long "phase two" program involving more moderate economic controls. Thus in a scant four years, the economic situation had changed completely.

New ways of thinking about investing evolved during these years of change. Speculators still liked growth-type stocks. Other investors were attracted by the chance to buy high income through purchase of bonds selling at discounts from par value (see page 21). Worried about the outlook, some investors turned again to the blue chips, the shares of well-known, sound, growing companies like Du Pont, AT&T, and others.

These swings in the stock market make it important for the woman investor to keep abreast of changes in investment practices — just as she keeps herself informed about her children's schools or her community's political scene.

All of the key business indicators that analysts and economists watch are reported in major daily newspapers, and are easy to read once their significance is understood.

GROSS NATIONAL PRODUCT. This is called GNP, and despite its complicated-sounding name it is simply the dollar value of all goods and services in this country, a massive figure issued four times a year equated to an annual rate by the government, and a figure that, I believe, leaves a wide margin for error and unknown factors.

Period	Consumer Prices*	Period	Consumer Prices*
1952	79.5	1971- Jan.	119.2
1953	80.1	Feb.	119.4
1954	80.5	Mar.	119.8
1955	80.2	Apr.	120.2
1956	81.4	May	120.8
1957	84.3	June	121.5
1958	86.6	July	121.8
1959	87.3	Aug.	122.1
1960	88.7	Sept.	122.2
1961	89.6	Oct.	122.4
1962	90.6	Nov.	122.6
1963	91.7	Dec.	123.1
1964	92.9	1972- Jan.	....
1965	94.5		
1966	97.2		
1967	100.0		
1968	104.2		
1969	109.8		
1970	116.3		
1970- Dec.	119.1		

*Prices are not seasonally adjusted.

Table 4

The point to remember about GNP is that it tends to grow each year partly because we have inflation and partly because the population keeps increasing. However, if the rate of increase slows considerably from one period to another, it can be an indication that a business boom is approaching an end. If the rate of increase rises sharply a booming economy is present.

PERSONAL INCOME. This is a component of GNP. It is the dollar average of what you and millions of other Americans receive each year from salaries, dividends, pensions, interest on savings accounts, social security payments. If personal income is noticeably on the rise, it shows a strong and growing economy, although one such as we have had in the late nineteen sixties and early seventies also indicates dangerous inflationary pressures.

CONSUMER PRICE INDEX. This has a basic importance to the average family, and more specifically to the typical housewife. From its components she can determine how much the cost of living has risen and where the increases have come, whether in food, services, housing costs, medical costs, appliances, cars, etc.

The government publishes its consumer price index each month, breaking it down into categories, with the price in 1956 taken as the base year 100. Table 4 gives the story for the last twenty years.

If the index rises sharply, as in 1968–1969, consumers know that inflation is progressing at worrisome levels. To compensate they may have to withdraw savings, cut back spending, borrow, or obtain more money through salary increases or through investing in securities that appreciate in value or pay higher dividends. Some people habitually seek other sources of investment such as real estate, art objects, etc.

INTEREST RATES. These rates reflect various forces on the economy at any moment. If consumers are optimistic and willing to spend their money for cars, appliances, houses and such, interest rates are apt to be high, mirroring the heavy demand for credit both from individuals and corporations. At times of pessimism the interest rates may move lower as banks and the government attempt to stimulate more spending and growth for the economy.

In a sense, interest rates measure the price of money based on the supply and demand for it. However, the Federal Reserve system can, by buying and selling hundreds of millions of dollars' worth of government securities, influence the money market. Money, like most everything else, has a price. Its price in recent years has changed considerably in terms of various types of money, as Table 5 illustrates.

BALANCE OF PAYMENTS. Anyone who reads a newspaper probably has become aware and even worried about the U.S. position internationally.

A nation like the United States exports billions of dollars' worth of goods each year — machinery, computers, drugs, chemicals, wheat, cotton, and many other items. We import billions' worth in the form of coffee, cocoa, sugar, textiles, shoes, toys, cameras, cars, and other goods. For years, however, this nation has enjoyed a surplus of exports over imports.

However, in recent years we have been sending large amounts of money abroad to maintain troops in Europe and Korea, and to fighting forces in Vietnam. Billions have also been spent helping underdeveloped nations. Millions of Americans travel abroad, spending dollars. And American business has invested large amounts in building factories and launching new companies abroad. For example, Colgate-Palmolive Company now makes more sales and earnings from its international operations than it does from domestic plants in this country. American Standard, a large producer of plumbing equipment such as bathtubs and heating units, is another that reports more sales and earnings from foreign operations than from activities at home.

The result of all this has been an unfavorable balance of payments for this country: Americans have been lavishing more money overseas than they have received from foreign nations. What is the effect?

The difference has to be made up by payment in gold, since gold has long been the internationally accepted way for nations to settle their balances. We can liken the position today to a prodigal man who is spending more than he earns each year, and therefore has to use up some of his capital. Worried about the gold drain, the government has asked businessmen to reduce new spending abroad. It has urged travelers to use fewer dollars when they leave the country and has restricted the amount of goods they can bring home free of duty. Some troops have been

	Government bonds			
	United States (long-term)	State and local		
Period		Total	Aaa	Baa
1962	3.95	3.30	3.03	3.67
1963	4.00	3.28	3.06	3.58
1964	4.15	3.28	3.09	3.54
1965	4.21	3.34	3.16	3.57
1966	4.66	3.90	3.67	4.21
1967	4.85	3.99	3.74	4.30
1968	5.25	4.48	4.20	4.88
1969	6.10	5.73	5.45	6.07
1970	6.59	6.42	6.12	6.75
1971	5.74	5.62	5.22	5.89
1971- Jan.	5.91	5.34	5.08	5.65
Feb.	5.84	5.28	4.92	5.73
Mar.	5.71	5.26	5.00	5.56
Apr.	5.75	5.49	5.22	5.85
May	5.96	5.99	5.71	6.36
June	5.94	5.98	5.65	6.36
July	5.91	6.12	5.75	6.58
Aug.	5.78	5.84	5.56	6.21
Sept.	5.56	5.45	5.09	5.86
Oct.	5.46	5.05	4.75	5.38
Nov.	5.44	5.20	4.94	5.53
Dec.	5.62	5.24	4.99	5.55
1972- Jan.	5.62	5.13	4.84	5.49
Week ending-				
1971- Nov. 6	5.33	4.98	4.75	5.25
13	5.37	5.15	4.90	5.45
20	5.46	5.25	4.95	5.65
27	5.56	5.41	5.15	5.75
Dec. 4	5.58	5.50	5.20	5.85
11	5.59	5.25	5.00	5.55
18	5.63	5.21	5.00	5.35
25	5.68	5.18	5.00	5.40
1972- Jan. 1	5.60	5.04	4.75	5.40
8	5.61	5.05	4.75	5.40
15	5.57	5.00	4.65	5.40
22	5.61	5.16	4.90	5.50
29	5.67	5.31	5.05	5.65

Table 5. Bond and Stock Yields. (Per cent per annum)

| | Corporate bonds ||||| Stocks ||
| | By selected rating || By group ||| Dividend/price ratio ||
Total	Aaa	Baa	Industrial	Railroad	Public utility	Preferred	Common
4.62	4.33	5.02	4.47	4.86	4.51	4.50	3.37
4.50	4.26	4.86	4.42	4.65	4.41	4.30	3.17
4.57	4.40	4.83	4.52	4.67	4.53	4.32	3.01
4.64	4.49	4.87	4.61	4.72	4.60	4.33	3.00
5.34	5.13	5.67	5.30	5.37	5.36	4.97	3.40
5.82	5.51	6.23	5.74	5.89	5.81	5.34	3.20
6.51	6.18	6.94	6.41	6.77	6.49	5.78	3.07
7.36	7.03	7.81	7.22	7.46	7.49	6.41	3.24
8.51	8.04	9.11	8.26	8.77	8.68	7.22	3.83
7.94	7.39	8.56	7.57	8.38	8.13	6.69	3.14
8.04	7.36	8.74	8.57	8.70	8.17	6.53	3.32
7.75	7.08	8.39	7.24	8.39	7.94	6.32	3.18
7.84	7.21	8.46	7.36	8.39	8.08	6.48	3.10
7.86	7.25	8.45	7.43	8.37	8.05	6.59	2.99
8.03	7.53	8.62	7.68	8.40	8.23	6.82	3.04
8.14	7.64	8.75	7.80	8.43	8.39	6.99	3.10
8.14	7.64	8.76	7.85	8.46	8.34	7.03	3.13
8.12	7.59	8.76	7.80	8.48	8.30	7.04	3.18
7.97	7.44	8.59	7.64	8.39	8.12	6.90	3.09
7.88	7.39	8.48	7.58	8.25	8.04	6.75	3.16
7.77	7.26	8.38	7.46	8.13	7.96	6.78	3.31
7.75	7.25	8.38	7.42	8.12	7.92	6.81	3.10
7.66	7.19	8.23	7.34	7.98	7.85	6.57	2.96
7.78	7.25	8.43	7.46	8.15	7.97	6.76	3.24
7.77	7.24	8.37	7.43	8.13	7.96	6.66	3.29
7.77	7.27	8.36	7.46	8.10	7.95	6.83	3.31
7.78	7.28	8.39	7.48	8.11	7.94	6.85	3.39
7.79	7.28	8.42	7.47	8.14	7.96	6.78	3.21
7.79	7.27	8.42	7.46	8.15	7.97	6.76	3.17
7.76	7.24	8.39	7.43	8.14	7.92	6.87	3.12
7.74	7.23	8.36	7.41	8.12	7.89	6.83	3.02
7.70	7.22	8.31	7.37	8.06	7.88	6.79	2.99
7.67	7.19	8.27	7.36	8.02	7.86	6.68	2.97
7.65	7.17	8.21	7.33	8.00	7.84	6.52	2.95
7.63	7.16	8.18	7.31	7.95	7.82	6.49	2.94
7.67	7.22	8.24	7.36	7.95	7.87	6.57	2.99

withdrawn from Europe; and well-publicized efforts are being made to lighten the financial load caused by Vietnam.

Yet the balance of payment problem continues to grow worse. No simple solution exists: the problem is inextricably meshed with the political and economic life of corporations, of you as an investor, and of the nation and the world at large.

Mindful of the intricacies of basic economics, the clever investor seeks to keep current with the trends, realizing that she can profit by the old adage: "Buy low and sell high."

Where can the average woman find out about basic economics and the rapid changes? Books on basic economics can help. (see Bibliography). A good newspaper such as the *New York Times*, the *Wall Street Journal* and others, if read with regularity, will keep anyone up-to-date. Also helpful are good news magazines like *Time, Newsweek, U.S. News & World Report*.

Many leading banks such as the Federal Reserve Bank of New York, the First National City Bank, the Chase Manhattan Bank, and Manufacturers Hanover Trust Company publish bank letters, usually monthly, available free to anyone.

Leading brokerage firms publish newsletters of a general economic nature, and so do some investment advisory services. Generally, the brokerage firms offer their letters free of charge to persons on their mailing lists, while the advisory services charge fees, although their publications can often be read in brokers' offices or in public libraries.

4 | Getting to Know You

"Women are different from men." This statement made by a man usually with a smile, but sometimes with a smirk, can be irritating. It's an idea inscribed permanently in men's minds, as deeply engraved as the writing on a stone tablet. True physically and sometimes emotionally, it need not be true intellectually, or in relation to investment ability.

There are wide ranges of personalities among women. Remember cold but passionately ambitious Lady Macbeth, who was the driving force behind her husband, impelling him to kill to obtain the ruling position he wanted? In business we see many successful men at the top partly because their wives are passionately ambitious — although not, hopefully, actually murderous.

There are wives who pursue their own careers with a vengeance, intent both on financial security and on self-achievement and independence. And there are wives who scrimp a few dollars out of food money year by year to build up estates for themselves in their old age and for their heirs. Hetty Green was an extreme example of a wealthy woman who lived penuriously (one black dress so aged that it looked green), and yet by her death she had parlayed $1,000,000 into more than $100,000,000. .

There are wives who watch their husbands grow beyond the companionship of the early days of their marriage, and these wives wake up one morning to find their husbands want a divorce to marry someone more in tune with their mental, social or political aims. Perhaps the divorce of Governor Rockefeller by his wife so that he could marry a younger woman exemplifies a situation like this.

There are wives of ever-loving, indulgent husbands who like to keep their wives and children from the harsh realities of life and who never teach them how to handle money. These women can be the most pathetic of all when hardships like death and expensive illnesses befall a family.

There are many women who don't get married, or who marry and then find themselves divorced or widowed unhappily at young ages. How many Vietnam widows are there?

All types of women can profit by developing a sound approach towards investing.

Know yourself, said Socrates, calling it the beginning of wisdom. Oddly enough it is very difficult to look at ourselves dispassionately. Yet, to do well in the stock market, knowing yourself is a cardinal rule for success.

Psychiatrists and psychologists make thousands of dollars from women (and also men) because these patients do not know themselves and are struggling to develop their identities. Many young people today have joined the ranks of patients, an age group where it could be expected that mental stability would be easy. The difficulty of knowing yourself apparently has nothing to do with age, financial condition, heritage, or social position.

Yet for a bored, frustrated, or puzzled woman, successful investment could be described as preventive therapy. It's a great ego builder. One of the basic principles is the simple prescription to know yourself financially; and that could be an approach to a larger more important self-knowledge touching every aspect of yourself.

Obviously every woman except the very wealthy or the very insulated should live by a budget, or at least attempt to do so. In knowing herself financially she must consider first the sources of her family's income — salary, dividends, outside money from gifts, inheritances, royalties, bonuses, and others.

Usually the largest expense involves housing, whether a family rents or owns its own home, along with maintenance — heat, light, water, telephone, repairs.

A second major expense for many families is one with which most housewives are well acquainted — the food budget, including a little extra perhaps for the peripheral expenses in a woman's domain like children's allowances, household supplies and cleaning expenses, her own pin money, the newspaper boy. These days a family of four probably cannot eat comfortably on much less than $45–$50 a week, not counting the little extras mentioned before. A couple probably has to allot at least $20 a week for comfortable eating, and a single woman cannot manage on much less — and eat well — than $15, and that probably doesn't include her lunches if she works.

Table 6 shows some sample budgets of families in various income categories, plus a government breakdown of the typical portions of income after income taxes (the take-home pay, in other words) allotted to various consumer items — and, more importantly, to items under the category called savings, such as life insurance. If your take-home pay is higher than these examples, you should have ample money to start investing.

For an investment program out of income there must be some surplus available representing the difference between income after taxes and outgo. Cuts often have to be made somewhere to achieve a surplus.

Many wives prudently insist that their husbands carry large amounts of life insurance, partly because they are worried about enough money for the financially dangerous years when children have to be sent through college; also for their old age. After all, a married mother of children who returns to the labor force upon the sudden death of a middle-aged husband generally cannot command a very good salary. If she has a profession (nursing, teaching, law, medicine) she probably could command a good salary; but otherwise, no.

The rule of thumb these days for sufficient life insurance for a husband might be about four times the man's annual salary.

Take-home pay	$600			$700			$800			$900			$1000		
Number in family	2	3	4	2	3	4	2	3	4	2	3	4	2	3	4
Housing	175	185	185	180	195	195	200	210	210	220	230	230	240	250	250
Food	135	150	155	150	175	180	190	195	200	200	210	220	210	220	230
Clothing	60	65	70	65	70	75	80	85	90	85	90	95	90	95	100
Transportation and insurance	65	65	65	90	90	90	100	100	100	110	110	110	125	125	125
Personal	70	75	75	85	90	90	90	95	95	95	100	105	110	120	125
Savings	60	38	33	90	53	50	95	73	65	135	110	95	145	120	115
Gifts and contributions	35	22	17	40	27	20	45	42	40	55	50	45	80	70	55

Table 6

The average insurance coverage nationwide is only about $18,000 per family, or less than twice the average income these days of a middle-income family. Thus the man earning $10,000 yearly should carry about $40,000 of life insurance, the man earning $20,000 should carry at least $80,000, and so forth.

Behind every family should be a month's salary in the bank collecting interest and biding time for emergencies.

If the family lives in a house the mortgage payments each month, plus real estate taxes (often included in mortgage payments) and utilities should come to about one-fourth of family income after taxes. Apartment dwellers can afford a little more, perhaps, than the usual one-fourth because of savings on heat, repairs (most apartments include basic maintenance), and other utilities (if paid by the landlord).

Also, many city families can count on another big saving not available to country dwellers or suburbanites — no car and the heavy operating and repair expenses involved. Probably more families underestimate the cost of owning cars than any other item in the family budget. In the first place, most families overlook the item of "depreciation." A car ages and sooner or later it must be replaced. Buying a car for most families is a major expenditure, usually financed by monthly payments carrying a high rate of annual interest.

In figuring the cost of a car to your family take the sales price and divide it by five or six years, if you can expect to keep the car that long. Find out from someone — your husband, a local bank officer, or your auto dealer — how much a five- or six-year-old car will bring when traded in on a similar new car.

For example, it might work out this way. If you have bought a car that cost about $3,000, it would be worth about $400 after six years in terms of buying a new car for about the same amount of money as it originally cost. Therefore the depreciation over the six years would amount to $2,600 divided by six, or about $430 a year. Ideally you should be putting this amount in the savings bank each year toward the purchase of the new car. Repairs to the car you have constitute an operating expense which you have to pay out of income; again, the ideal is to make a rough estimate of repair expenses and budget for them out of income each month. For example, $200 a year might be set aside for repairs, including new tires, brake linings, and so forth. Don't forget a sum required almost weekly for basic maintenance, such as gasoline. The first year of the car's life repairs would be minimal.

These costs, overlooked by many investors, explain their presence in the income budgets in Table 6.

If a budget is tight where can a wife find the money to invest? It's difficult. Very lucky are women who have a little sum of money left over from working days or can accumulate some out of their salaries, or luckier yet are those who have inherited money, either a small or large amount. Even so, a woman on an apparently tight but effective budget possibly can find some sources of money. Perhaps the food budget by dint of more careful buying can yield a few dollars a week; perhaps the money being set aside for a new car or other large purchases could be invested for a period of time; perhaps some major spending could be delayed for a while.

A husband might object to such an idea, pointing out that a new car might have to be bought when the price of stocks was down. A sophisticated wife can give a good answer. If she take household money and invests in a sound stock like American Telephone & Telegraph or E. I. Du Pont, she will receive good dividends each year pending the purchase of the new car or other major item; and the stock certificates can at any time be taken to a bank and used as collateral for a loan at a lower interest rate than a regular car loan. But more about this in future chapters.

Unfortunately there are still many wives who might find it hard to make out an accurate budget income statement because their husbands keep them in the dark about family finances.

One woman, the wife of a top executive, knows how much her husband earns, but little else about his finances, because his company has to issue a proxy statement each year before the annual stockholders' meeting. She has roughly $100,000 in money she inherited, and this she keeps invested continually in the market in good growth stocks. She does know that her husband carries little insurance beyond the coverage his company provides.

Another woman married to a top executive of a major company, also with a large salary, knows that he has set up a trust for her, enough to provide a comfortable income during her lifetime and to pass something substantial on to their children. However, a cautious woman, she has for years saved a little each month out of a generous household allowance and stashed it away unknown to her family. She now invests these amounts, after they accumulate to about $500, in stocks.

The wife of a middle-level executive, with a good salary of more than $20,000 a year, has long been haunted by memories of the depression. Shortly after their marriage she urged her husband to start a very sound life insurance program, which has been increased over the years. She can count on about $200,000 if anything should happen to him. With that accomplished she has been saving small amounts each year to make investments, so that each member of the family including the children own stock in their own names. Her aim is to continue and increase the pace of this program.

Another woman has gone back to work as a teacher for two reasons: 1) to help her husband during the heavy expense years when their children will be in college, three of them at about the same time; 2) to build up investments that will help by paying high dividends and offering borrowing power during those difficult years, and also provide a source of capital for retirement later.

A single woman often finds it hard to save, especially if she is young and her salary is low. Clothes, travel, entertainment appear to be much more important. One woman got into the investing habit when her company offered a stock purchase plan and she allotted $10 a week for the shares over a year's period.

She found by cutting out some frills — expensive lunches, more careful buying of food to be eaten at home, less money spent on clothes — that she could absorb the difference. Since then she has received a small raise of $5 a week and expects to continue saving, funneling the money into a monthly investment account with a brokerage firm. Under such plans as little as $40 a month can be mailed by check to a broker who in turn buys stock for the investor — as many shares that month as the money will cover, even if fractional shares are involved (see pp. 137–138.)

These case histories, all true ones, give an idea of how some women have found money within (or outside of) their budgets for investment. Certainly they couldn't have done this if they had not analyzed their financial status closely and come to a dedicated decision about investing. It does take dedication like almost anything else worthwhile.

Besides the income statement there is a second most important aspect of financial planning — the balance sheet.

While most women are so used to budgeting that an income statement is easy to make out and understand, a balance sheet is something hazy. It looks a little more complicated and the terms used — "net worth," "earned surplus," "current assets" — sound difficult, but oddly enough it is even more revealing of a family's progress than an income statement.

Like a page in a diary, a personal balance sheet is a moment stopped in anyone's financial life — and a very telling one when compared over a period of years. It details a person's financial progress. The reason is that a balance sheet summarizes a person's assets and liabilities at a particular time. Once a person has listed his assets carefully on one side of a page and his liabilities on the other, he can find a key figure: his net worth, namely the sum of all assets minus all liabilities at a given date. Most corporations report on a calendar-year basis and thus use December 31 (or the last working day of December) as the date for figuring their balance sheet. For an individual this date is also convenient. Then, year by year, he can compare his financial progress at the particular date.

Recently the National Consumer Finance Association disclosed that the nation's top wealth holders, defined as those with gross assets of more than $150,000, totaled about 4,500,000 Americans. Their net worth ran about $55,000 apiece.

With inflation rising so fast, the figure probably has moved upward quite sharply since this estimate made some years ago. Still, it gives a target for anyone making out a balance sheet. Whereas an income statement revealing that a family is living right up to its last penny of income and perhaps going into debt can be disconcerting, a balance sheet for the same family often is surprisingly encouraging.

The reason is twofold. Many people do not realize the value of assets until they sit down with pen and paper in hand and think; and many assets have built-in growth factors that often can be overlooked.

Let's make out a typical balance sheet of a middle-income family. The start is easy — one of the biggest family assets on a long-term basis is a house. Table 7 is an illustration of what the balance sheet might show.

One side of the balance sheet — the assets — adds up to $61,200, perhaps a more impressive figure than you thought. The liabilities total $19,265. The difference between the two is the important one for any family — the net worth. In this case $61,200 minus $19,265 equals $41,935. The net worth belongs to you — to your family.

Later, when you start reading corporate balance sheets regularly you might at first be puzzled because the total assets always equal the total liabilities. However, that is because the net worth belongs to a group outside the company — you the stockholders. In a corporate balance sheet your net worth as a stockholder is often lumped under liabilities, under the headings "available for the common," "earned" and "capital surplus." More about these items later.

In other words the stockholders' ownership in the business appears on the liability side of the balance sheet because they own the difference between the total assets and the other liabilities, just as your family owns the net worth involved on the family balance sheet.

Assets		Liabilities	
Long Term:			
House, market value	$35,000	Mortgage	$18,000
Furnishings – rough market value	8,000		
Cars – two, market value	3,000	Repairs, tires needed on cars	200
Shorter Term:			
Cash in savings bank	2,500	Current bills owed including mortgage payment, department stores, light, heat, telephone	1,000
Stock – market value	10,000		
Cash value, life insurance policies	2,000		
Cash in husband's profit, bonus plans	500	Estimated income tax due next quarterly payment date	35
Cash in checking accounts	200	Allowance due children	30
Total Assets	$61,200	Total Liabilities	$19,265

Table 7. Family Balance Sheet

Over a period of years net worth of a family tends to grow. In fact, a balance sheet is the quickest way for you — or anyone interested in your credit standing — to judge your financial progress.

Let's see how some assets grow and change.

House. Each year it grows in value to you possibly for two reasons. Year by year you pay off more of the mortgage debt, so you own a larger part of the house. Thanks to inflation the value of many houses has risen in dollars. Also, land values have been increasing faster than the price of houses.

Cash value of life insurance. This is another item that tends to increase each year.

Personal property. Despite wear, some household items like antique furniture, silverware (such as sterling), stamps, other collections grow in value.

Capital items. Such big items as refrigerators, television sets, air-conditioners, lawnmowers probably decline in value each year owing to usage and the advent of new models.

Pension and profit-sharing plans. Your husband's or family's participation in these usually becomes more valuable each year.

Securities. With a rising stock market or additional investments, your securities can be worth more year by year.

Installment debts. As they are paid off month by month such liabilities decline, possibly faster than the depreciation in the items purchased by the loan.

Cars. In the first years of ownership, new cars depreciate sharply in value. A $3,000 automobile might lose almost $1,500 in value the first year, if you tried to sell it.

While an income statement tells you how you are faring in managing income in relation to outgo, a balance sheet kept up to date year by year details your financial growth. Certainly anyone finding himself with lower net worth from one year to another should take remedial action.

After you have made out a personal balance sheet and income statement, you should not have trouble reading and understanding the corporate financial statements of companies in which you are interested.

5 | To Auction, to Auction, to Buy a Fat Stock

Most every woman enjoys an auction, and perhaps it's in our blood. There's an air of excitement about an auction, even when prices appear to be high in relation to value, or even when the auction goer has no money of her own to spend.

At an auction it is interesting to watch the interplay — the agility of the auctioneer as he tries to obtain the highest price for sellers, the pitting of buyers against each other while the tension mounts, the feeling of anticlimactic relief when suddenly the cry "sold" is heard.

The New York Stock Exchange, the biggest center for trading stocks, likes to consider itself an auction market. Prices, just as at an auction in a gallery or the backyard of a farmhouse, are set by open outcry between brokers who represent sellers or buyers.

Perhaps the best way to understand the exchange and its system of operation, and understand why it continues to be the nation's financial center can be found by looking at the history of the Wall Street area.

Often described as a "canyon" amid skyscrapers, Wall Street stretches only about eight hundred man-sized paces from Trinity Church at one end to the East River at the other — or from a scourge of the devil at one end and the not so deep, not so blue sea at the other. Wall Street is crossed at right angles by Broad Street (which once had a canal running down the center) and by other streets. Solid gray skyscrapers loom over the street levels, their noncommittal gray skins stretched taut; behind them throbs life, along with hopes, dreams, moments of despair in the offices of hundreds of financial firms.

Wall Street got its name because once there was a wooden barricade along it, built by the early Dutch to keep out the Indians — and possibly the British — who coveted the small colony the Dutch West India Company had settled at the tip of Manhattan Island early in the seventeenth century. Thus Wall Street existed before New York. Perhaps today it is a commercial center because of the trade-minded Dutch.

The Dutch settlers, epitomized by peg-leg Governor Peter Stuyvesant who tried to keep order with a kind of fierce and rugged justice, came to this country not for political reasons such as escaping tyranny at home, and not for religious reasons such as the Puritans' desire to find a place to worship in their own way. The Dutch arrived for a very basic reason — to trade and to make money. Their nation in the seventeenth century ranked as a leading commercial nation with a strong navy and many merchant ships. Hence the settlement they called New Amsterdam at the tip of Manhattan was soon a bustling seaport and financial center, where more than a dozen foreign languages could be heard in a walk along its dirt streets. Trade and money have long been closely allied because cargoes have to be financed for the long trips abroad and the goods have to be sold.

New York City grew lustily in the nineteenth century and the residential sections gravitated uptown, but the financial center remained largely in Wall Street, partly because of tradition and convenience and partly because people preferred to live away from their businesses.

As the nation grew, putting out fingers of conquest into the wilderness in the West, canals were needed to carry goods and settlers inland, along with roads and later railroads. Ever-growing needs for financing became apparent. In the early years much of the capital came from Europe at high rates of return; but the need for money was always urgent enough so that many new financial ventures were begun, to attract capital and funnel it into development. For example, the Bank of the Manhattan Company (later merged with the Chase National Bank) began as a water company founded by Alexander Hamilton. It built wooden pipes to carry water in the city. The Chemical Bank, another early company, was founded as part of its name implies to make chemicals. Such organizations often discovered they could make more money as banks lending money to help other new businesses.

The new businesses were many, and when they were formed they often sold shares. In the late seventeen hundreds, even quite a few years before the Revolutionary War, about two dozen men used to meet regularly under a buttonwood tree on Broad Street.* A tree makes a logical gathering place, on a hot day as well as on a rainy one. It's also easy to describe; as much so as an office with lettering and a number on the door.

At first the stocks traded under the tree were not many in number. Most brokers bought or sold for their own accounts or for a few friends busy elsewhere. The general public had no money in those days or time to spend on stocks, or even the credit to do so. In such a simple market many brokers could keep records of their day's trading on a few slips of paper stashed in their pockets or in their hats.

After a while the traders, perhaps bothered by weather changes or needing privacy to escape from the curious, decided to move their meeting place indoors. A local tavern was a logical choice. Eventually, in 1865, the group which began to call itself the New York Stock Exchange moved into quarters in the area where it has remained — with alterations — up to the present. Now it has plans for a new trading center somewhat south of its present quarters.

Over the years the auction idea remained. Billions of dollars of securities are traded each year between brokers, acting for

---

*There's a plaque marking the spot which you may see when you visit the New York Stock Exchange. The original agreement to trade was signed by twenty-four brokers on May 17, 1792.

customers or themselves, on verbal acknowledgment alone — the tradition that began under the buttonwood tree. Computers and automation have speeded the process and will change it, but it is still a market where men stick by their word. If mistakes happen, as they do in any business, or differences of opinion arise, the problem is often solved under the eye of a stock exchange committee by the flip of a coin.

How does the intricate stock auction market work for you in this highly computerized, pushbutton age?

Suppose, after consulting your broker you decide to buy 100 shares of General Motors. Perhaps you are sitting at your broker's desk in a suburban Illinois office of a big brokerage firm, or perhaps you are talking to him by telephone from your home. On his desk or nearby there may be a little machine with buttons; when he presses certain buttons the machine almost instantly either prints out or shows him on a screen the latest price quotation of General Motors. Let's say the last sale was at a price of 74¾, meaning $74.75 a share.

After he tells you the price you might say, "I'll buy it." "Okay," he replies, "we'll buy at the market — 100 shares." On a pad he jots down your order. A market order indicates that the shares will be bought at whatever price is going when the order reaches the floor of the exchange.

Or your broker may suggest that you place the order at 50 cents a share lower than the 74¾. "Let's put it in at 74¼ and see if we can get it. I have a feeling the market might go down a little today." He will mark the order GTC, which means "good till canceled."

Basically, you should remember three types of orders:

The *market order* means you will get the stock at the price quoted when the order reaches the floor of the exchange. This is the type of order you might use if you don't want to quibble.

The *GTC order* — good till canceled — represents a bid by you to buy the stock at a specified price. Usually these orders last about six months, and then the broker might ask if you want to renew it.

Or you can put in a *day order*, which is good for that day only. If the stock doesn't reach your price you would have to put in the order again for the next day, or the next and so on. If you are afraid of the market's direction, you might use this type of order.

What happens to your order when it leaves the broker's desk still fascinates me, although I've been writing about securities for twenty-five years. It goes to his office's order room — perhaps he takes it himself, perhaps an office boy does it, or even a conveyer system. Then it is "wired" either directly to the broker's representative on the floor of the exchange or through the head office of the firm in New York, and then to the exchange floor. Only minutes are involved.

On the floor the order is received by a clerk of the firm, who in turn hands it over to a floor broker for the firm. He walks, or speeds (most brokers walk so fast on the floor that it's more than a walk, but less than a gallop), possibly a few dozen steps to the trading post where that particular stock is handled.

The exchange, which trades some 1,941 different stocks these days, allots the stocks to each of its twenty-two trading posts.

General Motors is traded at Post Number 4. At this post your broker joins a group of men around a specialist, a broker who makes a market in GM and a few other stocks. This means that at any time he stands ready to buy or sell GM at reasonable prices in relation to recent market quotations. If ever he doesn't "make a market" then an exchange committee investigates. It might halt trading if prices get too far out of line temporarily. It might conceivably appoint another specialist to handle the job if he does not perform satisfactorily.

In this group around the specialists brokers come and go, asking the latest price at which the specialist quotes the market. Once they have heard the market price your broker and others will tell the specialist the price at which they want to buy or sell. This he writes in a little book.

TO AUCTION, TO AUCTION, TO BUY A FAT STOCK | 61

If it happens that the order calls for buying at the market (like your order for 100 shares of GM) then the broker says to the specialist he will take 100 shares at the quoted price. Or there may be another broker in the group willing to sell at the market, in which case your broker can buy directly from him.

However, if the order is a day or GTC order at a price under the market it will go into the specialist's book and it will be filled when prices reach that level.

Meanwhile, let's assume the market order has been filled. Your firm's floor broker reports back to the clerk, hands him a little slip noting the filling of the order. The clerk notifies the head office or your brokerage firm or contacts your own broker directly. In a space of less than five minutes your broker can tell you that the order has been filled and you have bought 100 shares of GM. The sale has been consummated, but you have five trading days after the date of purchase to present your broker with a check covering the transaction. Usually you will receive a confirmation statement of the trade a day after it took place, although mails might delay it another day.

If the speed of the transaction in this auction market astonishes you, remember it has evolved over a few centuries, based partly on trust. Along the way Wall Streeters have developed shortcuts to speed the process, such as the ticker system which carries reports on each trade of 100 shares. Almost every brokerage firm in the country has a ticker in its office. If you are in your broker's office you possibly will see your trade appear on the ticker a few minutes after it arrived on the floor. It might look like this:

$$GM$$
$$74¼$$

GM is a shorthand symbol, standing for General Motors. When this moves across the tape with a price under it, it means a trade has been completed for 100 shares at this price. If you had bought 200 shares it would look like this:

GM
2s   74¼

Each stock has a different symbol, which brokers use when they place an order. For example, suppose you are a big buyer and purchase 1,600 shares of Sears, Roebuck at 67½. It looks like this on the ticker:

S
1600s   67½

In the case of a big order like this the 1,600 is on it, but the more usual trade involves 100 shares, 200 shares, and so forth. After all, even with 100 shares priced at 74, a lot of money is involved — $7,400 and more.

On your next trip to the Wall Street area pay a visit to the exchange's visitors' gallery and museum on Broad Street. The floor of the exchange has often been described as almost the size of a football field, and actually it is about 30,000 square feet.* Scattered around the floor like players are the twenty-two trading posts mentioned previously. Instead of having colors and numbers like players, they sport symbols of stocks traded around the post and post numbers. Stock exchange clerks man the center of the posts to collect and transmit the transactions as soon as received, so that the trade shortly appears on the ticker — clicking out during the trading day in thousands of offices throughout the world. A large numbering board alerts brokers when their clerks, stationed around the edge of the trading floor, need them. Meanwhile, there's a ticker projecting the prices high above the floor, so that visitors can see them from the gallery. The brokers generally are too busy for more than hasty glances.

Until you become well versed in investing — beyond the

―――――――
*An official football field is 300 feet by 150 feet.

ABC's — you probably should avoid stocks on other exchanges, such as the American Stock Exchange, the nation's second largest trading center. If you are old enough you may remember it was once called the Curb Exchange.

The name dates from the days in the previous century and until 1921 when brokers who traded on the "curb" did so in groups gathered on Broad Street. Often in those days clerks in brokerage firms would call out customers' orders from windows of their offices overlooking the street. Just as on the New York Stock Exchange, the business was conducted mainly by word of mouth.

The ASE, however, has always lacked the prestige of the New York Stock Exchange, even after it moved operations indoors. The reason is that its listing requirements are not quite so strict as the Big Board's. Therefore, the ASE has attracted companies that are not so large, nor so prestigious as the ones listed on the Big Board, also companies that for various reasons can not or do not want to report their financial activities as fully as companies listed on the bigger exchange. Many conservative investors look down their noses at some stocks listed on the ASE, considering them to be much more highly speculative, unseasoned newcomers; these tend to be lower-priced, volatile stocks. Remember that price alone is not a criterion for safety or growth possibilities of a stock, but generally speaking few prestigious companies have stocks that sell for $1, $2 or even pennies a share.

But every investor — even the novice — should be aware of the ASE and its stocks. In any market boom many of the high fliers — the purely speculative stocks — have their homes on the ASE. Often small companies that make the grade becoming large and famous season their shares first on the ASE before they move to the Big Board.

Trading procedures and rules on the ASE are very similar to those on the Big Board.

An interesting point of reference for the average investor,

especially one with speculative interests, is to follow the new ASE stock market average. It tends to move up faster during periods of speculative activity than the Dow and other averages.

Over-the-Counter

Shares of a vast number of companies are traded in another market called the over-the-counter market. In fact, what many people do not realize is that it's a much bigger market than those offered by the exchanges. No one, not even the smartest broker equipped with the largest computer, can estimate how many billions of dollars of stock exist in the over-the-counter market.

We know, for example, that the New York Stock Exchange lists about 1,941 companies' stocks currently, the American has 1,260 and the regional exchanges such as the Midwest, the Pacific Coast and Boston exchanges list about another 2,000 shares, some duplicating shares listed on the two biggest exchanges. We can roughly measure the value of listed shares traded by multiplying the average price of the shares on each exchange by the number of shares traded.

Consider for a moment how many small companies there are in this country, even judging from your own community. Some of them, like the local drugstore, are too small to sell their stock to the public. Perhaps the shares are owned by the pharmacist, his family and a businessman or two who have supplied him with some capital. Other companies in your home city have grown beyond such family ownership and yet are local in nature — banks in the area and the local electric light company (if not part of a big utility), for instance.

It is obvious that most small, localized companies like these have little desire to become listed on an exchange; in other words, there are many fine, solid companies on the over-the-counter market. And many of the best fast-growth candidates appear in the ranks of over-the-counter securities.

Quotations of the more popular and well-known of the over-the-counter stocks are carried in major newspapers such as the *New York Times* and the *Wall Street Journal*. If such quotations are not readily available in newspapers then they might appear in the sheets published five times weekly by the National Quotation Bureau, and most brokerage offices carry such sheets.

Trading in over-the-counter securities is regulated chiefly by an organization called the National Association of Securities Dealers, more familiarly called NASD. Membership in the NASD is held by most brokerage firms, and also by firms that trade solely in the over-the-counter market. Some of these over-the-counter dealers specialize; they might deal only in bank stocks, insurance stocks, or other kinds of issues.

The method of trading in the market for over-the-counter shares is somewhat different from the auction system of the New York Stock Exchange. Dealers make the market, standing ready to buy or sell from their inventories. They regularly quote a bid and ask price for the stocks which they handle. Thus often buyers of shares in the over-the-counter market find that they don't pay commissions in the sense that they do for the listed stocks, but pay a markup.

For example, suppose you live in a city called New Hope, Wisconsin, and reliable persons have advised you to invest in the local water company. The area is growing, more water is needed for home use and irrigation and the company has shown good earnings. You go to your broker, who works for a member firm of the New York Stock Exchange and also has a big over-the-counter trading department, and you ask him to buy the shares for you. He will quote you the latest bid and ask price. This means the price at which dealers will buy shares from you for themselves or for their customers (the bid price); and the price at which they will sell shares to you (the ask price).

Then he may tell you that the brokerage firm itself makes a market in the issue (that is, keeps it on hand) and that the price at which he can buy it for you is "flat," or net, meaning no commission is involved. If the firm's over-the-counter department does not make a market in the issue, it may have to contact another over-the-counter house that specializes in that stock. In this case, you probably would have to pay a commission above the price quoted.

One problem with over-the-counter shares is that often the market for them is "thin." For example, a woman might inherit from her father or grandfather several thousand shares of a local water company or bank stock, only to find that it is a little hard to sell the shares, because of the fact that the market is thin. Perhaps there are few shares outstanding; perhaps many have been tied up in portfolios and estates by people willing to hang on to them for years because of family interest, pride, large capital gains, etc. Then the sale of a few thousand shares could take time and might force the price of the shares down.

Still another difficulty encountered by some investors involves bank loans. Generally banks will not lend as much with over-the-counter securities as collateral as they will on stocks listed on the major exchanges. Here again they consider that over-the-counter markets tend to be thin, and prices more volatile in the case of sudden liquidation.

In summary, remember that price is no indicator of a stock's value. Shortsightedness has often led some brokers and even more investors to ignore economic forces constantly at work at the edge of the stock market, like the ebb and flow of waves along a beach. Two examples (and there are hundreds of others) help illustrate this point.

I have hundreds of shares in a little company now gone into oblivion called the Port Ewen Ice Company, a once profitable venture. Years ago its operations involved cutting blocks of ice from the Hudson River each winter and shipping it insulated with sawdust by train or barge to New York where it went to hotels and private homes. Then came the electric refrigerator which virtually killed the company's one-product market, plus the fact that by then icebreakers kept the river open during most of the winter, making it difficult for ice to form in large blocks. Economic progress spelled the end of the company.

A more recent and better-known example involves a company that managed to remain in business despite its failure to move with the trend for many years. Its name: Montgomery Ward. After World War II Sewell Avery ran the company with the singlemindedness of a dictator. An elderly man in the nineteen forties and a successful business leader when the war ended, he was imbued with the idea that serious depressions always followed major wars. He insisted the company keep millions of dollars in cash and easily liquidated securities such as low-paying government bonds.

Meanwhile, the company's chief rival, Sears, Roebuck, foresaw the growth in the economy, answering the needs of people who had saved up money from good jobs during the war and now wanted to spend on scarce consumer goods. Furthermore, Sears top officials reasoned that the built-in stabilizers in the economy launched during the New Deal years, such as social security, unemployment insurance, public works, would blunt any depression into a mere recession. So they moved ahead and spent hundreds of millions of dollars on improvements, new stores, a wider variety of products for sale, training young executives.

The Sears management judged the economy correctly. There was no depression because the world's needs for consumer goods proved too great, and the war had been better financed so that Americans had money to spend and jobs with which to earn more. Sears moved ahead — far ahead in sales and earnings — while Montgomery Ward lagged so badly it took a proxy fight to wake up management to the realization that it could not remain out of step with progress.

Change is the key word in business, and the investor has to be flexible to keep up.

6 | Figures, Straight and Not Curvy

Figures can be as dull as dishwater, but a smart woman investor learns to handle them with discrimination just as she learns to separate the silverware from the kitchen utensils and the good china from the expendable variety. To do this she does have to absorb some boring details but after a while they become a part of her daily investment life.

The first step is to keep up with the stock quotations in newspapers. Soon they will become as easy to read as prices of canned goods in a supermarket.

Figures 2 and 3 are from the Monday, March 27, 1972, *Wall Street Journal*, showing the results on the New York Stock Exchange for the previous Friday.

In the top left-hand corner of Figure 2 you will note Friday's volume figures: 15,390,000 shares that changed hands that day — a reasonably busy day. In 1971 brokerage firms on the average broke even or made a little money each day the volume of trading was 12,000,000 shares. So the day proved to be a profitable day for your broker.

Below the volume figure in smaller type is another that investors follow: total trading for the year to date. It shows volume of 1,103,785,790 shares compared with 1,063,099,671 in the same 1971 period and 1,634,654,324 in the 1970 period. This indicates that trading activity during the first months of 1972 ran somewhat ahead of 1971, which had been a good year for

24
THE WALL STREET JOURNAL,
Monday, March 27, 1972

Friday's Volume
15,390,000 Shares; 181,500 Warrants

Volume since Jan. 1:	1972	1971	1970
Total shares	1,103,785,790	1,063,099,671	634,654,324
Total warrants	14,420,500		

MOST ACTIVE STOCKS

	Open	High	Low	Close	Chg.	Volume
Braniff Air	18½	18⅝	17⅞	18⅛	−½	417,100
Block HR	29½	29⅝	25¼	26½	−3½	297,900
Fedders	42⅞	43⅛	40¾	41¼	−1⅝	211,000
Gulf Oil	25¾	26	25½	26	+⅜	186,300
Memorex	33⅜	33⅜	29½	29¾	−2¼	178,300
Am Cemen	7⅞	8⅛	7⅞	8	+¼	134,800
Wheelb Fry	8¼	8½	8	8½		126,200
Am Tel&Tel	43½	43¾	43⅛	43¼	−⅜	116,800
Grant WT	42½	42⅞	41	41	−1½	107,100
Royal Dut	35⅞	35⅞	35⅜	35¾	−⅛	106,000

Average closing price of most active stocks: 27.77.

A-B-C

[Stock tables truncated — illegible newspaper fragment]

Figure 2

trading volume. Generally, a rising stock market will go hand-in-glove with heavy volume.*

Now for the table below these figures of the ten most active stocks, to which you should give some regular attention.

the Market

MARKET DIARY

	Fri	Thur	Wed	Tues	Mon	(a)
Issues traded	1,760	1,772	1,760	1,762	1,764	1,926
Advances	606	1,029	684	286	571	595
Declines	808	440	738	1,199	914	1,146
Unchanged	346	303	338	277	279	185
New highs, 1972	73	80	40	30	108	182
New lows, 1972	49	55	67	97	52	215

(a) Summary for the week ended March 24, 1972.

DOW JONES CLOSING AVERAGES

-----FRIDAY-----

	1972	—Changes—	1971
Industrials	942.28	− 2.41 −0.25%	903.48
Transportation	259.92	+ 0.64 +0.24%	198.77
Utilities	113.24	− 1.12 −0.97%	123.69
Composite	324.10	− 0.68 −0.20%	296.52

Dividend yields last week on the stocks used in the averages: Industrials 3.30%, Transportation 2.95%, Utilities 5.83%.

Ex-Dividend of Pacific Gas & Electric Co., 43 cents, lowered the Utility Average by 0.13.

The above Ex-Dividend lowered the Composite Average by 0.06.

OTHER MARKET INDICATORS

	1972	Change	1971
N.Y.S.E. Composite	59.86	− 0.13	55.19
Industrial	65.04	− 0.11	58.73
Utility	38.20	− 0.24	41.80
Transportation	53.58	+ 0.13	41.49
Financial	78.68	+ 0.02	71.69
Standard & Poor's Industrial	119.56	− 0.25	109.96
American Exchange Price Index	27.84	− 0.03	26.04
NASDAQ Over-Counter Composite	127.55	+ 0.17	....
Industrial	135.75	+ 0.36	....
Insurance	136.02	− 0.17	....
Banks	106.35	+ 0.42	....

Volume of advancing stocks on N.Y.S.E., 4,870,000 shares; volume of declining stocks, 8,410,000. On American S.E., volume of advancing stocks, 1,440,000; volume of declining stocks, 2,260,000.

Figure 3

An astute investor would note that a conservative growth stock like AT&T was on the list as a volume leader, an indication

---

*Also note that 181,500 warrants were traded that day. A warrant entitles the holder of it to buy a stated number of shares of a company's stock at a stated price. Warrants fluctuate in price.

(if it has been occurring regularly) that investors might be moving into AT&T and other such stocks and out of the speculative growth issues. However, AT&T was down a little in price.

Look at some of the other very active stocks that day: H. & R. Block, Braniff and Memorex, all speculative issues. However, along with AT&T there were some other blue chips such as Royal Dutch and Gulf Oil.

One day's look at the most active list cannot indicate a trend usually. The two big oil companies for example, were in the headlines for various reasons during part of 1972. Thus specific news items, such as earnings, discoveries, merger talks, can stimulate activity in a stock.

The important thing is for the investor to keep watching the most active list over a period of time — to spot trends, to associate news items with their impact on particular stocks.

Let's look down the list of stocks mentioned in the "A" column to the second stock listed — a well-known, sound, chemical and pharmaceutical outfit called Abbott Laboratories. At the left, the reader can see the list of numbers headed

—1972—			
High	Low		
$73^3/_4$	$64^1/_8$	Abbt Lab	1.10

This indicates simply that the high price for Abbott during the year to date was 73¾ and the lowest price traded was 64⅛. The figure following the name of the stock refers to the dividend paid on a year's basis — $1.10. It doesn't provide the quarterly rate, unfortunately, so that the investor interested in such a stock must do more research on that. Sometimes the dividend is followed by a small letter referring the reader to an explanatory footnote.

Next comes a heading dubbed "sales in 100s," which means the number of round lots (100 shares) traded that day. The figure is 92, meaning that 9,200 shares of Abbott changed hands, not an active day compared with AT&T's 116,800 shares traded.

The next headings for Abbott are quite obvious — an opening price of 69¾, on the first transaction, a high price during the session of 69⅞; a low of 69⅜, and the final quotation of 69⅝. It could be described as trading in a narrow range. Furthermore, under the heading "net change" the investor can take note that the price showed no gain in comparison with the closing price the previous day.

A rise of even $1 a share in a stock selling in Abbott's price range would be considered good. Naturally a $1 a share rise in a stock priced at $20 would be even more significant, just on a percentage basis. Just think that if you own 100 shares of a stock that rises $1 you are $100 richer — on paper — than the previous day.

Why virtually no change in Abbott that particular day? It's impossible to say without knowing more about the company itself. The stock market generally tended to be weak that day, a factor to consider as your eyes run down all those little plusses and minuses in the right-hand column under the "net change" heading.

By reading the daily news columns of the newspaper you might be able to find a reason for a stock's relative strength on a particular day. Perhaps a brokerage firm has issued a favorable comment about the company; perhaps the company came out with favorable earnings or a new product. Perhaps merger rumors have been surrounding the company. You the investor have to ferret out such news if you want an explanation. Stocks only talk to you through figures and news items.

Late in 1972 some newspapers added a new category to their quotation tables, price earnings ratios. The "p-e" ratio is the closing price of the stock that day divided by the per share earnings. Example: If a stock closes at 20 and the latest 12 months earnings reported by the company are $2, the p-e ratio is 10.

Once you have perused the stock market quotations of companies whose shares you own or in which you might be interested, you will want to turn to find out how the averages fared — namely the Dow Jones industrial average, since that is the best known and most widely quoted (see Figure 3). It closed at 942.28, down 2.41 points; so Abbott in holding steady was showing ability to buck a market trend. In an adjacent column the investor can find out where the same average was a year earlier in 1971 — 903.48. Stock prices are up generally — that conclusion can be drawn from the difference in the average for Friday, March 24, 1972 and the comparable date in 1971.

Then the investor's eye would drop to the other market indicators. He would find that the New York Stock Exchange's industrial average closed at 65.04, off 0.11 of a point. At the same time he would note that Standard & Poor's industrials (500 stocks) closed at 119.56, down 0.25 of a point.

In view of the general stock market trends, an investor might find the NASDAQ* index of over-the-counter issues more significant. That particular day the figure was 127.55, up 0.17 of a point. An alert investor might conclude that there was a slight swing into the speculative issues on the over-the-counter market, which showed a gain and a swing away from listed shares.

This is the kind of detective work that a smart investor does, and by following such prices, averages, and the news items each day, you can become quite sophisticated about trends.

Figures for the American Stock Exchange issues are quoted similarly to those of the Big Board, although some of the smaller city and town newspapers carry only an abbreviated list of stocks, often limiting their quotations to the Big Board issues.

Then, the investor must be cognizant of the lists of over-the-counter issues, regularly carried each day by the major newspapers like the *Wall Street Journal* and the *New York Times*.

For space reasons the highs and lows sometimes are not included in the lists of the over-the-counter shares, nor by any means are all unlisted securities quoted. Remember that they constitute an army of thousands of companies with stocks out-

---

*NASDAQ is the shortened form of National Association of Securities Dealers Automatic Quotation.

Figure 4. Over-the-Counter Markets

standing, such a vast list that no complete count has ever been made. Only the bigger, more active, and sometimes controversial ones are listed.

The prices, unlike the quotations for the listed securities, are given in the form of bid and ask prices. Figure 4 is a list of prices from the *Wall Street Journal* for the day mentioned.

One company familiar to many women is Can Mills B, meaning Cannon Mills Class B stocks.* Cannon makes towels, sheets and other textile products. From the price range the investor can see that it was quoted at 94½ bid, 96½ asked that day. It pays a $3.76 dividend. (Cannon is an interesting example because it's a company that once was listed on the New York Stock Exchange. However, a few years ago the management refused to meet certain requirements of the New York Stock Exchange about proxy statement material, and it chose to give up its listing on the Big Board.)

Or take a look at Butler Manufacturing, paying 70 cents dividend, a maker of preengineered buildings and agricultural equipment. Its price range was a narrower 34 bid, 35 asked.

The wider range in the case of Cannon Mills indicates that a gap between the two must somehow be closed. Hence a buyer would do well if he really wants the shares to make an offer under the 96½ but over the 94½ price, and then wait to see if he can obtain it. And since the bid and ask prices and the commissions on over-the-counter issues are a little bit different from those of listed securities, you should be sure to ask your broker when you place the order what the price and commission arrangement will be, so that there will be no misunderstanding.

Now for a look at the bond market quotations carried under the heading of New York Stock Exchange Bonds. Remember that the Big Board only lists relatively few of the leading bond issues; most of them are traded over the counter.

Looking down the list in Figure 5 you will find Allied Str

---

*Some companies have two classes of stocks — Class A and Class B. Often one of the classes has no voting privileges, a reflection of the desire of management to keep control of the company in a few hands.

New York Stock Exchange Bonds

Friday, March 24, 1972

Figure 5

cv 4½ s 81. Allied Str is Allied Stores Corporation, a large retail store chain that operates Bon Marche, Gertz and Jordan Marsh, among others. Its sales run about $1.4 billion yearly. The quotation with the "cv" means the company has an issue of convertible bonds paying 4½ percent, or $45 per year per $1,000 bond, which mature in 1981. The maturity date is the year in which the company has promised to pay off the bond — to pay you $1,000 for each bond, in other words. (Most bonds provide for some sort of redemption, unlike Elsie's perpetual bond.) Generally, if a company redeems a bond before the maturity date, the indenture calls for some few dollars of extra payment for the right of "calling" your bond.

Remember that since bonds are traded in terms of 100 dollars but come in multiples of $1,000 and up, the quoted price of 94 actually means $940 for the face value $1,000 bond. Every time a bond declines a point in price it means a drop of $10. A one-and-a-half point decline therefore means $15.

Once you become accustomed to reading the price quotations, study the footnotes because they give you helpful additional information. Another important point to notice is the little letter X that often follows a stock. This means that the stock is trading ex dividend: in other words, buyers of the stock that day are not entitled to receive the next dividend, possibly because it is about to be mailed. (Usually dividends are declared well in advance of the day they are mailed out.) Sometimes when a stock goes "ex dividend" it will weaken in price, but don't be bothered about that. It's a technicality that has nothing to do with the underlying value of the stock.

Still another important group of figures for the investor to consider is the commission rate schedule of brokers trading on the New York Stock Exchange. The rates charged in 1972 are given in Chapter 18. In the table of commission rates (Figure 16) note the difference between the commissions charged for round lots (multiples of 100 shares) and odd lots (meaning 1 share, 10 shares, etc.). It is usually advantageous for the small investor to buy in round lots if possible.

The New York Stock Exchange has increased the commission rates for small investors. (In 1969 it decreased the volume rates available for large investors.) I think the argument is based on convoluted reasoning since the head of the stock exchange claims that he wants to broaden the market and offer better services to small investors, but charge them more.

In 1969, a year during which the stock market dropped sharply following a speculative binge in go-go stocks, the brokerage firms created much bad feeling with small investors (and with large ones, too) because of their inefficiency in handling orders. No doubt you and your friends were angered by uncompleted orders, straying stock certificates, inaccurate billings, prices that did not seem to be correct, etc. The problem apparently stemmed from bad planning by many brokerage firms whose clerical force could not keep up with the unprecedentedly huge volume of trading, confusion brought about by the changeover from manual operations to computerization, and the sharp drop in prices in that year. All of these combined to cut profits of brokerage firms, forcing some to cut back their personnel and offices, others to merge, others to absorb heavy losses with the hope that next year would be better. Some of the big brokerage firms such as Merrill Lynch, Pierce, Fenner & Smith did not believe that increasing the commission rates charged small investors was an answer. However, higher rates generally were put into effect.

This difficult situation in Wall Street means that the small investor has more difficulty than ever finding sympathetic help. More on this in the chapters ahead.

What is happening in the world influences our lives; in the same way, what is happening in the stock market affects you as an investor. Still, the company or companies in which you are interested must stand on their own merit as investment prospects. This means that every investor should follow closely the figures basic to a company he owns or wants to own. These basic figures are:

SALES. Most women care very much whether their families have high salaries. Yet, I think, both salaries and sales can be overemphasized. For example, the big supermarket chains have billions of dollars of sales *volume* each year, but they measure their *profits* in pennies — in very small percentages. So, too, the man down the street may be making a much larger salary than your husband, but his expenses can take a much higher toll, so that perhaps his family doesn't eat as well as yours, travel as much or even drive as fancy a car.

In other words, a company with $10,000,000 sales, growing fast, might be a more interesting investment than a company with a $1 billion in sales.

NET INCOME. This is a figure most important for you as an investor. It's the amount left over for the common shareholders after all expenses, taxes, interest on bonds or loans have been paid. In terms of the individual, net would be the money you could put in the bank for savings or use for fun, or for self-improvement, like a college course.

You should examine your company's net income in relation to sales. Did sales grow and did net income increase at the same rate as sales? Or did net increase at a faster rate than sales, usually a good omen? Then a careful investor would study these relationships a step further: how do these figures compare with other companies in the same industry? Is your company doing as well as the others, or better?

PRICE OF THE STOCK. How much are you paying in relation to these earnings each year and what kind of a dividend are you getting? If the company is a fast-growing one, it may be plowing back the earnings into new plants, factories, etc., and paying a tiny cash dividend, or none at all; yet perhaps the price of the stock is growing at a good pace.

At this point turn to a write-up on page 253 on the magic number 72. It will show you how to relate the return you are getting in your growth stock in terms of any slower moving stock that pays higher dividends.

Take a look at the earnings statement and the balance sheet of a company that most housewives know intimately, at least

Statement of Consolidated Financial Condition

Assets	December 31 1971	December 31 1970
Current Assets		
Cash	$ 3,224,892	$ 2,166,240
Marketable securities, including certificates of deposit- at cost (approximately market)	24,449,474	28,841,988
Trade accounts receivable, less allowance of $93,000	8,384,654	7,780,923
Inventories- Note B	30,469,703	30,456.421
Deferred federal taxes on income	1,591,600	1,483,700
Total Current Assets	68,120,323	70,729,272
Other Assets	523,218	701,204
Property, Plant and Equipment- on the basis of cost		
Land	823,590	823,590
Buildings and improvements	27,339,951	26,852,086
Machinery and equipment	54,378,930	52,993,980
	82,542,471	80,669,656
Less allowances for depreciation	49,214,641	45,013,644
	33,327,830	35,656,012
	$101,971,371	$107,086,488

Liabilities and Shareowners' Equity	December 31 1971	December 31 1970
Current Liabilities		
Trade accounts payable	$ 2,565,990	$ 3,285,757
Compensation to employees	2,825,337	2,728,049
Miscellaneous accounts payable	936,427	1,308,304
Accrued liabilities	3,386,483	2,885,740
Federal and state taxes on income	6,520,751	5,887,103
Total Current Liabilities	16,234,988	16,094,953
Shareowners' Equity - Notes A, C and D		
Common stock (par value $2.50 a share). Authorized- 20,000,000 shares. Issued (including shares in treasury) 1971- 13,412,050 shares; 1970- 13,407,100 shares	33,530,125	33,517,750
Additional paid-in capital	129,309	71,177
Retained earnings	52,474,266	57,860,971
	86,133,700	91,449,898
Less cost of shares of Common stock in treasury (1971- 13,400 shares; 1970- 16,250 shares)	397,317	458,363
	85,736,383	90,991,535
	$101,971,371	$107,086,488

Statements of Consolidated Income and Retained Earnings

	Year Ended December 31	
	1971	1970
Statement of Consolidated Income		
Income		
Net sales	$132,309,728	$174,246,707
Interest	1,174,774	1,988,197
Miscellaneous	265,359	805,452
	133,749,861	177,040,356
Costs and Expenses		
Cost of products sold	88,482,457	107,312,542
Selling, administrative and general expenses	22,180,866	25,347,987
	110,663,323	132,660,529
Income before taxes on income	23,086,538	44,379,827
Federal and state taxes on income, after reduction for investment tax credits (not material) on the flow-through method	11,060,000	21,565,000
Net income	$ 12,026,538	$ 22,814,827
Net income per share of Common stock	$ .90	1.70
Statement of Consolidated Retained Earnings		
Retained earnings at beginning of year	$ 57,860,971	$ 52,072,530
Add adjustment resulting from consolidation of subsidiary- Note A		377,614
as restated		52,450,144
Net income for the year	12,026,538	22,814,827
	69,887,509	75,264,971
Cash dividends- $1.30 a share	17,413,243	17,404,000
Retained earnings at end of year	$ 52,474,266	$ 57,860,971

Figure 6. The Maytag Company Financial Report

as far as its products — washing machines and dishwashers — go (see Figure 6).

Maytag is a relatively small but very profitable company, and yet for the year 1971 the annual report (published early in 1972) shows lower earnings and a drop in total assets. How come?

There was a hundred-and-fifty-day strike at the company's main plant. The point is that figures alone do not tell the full story; they must be studied in relation to what is happening to a company. Now Maytag is back at work and earnings are on the rise. Hence the stock, also, has risen quite sharply.

Just reading and analyzing financial statements is hardly enough for an investment decision. A prospective investor should also read what the company chairman and president say in the written — or essay — part of an annual report. Often their remarks can be revealing. The management will comment on the year's results, either indicating satisfaction or explaining why profit and/or sales were not better. It may talk about industry trends, about competitive products, about labor relations, about new developments, and sometimes even the state of the economy.

Meanwhile, your brokerage firm might provide you with its latest analysis of the company, in all probability based on much more expert judgment than you have. For example, the analyst might think that the management of the company was 1) exaggerating its bright future, or in some cases 2) underestimating it. The president or chairman of a company is an individual and often his personality — hopeful, overconfident, cautious or pessimistic — can come through in the annual write-up. Analysts know or should know the particular personality involved.

More than you are able to do, the analyst has some convictions about the growth rate of the company, and this is vitally important to an investor. In a company that is doing well the current price can be high because the buyer of such a stock is in a sense purchasing tomorrow's earnings.

No analyst can guarantee a company's growth rate, but generally he will be able to make an informal prediction. This is his job essentially — the most important job he can do for you, I think, except provide information as to when you should sell a stock.*

Even if he forecasts good future earnings for the company, you must realize this point: the stock's price may not necessarily rise in line with higher net.

Why not, you will ask quite logically? The answer has several facets:

1. Stock prices don't trend up with higher earnings if the stock market itself is in the doldrums, such as during the reactions following speculative binges in 1962 and again in 1969.

2. Stock prices might not move upwards in line with better earnings if the government is trying to curb inflation, as it has been doing since 1969. Pressures to halt inflation eventually lead to a company's cutting back on capital improvements, cutting costs, and perhaps losing some sales.

3. Stock prices might not follow earnings upwards if the threat of war, civil disturbances, or increasing taxes discouraged investors in general.

4. Stock prices might not move upwards if other forms of investment appeared more desirable. In 1969 for example, some investors sold their shares and bought bonds for high yields; real estate as a hedge against inflation; or silver because of expectations it might show a sharp increase in price. As the stock market continued to decline, more people withdrew money and put it into savings banks. Yet by the end of 1971 and early in 1972 the market was strong once more.

To summarize, even though an analyst tells you that SuperduperCompElectronics might increase earnings twenty percent — and be correct in his estimate — the stock's price might not rise by that much if any one or more of the various reasons mentioned above was influencing the thinking of other investors. Remember that the law of supply and demand rules the market.

*Here, I believe, many analysts fall down. They are good at forecasting growth, but are often too slow with sell recommendations.

7 | The Man in Your Investment Life

Like oil and water, male brokers and women investors don't mix well unless there is some effort on the woman's part. Let's face it: brokerage firms basically don't like female customers — with a few wealthy and knowledgeable exceptions.

Yet the selection of a broker (or brokers) ranks as the first most important investment decision you make. A good broker interested in your welfare can teach you as you go along, and his advice can make the difference between success and mediocre results in the stock market. The New York Stock Exchange likes to think that no broker working for one of its member firms could possibly guide you into failure, but even that has happened occasionally. And women unfortunately can be more gullible than men.

There are some good reasons why male brokers tend to treat women customers charily and sometimes contemptuously. First, of course, is the fact that men have the opinion that women often are overemotional. No broker, or any other businessman, likes to visualize an indignant woman making a noisy scene in the firm's office, if her investments turn sour or mistakes are made in her account. Secondly, male brokers have the deeply ingrained feeling that women just don't know anything about finance, anyway.

There's another thought that makes them chary about women:

it might be categorized as "sentimentality." For example, a few years ago Bache & Company officials laughed ruefully about one of their fellow vice-presidents. He was sued by a woman customer who claimed that she gave him her investment account because he led her to believe that he had marriage in mind. Not only was she disappointed in love but she also charged that he had not fared well with her account. The moral is that thoughts of romance should be kept out of a brokerage office relationship. Lonely women should not look upon their brokers as a possible source of companionship or a listening post for their troubles.

Sad to say, there are many lonely women in the world. Many brokerage firms avoid having offices on the ground floor of buildings to discourage customers living or working in the vicinity from dropping in for a social hour or two as they would to a club. Other firms deliberately limit the number of chairs available for board watching.

All brokers encourage customers to do their trading by telephone, and most of it is done in this way. Even so, brokers often claim that women on the telephone talk too much. Whether you like it or not, your broker is in business to make money and he depends for his livelihood on the volume of shares he handles. In some firms he receives a salary; in others he works on straight commission, but in either case what he earns annually is based on a percentage of the commissions received from the trades made for you and other customers. In good volume years popular brokers can earn $100,000 and more a year, making them well paid and sometimes more prosperous than the officers of the brokerage firm who usually receive a straight salary plus bonus out of profits. In lean years the broker's $100,000 can decline sharply. And a woman who chats idly on the telephone can exasperate a busy broker. It prevents him from servicing adequately other customers to help him build up his commissions for the year. If you think about it, you would not subject your husband or other male relative to long conversations during his business day. He wouldn't permit it. Being related to you, he could afford to be abrupt, unlike your broker who often feels he must be polite even to difficult customers.

The woman who wants to make the most of her relationship with a broker should treat him in a businesslike fashion. She might ask him when is the best time to call him 1) to place actual orders and 2) to talk more generally about the market. Before telephoning, collect your ideas by jotting them down in orderly fashion on paper, including specific questions.

The fickle woman is another variety that brokers fear. She calls up, or pays him a visit, and he advises her at some length about what to buy or sell. Then without giving him any straight answer of "Yes, buy it" or "No, I don't want to buy now," she says she will think it over. Or sometimes she says "Go ahead," and then calls back a few minutes later and asks to change it. But by then the order has been placed, and she is out of luck — she either has bought or sold the stock in question. Remember that brokers — and the stock market — move fast because that is the nature of the business.

All of this brings into focus another type of woman that brokers find alarming — the reneger. In fact, the New York Stock Exchange has a blacklist made available to brokerage firms with the names of renegers on it, and other more unsavory types of customers.

The reneger might be the woman who places an order for 100 shares of Ford at the market, meaning the price when the order reaches the floor of the exchange. Let's say the 100 shares are bought for her at $45 a share. Then the next morning the woman reads in the paper that the stock has dropped quite sharply to 42. She tells her broker when the confirmation statement arrives that he misunderstood her, that she definitely remembers she put the order in at 42, not at the market. She probably tries the sweet approach first — her memory was good that day and she knows he must have been very busy and confused her order with another.

If she becomes insistent the broker, to get her out of his hair, perhaps forever, might settle the issue with her on her terms and then close her account or ask her to use another registered representative in the firm. He probably makes sure that the word goes around that she is a reneger.

Knowing that male brokers will look at you a little askance means that you are forewarned and can prepare yourself. You, as a new investor, have a little selling of yourself to do to this often charming, polite, cheerful (usually) but skeptical man who will be your broker.

First, before you approach a brokerage firm to open an account, think about your finances. If you have made out an income statement and a balance sheet as urged in Chapter 4, you will have a good idea of what you can invest. You will be able to answer quickly, without the embarrassment of "hems and haws," some of the basic questions that the broker will ask.

If you live in a small city and are well known, the broker perhaps will know you by name and income level. Possibly he will know something about your husband and his job, or about your family. Your name might have been on his (or his firm's) mailing list. No doubt he will ask for credit references, such as your local bank.

He will want to ask you about your income status, and possibly whether your family carries adequate life insurance coverage and has some savings in the bank (at least one month's family income after taxes is a good rule of thumb for bank savings). He will want to know what investments, if any, you already have. The key question, of course, is how much you want to invest at the moment you contact him, or in the future. Some women have a small sum to invest immediately; others count on regular amounts coming in at intervals, perhaps quarterly or once a year.

While his questions may appear to be prying, don't bridle at them. He can advise best if he knows your financial status and aims. The aims are very important.

Recently a leading brokerage firm ran an advertisement which showed a large butterfly. Under it the caption read:

Extinct Species
The no-risk, high dividend, fast-growth stock

A naive woman investor could be expected to say to her broker something along these lines: "Now I can't take any risk, but I want a high dividend and I must have a quick increase in price — growth you know."

If there were such an investment "butterfly" you can be sure that investors with much faster nets than yours would have captured it already. Such a statement by a woman — or even a man investor — indicates he or she knows nothing or next to nothing about the stock market for the following reasons:

RISK. There is always risk because stock prices rise and fall like a kite, wafted by winds of change in corporate fortunes, in political and economic conditions. What so many women don't understand is that a good stock like General Motors, for example, can drop in price even when car sales do well, as economic or political factors affect the market.

DIVIDENDS. Generally speaking, stocks that pay high dividends are not growth issues. They may be very fine stocks for investments, but the fact that they pay high dividends in relation to price indicates that investors are not buying them for growth. This, too, is a fact that many women find hard to understand. For example, they reason that if AT&T pays a good solid dividend without fail, isn't it a growth stock too?

For years after World War II, AT&T was anything but a growth stock. It was the widows' and other conservative investors' friend — a solid public utility offering a basic service to a growing population.

Then came a fixation by the public on the development of space age electronics. In the nineteen fifties a few brokerage firms such as David J. Greene & Company "discovered" AT&T. These brokers figured — and rightly so — that AT&T's research and development arm, Bell Laboratories, and its equipment maker, Western Electric, were deep in the exciting new technologies. Thus from a sound public utility AT&T suddenly switched from being called old Mother Bell into a glamorous go-go girl for a time.

The price of the share rose sharply in relation to dividends because of this new look as a growth stock. The widow who owned AT&T at a price of around $28 a share where it lingered in the early fifties suddenly found herself with a stock that rose to $40 in 1959, to $70 in 1961, to $75 in 1964, and fell to around the $50 level in 1969. (These figures are adjusted for some stock splits.)*

The decline in the years since 1965 came after investment men decided that AT&T had lost some of its appeal. One reason was that the government began to threaten antitrust action and also began to give the company trouble about rate increases. In 1969 the shares were back to a level where they paid high dividends in relation to price, and hence once more were the widow's friend, and not a growth stock with dramatic implications.

Thus the point to remember is that fast-growth stocks usually do not pay high dividends for the simple reason that shrewd investors have found them before their growth potential was widely realized, bought them in quantity and thus forced the price up, well beyond the point of a favorable yield. Their hope is that earnings will grow fast over a year or so justifying not only today's high price but also higher prices later.

IBM is a prime example of a growth stock that sometimes pays about a one percent dividend return each year, plus an occasional stock dividend. No investor would buy IBM for a high dividend yield the way widows bought AT&T in the early nineteen fifties. The advocates of IBM buy because they have faith that the stock price will rise as earnings increase. So far, IBM has justified their faith in most years.

Therefore before you approach a broker you should know your

*Dividends: 1959: $1.58; 1961: $1.73; 1964: $1.95; 1965: $2.00; 1966 and 1967: $2.20; 1968 and 1969: $2.40; 1970 and 1971: $2.60, adjusted for splits.

investment objective. You cannot have high dividends, no risk of price downturns and assured fast growth in the same stock. You should consider the following three points:

1. Do you want to protect your principal and receive a specific income each year? Then you may want bonds with fixed interest; or you might want to try relatively high dividend-paying stocks with a little expected growth as a sweetener, like AT&T in recent years.

2. Can you afford to take more risk and receive low or virtually no cash dividends in exchange for the chances that the price of the shares will increase to give you a capital gain as far as taxes go? (See Chapter 16.) Your tax bracket will be a matter of inquiry, perhaps, by your broker.

3. Perhaps you need a combination of the two investment approaches, mixed to suit your taste like a good martini. Your broker might suggest some pivotal shares paying satisfactory dividends, and then some fast-growth stocks to help achieve an increase in your total capital as a help to combat inflation.

So much for the amount you can invest and your aims. The broker will be sizing you up in other ways: 1) young, middle-aged or old; 2) married, or unmarried; 3) homemaker or career woman; 4) your psychology — whether you are prepared to take risks or are conservative. Are you the nervous, jumpy type? 5) Your investment know-how — whether you have ideas of your own and pick your stocks yourself, or whether you indicate you will rely on the broker, your husband or others.

Such factors — judgments, since they are based on educated guesses — will enter your broker's estimate of you as a customer and color his ideas about the stocks he might suggest. His suggestions may not turn out to be the shares, or the types of investment that you think you should own. Perhaps you have more experience, knowledge of the market and determination than he credits you with. If so, assert yourself.

These are matters you should think out before you approach

a brokerage firm. In fact, it's a good idea to write down your ideas or questions before you sit down at a broker's desk.

What will your broker be like — apart from the obvious physical makeup? Naturally brokers come in all shapes and sizes, all ages from about twenty-five up through about sixty-five when most of them retire. He may be happily married; he may beat his wife in which case he probably dislikes most women intensely. He can be humorous or earnest; forceful in personality or pleasantly shy. He probably dresses quite well, is clean shaven and does not look like a hippie. Brokerage firms do demand presentable appearances from their employees who deal with the public.

These days he probably has a college education behind him and perhaps has taken some graduate courses. Oddly enough, he may also have an unusual working background. Men from many different professions switch to the brokerage business, either because they become bored with their jobs or because they believe there is more money to be made in the investment field. The ranks of some recent brokerage firm training programs include former college professors, actors, publishers, engineers, accountants, clergymen, retired army and navy officers, newspapermen, businessmen who had their own firms. What lures them? The fascination of investments and the chance to make a larger income, plus the fact that as brokers they work, in a sense, for themselves.

Depending on the firm, a broker can be called a registered representative, an account executive, a customer's man or some other appellation. To the New York Stock Exchange he is a "registered representative," a title the exchange likes because it indicates that he has been "signed up" so to speak. It means that (if he is young or middle-aged) he has gone through a formal training program given either by the brokerage firm or by an educational organization, that he has taken formal exams after the training to prove his knowledge both of New York and American Stock Exchange regulations, and that he has acquired some general knowledge and experience. He also must take exams indicating his knowledge of over-the-counter transactions, under the jurisdiction of the NASD — National Association of Securities Dealers.

The fact that he is a registered representative does not mean that he can prevent you from losing money, or even put you into stocks guaranteed to perform the way you expect, especially if you have very elaborate aims such as doubling your money every time you buy a stock. He can point you in the right direction in accordance with your investment aims. Remember that he is not necessarily a keen judge of the market, a student of economics, or a creative thinker. To be a really fine broker he should combine these qualities with the ability to analyze a particular company. I am sorry to tell you that brokers with such ability are rare, so rare that one of my favorite brokers once said to me: "I know most of the leading brokers in New York, and I can count on the fingers of my two hands the number I think are superior." (Modestly, in naming them he did not include himself.)

All this makes it important for you to select your broker carefully, not on his looks, the cut of his suit, his golfing ability, or his friends. It also is another reason why you should learn as much as possible about investments yourself.

If it is so hard to find an exemplary broker, how do you pick one? To put it humorously, you should try to select a broker who will fit your ideas comfortably like an old shoe. Naturally you want someone who is pleasant to you, helpful, and doesn't growl with impatience if you ask questions. You know that some people appeal to you immediately because of their spontaneous enthusiasm about their job and their willingness to be helpful.

You want someone trustworthy and reliable. Most member firms of NYSE employ only trustworthy individuals as account executives (barring a small percentage of sour lemons or bad apples), and generally you should deal only with a member firm of the New York Stock Exchange. An account with a member firm provides you with some safety measure in that the exchange has a fund to insure against any losses to customers through the failure or financial embarrassment of a member firm. Also, the exchange regulates its member firms (surprise audits, rules about capital needed, etc.), and when you have a complaint it investigates thoroughly. It also provides for arbitration — an inexpensive way for disputes to be handled by impartial judges without the need for lawyers (see pages 256–259). Member firms must arbitrate a dispute with a customer if the customer chooses, and the decision is legally binding in most instances. The American Stock Exchange also provides for arbitration.

Almost every broker would be vitally interested in a wealthy widow who could invest $1,000,000; but you want a broker who will show interest in you as a small or novice investor (or both). Many of the big brokerage firms are well geared to handle the small investor; more so than smaller firms who make their money out of a few large accounts. Thus you may fare better with a big firm. All brokers hope that little investors will become big investors because as mentioned before their welfare lies in commissions; and after all, in a few years you might well inherit, receive as a gift, earn, etc., more than the small amount you have to invest at the present. If your broker does do a good job for you over the years but you yourself cannot bring in a big sum for him to handle, you can always recommend your wealthy friends to become his customers.

Beware of a broker who "churns" — a method of persuading you to buy and sell so often that you don't make much money and yet the rapid turnover of stocks in your portfolio brings him big commissions. This is unethical, and as you gain experience you can sense if a broker is advising you to trade too often. Generally the new investor doesn't have to worry about this because she plans to keep her shares for a while, and at least for the six months' capital gains period.

You want a broker whose firm has the reputation of turning out good research so that he can provide you with sound material on stocks. Generally a broker can be no more effective than the research his firm turns out, for a very simple reason. He has so many customers that he cannot spend much time doing research himself, beyond listening to rumors, reading his firm's research material, and keeping up with what's happening on the ticker and the news service. Good research by a brokerage firm is important to the small, inexperienced investor because she cannot afford or cope with the expensive advisory services available to big investors who can pay fancy fees.

If you are a new investor you probably want advice on specific stocks, on market techniques, as well as proper timing. You need a little fathering, but that doesn't mean your broker should be an older man. Often very young brokers building up their customer lists can give you more of the type of help you need than an older man who has plenty of wealthy accounts to keep him busy. A broker who is a little hungry for business might be your best bet.

As we pointed out earlier one of the worst mistakes a new investor can make is to buy the best stock at the wrong time. In other words the smart investor doesn't rush to buy a stock as it hits its record high price. I think this is the biggest mistake that small, unsophisticated investors make — the jump on the bandwagon psychology. If your broker tells you that a good stock like AT&T or Du Pont is too high priced at the time to buy, listen to him. If you insist he might weakly shrug his shoulders and let you buy it without further argument, on the theory that it is a good all-round, all-time stock; but you are making a mistake. A superior broker would give you a good dispute on the point.

Let's take a fine growth stock like IBM as an example. IBM could have been bought at a price of 70 in 1960. It dropped from 150 to 78 in the trough of the 1962 stock market decline — the so-called Kennedy market break (see page 37), obviously a good time to buy it. Then it rose again to reach a new historic high of 375 in 1968: not a good time to buy, since in 1970 it dropped to as low as 218. Today, in 1972, it sells at around 384.

Thus in a short space of a year or a period of years good stocks can swing widely in price. The company is the same; its earnings probably (as in the case of IBM) continue to be good. An effective broker would keep you from buying IBM shares at their high point. Yield to his experience. He has a "feel" for the market, based on experience, which (at the beginning at least) you probably do not.

What about women brokers? The New York Stock Exchange reports that its member firms have 49,000 registered representatives, and about 1,800, or less than 1 percent, are women. By these measurements the investment world still is very much a man's domain. However, don't overlook the possibility of having a woman broker. To compete in the business and keep her job a woman broker usually has to be more adept, I think, than the average male broker. True, the proportion of outstanding male brokers probably runs higher than it does among female brokers, but you can be sure that a woman broker has to be good, though she may not be the "superior" type of broker that is a *rara avis*.

It has long been my contention that the wise woman investor starting out should use two brokers. After all, advice from two sources can be better, or at least more educational, than from one. A woman likes the feeling of two men vying for her attention; well, why not two brokers? Or she could use a male broker and a woman broker. Naturally she should not mention the fact that she has two brokers to anyone because, quite frankly, brokers don't like the idea. But they need never know if the customer handles the matter with discretion. If your friends ask who your broker is, turn on an enigmatic, Mona Lisa smile.

Suppose you are undecided about investing in a certain stock. You can ask the question of each broker. If both consider the investment wise, then you have the advantage of a double green light, which could mean you are on the right road. If one reacts strongly against such a stock, then the caution light goes on. You should slow down and think before making a move. Which broker is right? Situations like this can happen more often than you think. It wakes the investor up to the fact that investment judgments vary widely; an eye-opener for the novice.

If you think of it on the basis that the stock market is an auction place where there usually is a buyer for every seller — at a price — you realize that differences of opinion make a market, and win or lose fortunes. It makes investment life that much more interesting. Often you will learn that one mutual fund, supposedly run by experts, is buying a large block of a certain stock, while at the same time another respected mutual fund is selling shares of the same stock. Similarly two brokerage firms can come out at the same time with diametrically opposite suggestions. For example, one broker might suggest Avon, a name familiar to many housewives because it makes cosmetics sold in the home by representatives. Avon stock has a splendid growth record. Broker number one who says "Buy" is contradicted by broker number two who says, "Too high," and shows you a chart like the one in Figure 7. Then he suggests another cosmetic company whose stock has not risen so high.

Which do you buy? You are faced with a quandary; but if you have been a customer of the two brokers for a while you probably have come to a conclusion about which one performs more efficiently and which one has ideas most suitable to your own.

One of my friends uses one broker because the firm publishes such fine research material. "As far as I'm concerned," she says, "the broker is only a glorified order taker." She has a second broker who occasionally provides her with interesting, creative ideas for growth-type investments. With two very different brokers she has been successful in her investing.

Be like this woman and don't expect too much from your broker, especially at the beginning of your relationship with him. At present member firms of the stock exchanges are so busy that many mistakes have been made — clerical errors — so much so that you probably have heard from indignant friends about the months they waited to receive stock certificates, about monthly statements that contained terrible errors in their accounts and the difficulty they had straightening out the trouble, plus the apparent lack of interest by sometimes irascible brokers.

Figure 7. Avon Products, Inc.

Unfortunately most brokerage firms did not computerize early enough to prepare them for the spiraling pace of business in the past five years and this has been the chief reason for their often inefficient operations. Another reason is the heavy load of clerical work traditionally relegated to "back office employees" not equipped to do the job. For years brokerage firms hired young and often unmotivated girls and boys right out of high school for the low-paid, dull clerical jobs. Their bright young people were channeled into jobs as registered representatives or as analysts where they could put their college education and personalities and ambition to work for the firm. This situation has caught up with many brokerage firms: now they are vying for good back office help and paying much higher salaries, as well as working such employees hours overtime to catch up with the flood of paperwork. In a few years, computerization and streamlined techniques probably will eliminate these headaches.

The subject of new corporate stock issues has caused many of the recent difficulties for brokers and bad relations with customers. Many new investors open brokerage accounts with the starry-eyed hope of participating in new issues, the hot-shot stocks they have heard their friends discuss. Don't be fooled. Most new issues are put out by small companies. Let's say Super Atomic Electronics offers 1,000,000 shares of stock at $10 each through a group of 50 leading brokerage firms. Suppose that each brokerage firm agrees to sell 20,000 shares of the stock. A big brokerage house has perhaps 100,000 customers; a moderate-sized one has 50,000 or less. If the 50 firms average 50,000 customers, then they could provide each investor on their lists with only 2/5 of a share of the new "hot" issue.

Do you get the point? New issues are usually so small that even big brokerage firms only have a few thousand shares to allot among their customers. Therefore they will give their old and large customers the first chance at the new issue. You can be sure that if it is a good issue and if you are a small, new investor you will not be given the chance to buy a single share at the offering day price. Knowing this, you won't be disappointed or angry if your broker shakes his head when you ask. It is not his fault that you cannot buy Super Atomic Electronics at the offering price of $10, even though you might see it rise to $25 in a day or a week.

You can help your broker and get better service by learning the ropes — a trite way of saying you should know some of the lingo of investing and the technicalities. Here are some of the basics to remember.

DISCRETIONARY ACCOUNTS. Some of your friends may tell you that they have turned over their money to a broker, Mr. So-and-So, and he has done *so* well with it. He doesn't let them know what he does but just sends them a monthly statement showing the status of the account. It's *so* convenient! Stop right there. What they have is a discretionary account. Don't ever turn your money over to the discretion of a broker. The only possible exception is if you are going to be away for a few months you could leave written instructions that he could buy and sell certain stocks at his discretion if they are in a certain price range.

	April 1955	Jan. 1958	Aug. 1958	Oct. 1958	July 1960	July 1962
Listed stocks	70	50	70	90	70	50
Convertibles	...	...	...	...	...	...
	Nov. 1963	March 1968	June 1968	May 1970	Dec. 1971	
Listed stocks	70	70	80	65	55	
Convertibles	...	50	60	50	50	

Table 8

Most brokerage firms do not permit their registered representative to handle discretionary accounts except 1) for close members of their family or 2) with special permission. Furthermore, a reliable broker would require you to sign a letter excusing the firm of any responsibilities if he exercises discretion.

In other words, you can take your broker's advice but you must make the decision on a particular investment, since you must accept the final responsibility in any event.

MARGIN ACCOUNTS. Buying on margin means buying on credit. The amount of credit a brokerage firm can extend depends mostly on the Federal Reserve System, which sets the margin rate. Table 8 is a list of the margin rates in some recent years.

When speculation is rampant, as it was during the early part of 1968, the rate is inclined to be high — such as the 80 percent level indicated. It means you must put up about 80 percent of the price of a stock you buy, and the brokerage firm can lend you 20 percent. However, if the price of the stock goes down the broker can call upon you to put up more cash or more securities to back your account. If you do not put up such cash quickly he can sell out your shares and recover the full amount he advanced you, and you have little recourse.

Some firms traditionally require somewhat higher margin rates than those set by the Federal Reserve. Many brokerage firms will not permit women customers to use margin accounts, a kind of discrimination against women. Some refuse to extend margin-trading privileges to unmarried women; others extend them to married women only with the written consent of a husband. The reason probably is that brokers have had some unpleasant experiences with certain women customers. New investors should avoid margin trading.

TYPES OF ORDERS. Your broker probably will ask you what type of order you want when you buy or sell shares, or he may assume that you know the differences. A market order means that you want to buy or sell at whatever price is going when your order reaches the floor of the exchange. A day order states a specific price to buy or sell, and must be exercised that day, if possible at the stated price, or better. It expires at the end of the day. You must contact your broker again, if you want to renew the order. And an "open" or GTC order carries a specific price at which you want to buy or sell the stock but remains open until canceled (GTC: good till canceled). Usually even a GTC order expires after about six months and then you must renew it if you still wish to buy or sell the shares.

A *stop order* is a useful tool for every investor. Suppose you own a stock and you have decided to sell if it falls a certain number of points; you can order your broker to put a stop order in at that lower price. Suppose you have bought a stock at 50 and in a short time it has risen to 55. You have made a 10 percent gain and you want to protect it. You can tell your broker to sell at a price below 55, say at 54 if it drops to that level. Suppose the stock fails to rise further and suddenly drops to 52. On the way down your stop order automatically becomes a market order and is exercised. Often it will sell you out at the hoped price of 54, but if the market happens to fall very swiftly and there are other stop orders dated ahead of yours at around 54, your order could be exercised a little lower in price, a disappointment naturally.

Still, the use of a stop order gives an investor a measure of protection against serious losses and often helps get her out of the market with some profit. As a stock price rises, many wise investors place stop orders a few points below the current market price. As the stock continues moving upwards in price they raise the price on the stop order, thus giving them protection.

Your broker will ask you whether you want the stock registered or not. By all means, because of the bookkeeping difficulties these days, ask that the stock be registered in your name. If the shares are registered in your name the company will mail dividends, interim reports, annual reports and proxy statements directly to your home — all important to keep you alert about your company's progress.

Your broker will also ask whether you want the firm to keep the shares or whether you want them delivered to your home. It is much better to leave the registered shares in the custody of your broker. It makes it easier to sell them. Also, unless you have an unusually safe place, like a metal safe or a nearby safe deposit box, keeping stock certificates can be worrisome. (If you are not convinced read in pages 265–268 about the expensive and time-consuming procedure if you lose stock certificates.) And even though the broker holds the physical certificates, all mailings from your company will come to you as the registered owner.

Usually only sophisticated stock traders who buy and sell constantly for quick profits leave their shares with the broker registered in the so-called "street name." This means that they are held by the broker in the name of the firm, though credited to the customer's account. The dividends are paid directly to the brokerage firm, which then credits them to the stockholder's account or mails a check covering them to the customer. Registration in the street name also means the customer may not receive all the written material the company issues.

Be sure to keep the statements that you receive each month from the brokerage firm, showing the price at which you bought or sold shares and the names of the shares, etc. You will need such statements for tax reasons. Also you should make sure they are correct, so check them carefully each month.

You must also learn the dividend dates for your shares and keep track, checking them off as they are received. Otherwise you might miss some payments, especially these days when the U.S. mail has become so tardy and inefficient. Some dividends arrive in envelopes with windows looking like bills, so don't throw them away by mistake.

The last and perhaps most timely hint for creating good relations with your broker: abide by the five-day rule. He will undoubtedly explain this to you when you place your first order because of its importance to his welfare — and his nervous system.

The rule is that you must pay by check or cash for stock within five business days after the date of purchase. Leeway is permitted for weekends. The five-day rule works like this:

Date of Purchase	Payment Date
Monday	Monday
Tuesday	Tuesday
Wednesday	Wednesday
Thursday	Thursday
Friday	Friday

In other words, you can forget about the weekends since they are not business days. Probably the day you place an order, if it bears a price at or near the market level, the trade of your stock will be consummated — either bought or sold. Your brokerage firm will put a confirmation statement into the mail that day which should reach you the following morning or a day later. Still, the five-day rule applies no matter how fast or slow Uncle Sam's mail delivery is. So you have to do your own counting.

If you fail to pay by the required time, the broker will telephone you in annoyance. If you continue to be tardy he can sell the shares without letting you know, not a happy situation. Don't try to wheedle extra days from him because it can spoil an otherwise pleasant relationship, get him into trouble with his firm, and even result in your having to pay interest for the late arrival of your money, or lose the stock. He could decline to continue handling your account. Make sure your check arrives by the required date, or take the money in person, which is what I often do. And if you are selling shares and you have them at home registered in your name you will have to take them to your broker within the five-day limit.

8 | Analysts without Couches

Behind nearly every successful husband there's a good wife; behind nearly every excellent broker there are efficient stock market analysts.

Good brokers are so busy contacting their customers, watching the market, and making investment decisions that they don't have time to do much basic analysis themselves. Thus they depend largely upon the research departments of their firms. If the firm is too small to have an adequate research department then a broker can utilize other investment advisory services for a fee.

Investment analysis has changed vastly over the last thirty years, so much so that the analyst today is quite a different breed from his counterparts before World War II.

Back in the nineteen thirties, many investors lost a great deal of money, partly because of the depression, but partly too because companies in those days did not have to provide their shareholders with much information. There were a few leading brokers in favor of tighter governmental reins on securities, after the 1929 debacle. One of them, the late Charles E. Merrill, founder of today's largest brokerage firm, Merrill Lynch, Pierce, Fenner & Smith, put into practice several ideas to protect the small investor and help Wall Street regain some of the respect it had lost because of the crash in 1929.

One of his ideas, carrying out the firm's slogan "investigate before you invest,'' was that a brokerage firm should build up a good research department and offer its services free of charge to small and large investors. Out of this research, of course, should come a large amount of published material, brochures on investing, analysis of various industries and companies, periodical write-ups of individual companies. Merrill even launched a magazine for investors called *Investor's Reader,* still published by the firm.

He also believed that analysts should go through a training program along with young brokers. Hence his firm was among the first to have a formalized training program for young men, usually right out of college or the armed forces, who were interested in making the securities business their profession.

The trainees were rotated among departments to get the feel of the business; they attended lectures given by partners of the firm and outsiders; they took a course in public speaking to teach them to think on their feet and develop poise to meet the public; they also passed an exam approved by the New York Stock Exchange. They were encouraged to study outside: to take graduate courses at local universities, for instance, for which the firm would pay the tuition. In other words the emphasis suddenly became education.

Other large firms took the cue. Those that at first couldn't afford such training programs often hired graduates of Merrill Lynch's program by offering them higher salaries or commissions.

Today, analysts usually go through such a training program. However, I remember as recently as the mid-fifties talking to a partner of a well-known brokerage firm which might be described as medium sized, with a few branches outside New York. The partner told me that only one man in the firm devoted himself to research, and only part time at that, because the analyst was allowed to have some customer accounts.

Handling accounts with one hand and doing research with the other could hardly result in much analysis on the part of that firm. Unfortunately, Wall Street brokers until very recently focused much more attention on where the money is — in the hands of investors who can be induced to trade — than on research to help insure good investments.

The point of this statement — and of the open cynicism it reflects — is that a new investor must make sure that the firm she deals with has a good research department or utilizes good outside services. Such information can be found by asking businessmen in your community, quizzing the local banker about his attitude towards various brokerage firms, judging for yourself.

The investment industry has taken a big step towards more professional research with the launching some years ago of a program which leads to a degree for analysts called Chartered Financial Analyst — CFA. This move was launched, many years after the death of Mr. Merrill, because some leading analysts thought that the profession needed more prestige and a little more formality, plus the nice-sounding letters to be placed after their names. Without a doubt, an analyst with the CFA degree can command a higher salary than a man without it. Furthermore it separates the very young analysts, still uneasy with their slide rules, from experienced men.

The training for the CFA calls for intensive study and the taking of three exams in a period of three or more years. Study doesn't necessarily make a great or even good analyst; there's a little more to it than that, such as creativity and imagination. But if your brokerage firm's analyses are issued by some men with CFA after their names, you can be sure that at least they have gone through about the best training that Wall Street offers at present.

The usual big brokerage firm's research department might consist of a large room filled with analysts — perhaps a dozen seniors assisted by another dozen trainees or assistants, plus an assortment of staff: a librarian (who perhaps has some assistants), one or two statisticians who keep charts and work on market averages; an economist who devotes himself to general trends (political, economic, world); perhaps some portfolio planners who answer inquiries from the public and analyze individuals' stockholdings; and often a writer or two, attached to the department to edit and improve the abundant publications issued by the analysts. The department probably is headed by a senior partner (or vice-president of the firm) assisted by several experienced men who also hold titles in the firm. They are the heirs apparent of the top job in the department.

Each analyst is assigned a particular area. Generally, brokerage firms break down the nation's businesses into some major groupings — railroads, public utilities, financial companies (such as banks, commercial finance, insurance companies) and industrials. One analyst, aided by an assistant, might cover the railroad business. On a par with him and probably sitting nearby would be a man assigned to cover other forms of transportation such as airlines, trucks, buses.

At one time the three transportation areas — railroads, airlines and trucks — might have come under the aegis of one analyst — a busy man. Today the importance of airlines and trucks has grown tremendously in relation to railroads, and the legal, political and economic factors governing their investment merit have become much more complicated than twenty years ago. At the same time railroads have been undergoing many changes, too. Some have withdrawn almost entirely from the passenger business, generally a losing proposition. Railroads know how to carry cattle profitably and even without making them change trains but they cannot make money from human cargo in most cases. Some have been forced by states to continue operating commuter trains despite their claims of heavy losses. Mergers have strengthened some railroads. Others have improved their finances by changing into conglomerates like Northwest Industries, which operates the Chicago & Northwestern Railway, and has some unusual sidelines like making men's underwear, chemicals, and electrical components.

In other words, railroad stocks these days have become much

more like industrial stocks, giving them an entirely new investment look, not to mention the difficulty in analyzing them.

The second major grouping consists of public utilities. They have not changed as much as the railroads in that they have not tended to diversify but have stuck pretty much to their own fields, serving consumers with basics like electricity, telephone, gas, water, atomic energy. In the typical brokerage firm a senior analyst would devote himself to utilities, including space-minded AT&T, which does have some elements of a two-headed company — a public utility in one aspect, a scientific instrument company on the other.

In the third group there are the financially oriented companies, which would also come under the eye of a senior analyst, perhaps with some assistants. These include a wide variety of companies like commercial banks, insurance companies, small loan companies, commercial loan companies, credit unions, pension funds, savings and loan companies — all money oriented. Such companies, including mutual funds, are important in many ways to a brokerage firm. Some offer investment opportunities for the firm's individual customers; all continually make investments themselves; some borrow in the money markets.

By far the largest and most disparate group falls into the all-embracing category of "industrials." These can range from a relatively new company like Kentucky Fried Chicken, which issued stock publicly a few years ago, to General Motors, the world's largest industrial company* with $14 billion assets and 286,000,000 common shares worth $84 each or a total market value of almost $24 billion during 1972.

Twenty years ago it was relatively simple to break down the industrials into subcategories that could be handled by an analyst. For example, one man might be assigned to the automotive companies, such as GM, Ford and Chrysler, and the many auto

---

*AT&T is the world's largest company in terms of assets because of its heavy investments in power plants, communications equipment, etc. But GM ranks as number one in terms of sales. Furthermore, AT&T is classed as a utility and GM as an industrial.

equipment-makers ranging from companies who make auto springs, to safety glass, to tires. Another man might handle the steel companies: the half-dozen major ones led by U.S. Steel; the more numerous specialized ones; other metal producers like Anaconda, and fabricators like Bridgeport Brass (now part of National Distillers, an example of diversification).

A young analyst might cover the vagaries of cyclical industrial groupings such as the machine and machine tool industry. The sale of machine tools often indicates economic trends since these companies receive the orders months in advance to build machinery for new products, to handle new processes or replace old equipment with more efficient inventions.

Entertainment companies would be another category. Rising interest in them in the past few years indicates that consumers have more leisure and more money to spend than some years ago. Broadcasting companies, moviemakers, and publishers are included in this group.

Tobacco and food companies constitute another very important part of any research department coverage, along with department stores, construction companies, etc.

Generally, when a young analyst is assigned to the investment research department he doesn't have a choice but is placed in an available slot. However, later he probably moves to other groups to widen his experience before he takes a final assignment.

Often as he progresses in a department he will become restless and look around for a higher paid or more responsible job elsewhere. There is quite a fluidity of movement among analysts who go from firm to firm until they obtain coveted status as senior analysts, or later a chance to head a department as a partner or vice-president. As a department head an analyst probably earns $40,000 plus a share in the profits. The pay is good, though not as good as the commissions a broker can make in an active market.

This, then, is how the research department of your broker's

firm works. It is a stimulating place, constantly changing to keep pace with business evolution; it makes for an atmosphere that encourages study and professional growth.

What are some of the tools the analyst uses? First, like you, he reads the annual reports of companies; but many more than you do, since he takes responsibility for a large group in his particular field of specialization. He also has available to him the regular reports published by Standard & Poor's — yellow sheets they are called — keeping facts about every company updated. Perhaps when you express interest in a certain stock he will hand your broker such a yellow sheet to give you. He also has at hand basic manuals published by Moody's and Standard & Poor's, kept up-to-date by arrival of daily sheets. These provide him with the latest statistical information on the companies he covers, including changes in management, dividend rates, etc. When you visit your broker, and have a little experience in investing, ask him to show you these manuals, used so regularly by him and the analytical department. (They probably are also available in your public library.)

In addition, the analyst keeps abreast of current changes by following the financial pages of leading newspapers, such as the *New York Times* or the *Wall Street Journal*. If he commutes by train to a big city like New York or Chicago, he probably starts his day with newspaper reading. The *New York Times* is important because of its national circulation, plus company stories, analytical opinion, editorial judgments.

Outside of New York, the analyst for a big brokerage firm probably also reads a leading local paper, in whatever city he works. Since most of the leading brokerage firms operate in New York close to the stock exchanges, their analytical departments generally are in the city, too, so analysts tend to be oriented to the two major newspapers mentioned.

When he reaches his desk the analyst usually finds a pile of mail — research reports from other brokerage firms on the companies he follows, possibly invitations from companies to attend talks by their officials, inquiries from brokers or customers of the firm about certain stocks. During each day he is peppered with news items from the Dow Jones news wire, and from Reuters if the brokerage firm carries it.* Wires from out-of-town offices come in during the day, requiring quick answers about the value of certain stocks.

At the same time the analyst probably is working on some longer-term study of an individual company or an industry he covers, so his desk is apt to be piled with reference books, annual reports, and other reading matter.

He may also have to take an hour out for a talk at the New York Society of Security Analysts which holds daily luncheons at which speakers from companies present their corporate story and answer questions from the floor.

There is a great deal of local pride in some areas of the country, where growing companies often arouse the interest of investors in the area, and the analyst must be aware of them, too. Unfortunately, since the research facilities in the big brokerage firms are centered in New York, some local ventures do not get the good coverage they deserve. In this case alert brokers in other cities sometimes do their own analyses of such firms. However, many New York-based brokerage firms are now sending their junior analysts on business trips to explore such opportunities. While older analysts do travel, too, much of the legwork falls to the younger men in the department, who then return and write reports.

To supplement his basic study of the companies he covers, an analyst must talk to the companies' managers frequently and must even try to go through their plants occasionally. Since most corporate presidents and treasurers periodically visit New York, the analysts do have plenty of opportunities to meet the managers. Also many growth-minded companies need periodic infu-

---

*Reuters is the leading British news agency with worldwide coverage of news, somewhat like the two major American agencies, Associated Press and United Press International.

sions of capital, and to tell their story and drum up investor interest they either are happy to talk to analysts or retain public relations firms who help spread the needed information.

The younger analysts' frequent field trips help increase their knowledge of a company or an industry, keep them up to date on new developments. Sometimes the trips are junkets financed by the companies wanting the public to know about their operations. Other times the brokerage firms pay the way for their men.

In addition, these days analysts make much use of computers. Some leading firms have sent at least one bright young partner from the research department to be trained in computer programming. Then the research department receives regular time on the computer — time now needed for the handling of orders, bookkeeping, making out payrolls, and other accounting procedures. Small firms, that cannot yet afford their own computer setups for research, use outside computerized research on a rental basis. Thus Standard & Poor's offers Compustat to update analytical information on listed companies that can be processed through a firm's regular equipment. Each day an analyst might receive some of this computerized material about his companies, and these he has to analyze and fit into his thinking about them.

Several times each week the analysts of a research department have a staff meeting at which they tell the top officials of the brokerage firm about important changes in the outlook of an industry or of particular companies which they cover. They discuss the reports they plan to make, and exchange information. The economist for the firm may give a little talk about the latest development in the government's economic policies which might affect the stock market. These general exchanges are important because an analyst is busy keeping abreast of his own field and needs the give and take of such a flow of ideas.

Another source of information is the frequent luncheon meetings the analysts attend. Some meetings at which company presidents speak are sterile in that the presidents talk more like advertising men, extolling the company, its management and its prospects. But some, and only a few, company presidents provide the analysts with the basic data they need. If the speeches are not all that productive, the chance to talk with other analysts from other brokerage firms can be helpful. Some analysts faithfully attend all luncheon meetings devoted to companies in their industries; others send their juniors with questions to ask, and require that they write up reports on the meetings afterwards. Often these reports are sent out to customers of the firm.

In general, what are some of the points that an analyst considers before he writes a recommendation to his firm's customer to buy a stock?

Remember first that if he is wrong, and the price goes down, he suffers in reputation not only in his own firm but among other analysts covering the same field; this is damaging to the male ego. (There are some good female analysts, too, and they also hate to be wrong.) Secondly, the head of his department is not likely to forget a bad error of judgment because the brokers on the firing line — the registered representatives handling the orders — will hear from their customers. Angry customers not only can be unpleasant but they can do a firm's reputation damage.

For one thing, the analyst must look at a company and consider the number of shares available for purchase by the public. A big firm like Merrill Lynch, Pierce, Fenner & Smith, with customers numbering in the hundreds of thousands, isn't likely to suggest to all customers generally that the stock of a small company with few listed shares be bought. A large number of eager buyers could send the price of the shares up too fast. The large firm with many customers has a problem in this respect, whereas the smaller brokerage firm has the advantage.

The analyst will also consider profitability. Is the company making a satisfactory return on its equity capital? Is the rate of profit going up, remaining the same, or dropping? Looking further into the future, the analyst may believe that the company will make an increasing return on equity capital. Equity capital is the amount of stock it has outstanding.

The price earnings ratio also merits consideration. This is the current price of the stock related to current earnings, either actual or estimated.

Suppose, for example, that a stock sells at $50 a share and its annual earnings this year are expected to be $2 a share, then its price earnings ratio is 25 to 1. Next year the analyst figures that the earnings will rise to $2.50 a share. Then the stock's price earnings ratio will be a more favorable 20 to 1. On the other hand suppose that the analyst figures that the earnings will increase by a large amount to $4 a share, then the price earnings ratio would be about 12½ to 1.

Naturally, the price earnings ratio, if accurate, is meaningful not only to a stockholder interested in a particular company but also in relation to the price earnings ratios of other companies in the same field. Perhaps there is a good reason for the stock to be selling at a lower or seemingly more attractive price earnings ratio than other companies in the same industry. These factors could be — for instance — a product losing its competitive place, management disputes, the possibility of a crippling strike. As a result some investors may be selling the stock, dumping it in fact, to get their money out. The analyst possibly can determine what is happening and advise investors.

Sometimes a stock can be temporarily neglected by investors too busy putting their money elsewhere, with the result that its lower-than-usual price earnings ratio might indicate it is a good time to accumulate the stock.

For example, a few years ago the Ford Motor Company suffered a bad strike and its shares dropped sharply in price. However, some astute analysts and investors realized that once the strike ended the Ford management with its aggressiveness would make a swift comeback, and these people bought Ford shares at low prices. The low in the stock, in 1967 when the strike began, was 39, in a year when earnings dropped to 77 cents a share compared with $5.65 the prior year. A year later earnings more than recovered to $5.72 in 1968, and the price of the stock rose sharply, ranging from a low of 48 to a high of 60 that year. A good buy at or near its low in 1967? Yes. In early 1972 Ford shares sold at 74, responding to a good sales outlook, after having fallen as low as 37 during the 1969–1970 downturn.

Studying a company's management and judging its capabilities is also important to an analyst. It represents a very difficult and intangible part of analysis. Sometimes it comes down to playing golf with or knowing socially some members of the top management of a company.

Some questions an analyst might consider are these:

Is management young enough, aggressive enough and yet experienced?

Has it adapted easily and quickly to ever-changing market conditions?

Has it achieved relatively stable labor relations, so that strikes are kept to a minimum?

Has it been willing to invest substantial amounts of money into research and development (R&D), and has this paid off with results?

Has it spent money to keep plants and equipment at peak efficiency?

How is it considered by competitors? Do other companies try to steal away its top men because they are so able? Has the company been able to make itself financially attractive to its top men so that they will remain? Analysts usually can find out quite a lot about management by contacting a company's rivals. Often they will speak about the quality and fierceness of competition they are getting in the market.

Fortune magazine does some fine stories on individual companies and is a good source for investors interested in growth possibilities and in managerial achievements and in unusual approaches to problems.

In recent years some developments have been disconcerting not only to analysts, but also indirectly to investors. These you should know about because they are changing the emphasis in Wall Street research.

As mentioned before, the trend towards mergers, especially the creating of conglomerates with a wide variety of interests, has made analysis difficult. How do you judge a company that operates in five or six widely different fields, especially if the company doesn't break down its sales and earnings from the component parts? Furthermore, it's even hard to determine sometimes which analyst in a brokerage firm should cover such a company. Example: National Distillers, maker of whiskey and wines, has a subsidiary called Bridgeport Brass. Should this company be analyzed by a metal expert or a food analyst?

In recent years presidents of corporations have told me that they are so hounded by analysts from many different brokerage firms wanting to talk to them that they cannot grant some interviews. The tendency has been for the president to turn over analysts to the financial officers such as the treasurer or financial vice-president. Unfortunately, analysts and newspaper reporters have found that few financial officers can speak with much authority or even know much about what is going on in the productive parts of the company. By nature, treasurers are conservative and willing only to talk about their own small area of a company. Also, they tend to speak warily because they fear offending the president and thus endangering their own chances of promotion to the top spot. The result: inconclusive, lukewarm interviews to analysts and the press.

In the past few years the Securities and Exchange Commission has begun to take a stricter view about what companies should tell the public. For example, there was the Texas Gulf Sulphur case in which some insiders including directors and top officers apparently took advantage of their knowledge of a major discovery by the company to buy stock either for themselves or for institutions with which they were associated. The SEC in this *cause célèbre* cracked down hard, promulgating some new rules of disclosure.

The whole basis of the Securities Act originally was to help make sure the public received disclosure of facts necessary to make a sound investment judgment. The Texas Gulf case highlighted the importance of immediate disclosure to the public, as fast as humanly possible, along with the idea that directors must lean over to be scrupulous about not taking advantage of their favored position as insiders. There were other significant cases before this one, such as a case involving Curtiss Wright Corporation a few years ago. This instance involved a director alerting a broker that the dividend was going to be skipped (a bad sign) before the news made the wire systems of news agencies, which alerted the public.

Disclosure of corporate news apparently means getting the information to the major news services such as Associated Press, United Press International, and Dow Jones, the financial news service.

The rule of immediate and equal disclosure has hurt the relationship of analysts and corporate executives in that many of the latter now are loath to speak freely with their favorite analysts, for fear that they might say something that would violate SEC's new, strict rules. Corporate lawyers have had a field day, advising no comments, no speeches, no interviews, etc. Wall Street observers cannot help concluding that these factors have a muzzling effect on analysis.

Inside information — which might consist of offhand remarks to friends by people working in a company, chitchat on the golf course or over a drink at a club — cannot be stopped by any regulations. The need to gossip is too deeply ingrained in human nature. Along with inside information exist false rumors, which abound in Wall Street and which can be used for specific purposes by whoever starts a good one. They can emanate, of course, quite innocently from one man's imagination, or from idle talk at lunch or from deliberate placement. The two — inside information and rumor — are as closely entwined as honeysuckle growing around the branches of small trees. It's hard to disentangle them. Certainly it cannot be done by the SEC.

By strangling legitimate sources of news like the corporation executives, the SEC plays into the hands of the rumor peddlers, I believe. At the same time analysts are relying more on computers and their statistical agility. The result, I think, will be analysis based too much on the computer or too much on rumor, not on the happy in-between that might have been possible if the SEC had taken a more liberal stand.

Such trends make it even more important for the average investor to be aware of economic and political factors at work in the market. He must be aware that with computerization and the SEC rules, analysis will tend to become more static, more technical, less based on actual observation.

The difference between good analysis and superior analysis will come from 1) creativity on the part of the research men — the searching out of special situations or new factors in old companies ahead of other analysts; 2) the quick comprehension of economic and political trends that can influence the stock market; and 3) the ability to persuade investors to sell — to get out of the market in time. This last has long been a great weakness of Wall Street.

Research departments are always equipped at a given moment with buy suggestions. But once you buy, your broker will seldom tell you when to sell. This is odd because he makes a commission on the sale, too. No investor can make profits while he holds on to a stock because capital gains are created only upon the actual sale. Profits on paper may sound good, look good and make an investor happy but they are not a profit in terms of good green dollars until the stock has been sold. Nailing down these profits is important and yet so neglected by most brokers and analysts.

9 | The Mysterious Mr. Dow

Once you become interested in investing, a shadowy man named Dow will enter your life, along with a companion named Jones. You can forget about Jones, but Dow is inescapable. You will hear his name almost daily if you read the newspapers, listen to the radio or watch television.

For the rest of your life, in fact, the enigmatic Charles Dow probably will be an influence. Comments like these will become part of your daily investment knowledge as well as know-how: "The Dow lost 2 points." "The Dow gained 7 points." "The Dow has dropped 10 percent and Wall Street is worried." "The Dow has edged up to a new record level." (The last statement will make you feel good, although maybe a little apprehensive.) Soon you will notice with regularity whether your stocks tend to go in the same direction as the commentators say the Dow has moved. Generally they will.

The Dow Jones industrial average is not literally an "average" but is the total of the prices of stocks in a certain 30 companies in any given day, weighted to take into consideration stock splits, etc. These big companies and trading in them account for about 30 percent of the volume on the New York Stock Exchange in a typical day.

Look at the names of the Dow Jones industrials in 1972: Alcoa; Allied Chemical; American Can; AT&T; American Tobacco; Anaconda; Bethlehem Steel; Chrysler; Du Pont; Eastman Kodak; General Electric; General Foods; General Motors; Goodyear; International Harvester; International Nickel; International Paper; Johns-Manville; Owens-Illinois Glass; Procter & Gamble; Sears, Roebuck; Standard Oil California; Standard Oil New Jersey (now called Exxon); Swift & Company; Texaco; Union Carbide; United Aircraft; U.S. Steel; Westinghouse; Woolworth.

Obviously most of the companies on the list are sound, prestigious companies whose shares would be good investments. But their movements, grouped together in the Dow average, don't begin to show what some of the fast-growth speculative issues are doing as a group. This, of course, is a basic weakness in the Dow.

In addition to the DJI, as it is called, there is also a Dow Jones railroad average and a Dow Jones public utility average. The Dow Jones Industrial is the one which you will be aware of most quickly. It gives an indication of the market movement as a whole, not perfect by any means but a measure of direction of basic strength or weakness. It also provides an available yardstick to measure the performance of individual stocks. The investor who can say that his stock is outperforming the Dow on the upside is usually very pleased. The person who watches his favorite stock drop more quickly and more sharply than the Dow knows that something has probably gone awry with his investment judgment.

The thing to remember about the Dow is that by nature it tends to be conservative. Why not? The stocks comprising it are those of solid, generally well-heeled companies. Perhaps some have even outlived the years of their fastest growth, like the successful businessman who can't increase his income much on a percentage basis because it is already so high; nor can he grab a much bigger share of the market in his particular business because the government's antitrust sharpshooter would take action.

Though some of the stocks composing the Dow Jones average at any one time are growth-type investments, their pace cannot be expected to match the rate of little growth companies who can double or triple their income and still be small. In other words the investor must not expect Du Pont, though constantly growing, to double its sales; but the investor can perfectly reasonably have such hopes for some newcomers in new fields.

A stock market average like the Dow can be called weighted in that the component stocks are changed periodically to reflect stock splits and stock dividends that change the number of shares outstanding. Occasionally stocks are dropped and replaced. A merger might be one reason; lessened industrial status of a company could be another.

The average is calculated several times each market day by — guess whom? — Dow Jones, Inc., which also happens to publish the *Wall Street Journal* and *Barron's* and operates a news wire which ticks out the latest news affecting business into almost every brokerage office in the country — and in the world.

Who was Charles Dow?

Born in 1851, he was a thoughtful, shy, ambitious man who began his journalistic career in Providence, Rhode Island. Like many newspapermen of the late nineteenth century, he moved around to various towns and cities gaining experience. He worked as far west as Leadville, Colorado. Then, in the year 1880, he came to New York. After working as a financial reporter for the Kiernan News Agency, he organized a service of his own in 1882 with an acquaintance named Edward D. Jones, who had published newsletters for investors. Three years later Mr. Dow bought a seat on the New York Stock Exchange, which gave him a close view of the market and also an entrée into a quite exclusive group.* Membership in the NYSE has grown less exclusive in the years since, but it is still costly.

In the year 1889 Charles Dow took a major step: he started to publish a newsletter called the *Wall Street Journal*, which became the most influential of the financial publications, except

---

*The year he bought a seat the price ranged from $20,000 to $34,000: a substantial amount in those days. In 1929 the cost of a seat was a record $625,000.

for some of the banking letters in the late part of the nineteenth century and the beginning of the twentieth. In those days, remember, the leading bankers (headed by the Morgans) dominated financial thinking, mainly because they controlled most of the major businesses of the country. Their money, prestige and supposed economic knowledge gave them power, not eclipsed until antitrust laws broke up their "empires."

Much of the financial writing in the period was still based on personal judgment, guesswork, and rumor, plus occasional planted news. It wasn't until 1895, for example, that the New York Stock Exchange required that all of the new companies who wanted their shares listed must publish annual reports. The rule was not retroactive, so the big old-timers could escape such reporting.

A public utility named Kansas City Gas Company became among the first voluntarily to publish its profits "not less than twice a year." Even in the early nineteen hundreds a man like Henry Huddleston Rogers would say haughtily, "Just tell those people [the stockholders] that our way of doing business is to send out reports when we decide it is time for them to be seen." And pretty sketchy reports they were.

It doesn't take much imagination to realize the amount of looting of corporate treasuries, the lavish spending, or other improprieties that could occur in those days.

Remember that you as a stockholder are one of the owners of the company: stockholders were in the same position in 1890 and 1900, too, but managements of corporations so dominated companies that they could ignore stockholders except when they suddenly needed new money for expansion. It has taken years to break down some of this arrogance and indifference on the part of managements, and you will still find it in some companies, especially those owned largely by a family or a few large stockholders.

The breakthrough has come partly because of the rules set by the exchanges and later by the Securities and Exchange Commission (which came into being actively in 1934), and partly because following a series of financial panics (especially 1929) corporations realized they had to live more amiably with the public and raise money from stockholders. Over the years pressure for better financial disclosure had come from some responsible organizations like Dow Jones, Moody's Investors Service, and Standard & Poor's.*

Mr. Dow did not spend all those years in Wall Street (he died in 1902) without developing some valuable ideas about the stock market — namely the so-called Dow theory, of which the Dow averages are an integral part. Over the years since his death a cult of Dow theorists has grown up, and many of them have used his ideas successfully in investing or advising others how to invest.

While Mr. Dow was an articulate writer he never spelled out his theory concisely, which may seem a little odd. But remember he was a pioneer, operating at a time when financial news was not very accurate, up-to-date or even available in any quantity. Many investors operated blindly, as did the writers. In fact, he could be likened to a pioneer who went West to discover a gold mine, but didn't quite have the ability or the equipment to dig deeply enough for the lodes he hoped to find. That was left to some of his followers. Probably the most able interpretation was made by Robert Rhea, who dug deep to refine and form the raw nuggets of Dow's thoughts into what became a golden theory, probably the most successful in its application to the stock market.

In my early days in Wall Street (as a copyeditor for the *Wall Street Journal* in the nineteen forties) I kept asking experts where I could find out about Dow's theory from original sources. The answer was always, "Well, you wouldn't understand what Dow was saying so the best way is to read Rhea." Even that gentleman, however, I found a little vague.

---

*Today Moody's is part of Dun & Bradstreet, while Standard & Poor's is a subsidiary of McGraw-Hill.

Here in essence is the Dow theory as expounded by Anthony Tabell, a leading Wall Street analyst* who liked to use an analogy about the ocean and the beach.

Imagine standing on a beach watching the waves. As you ponder their ever-changing sameness, you wonder whether the tide is going out or coming in. There are ripples, waves, and then an ebb and flow. To find out what is happening you might pick up a piece of driftwood and poke it in the sand at the edge of the water, and then wait to see whether the waves break and send fingers of water higher on the beach or whether the sand dries because the waves are pulling back.

"Dow's conception," says Mr. Tabell, "of the behavior of the stock market was simply that it was similar to tides — that it was composed of major trends analogous to the tides themselves, intermediate trends analogous to waves, and minor trends analogous to ripples. He believed it was largely impossible to predict the direction of minor and intermediate trends, but that a study of these trends could be used to determine whether the major trend was up or down."

Suppose that after a high point (measured by the Dow industrial average) the prices reacted by falling and then after a while rallied again to a point below the first high and then dropped back to a point below the previous reaction level. The investor might consider this a warning or indication that the tide was ebbing for the market and that a downturn had begun.

Under the Dow theory, the action of the Dow industrial average must be confirmed by similar actions in the railroad averages; and sometimes such similar action would not come at the same time or even near it. In fact, in recent years one of the weaknesses of the Dow has been the railroad average, in that it has lost much meaning these days because of the decline of importance of the rail industry.

Mr. Tabell summarizes his thinking about the Dow theory this way: "Most users would agree, however, that its ability to call major turning points in the market, e.g., 1929, has been

*He was a senior vice-president of Walston & Company, a large brokerage firm.

extremely good. A moment's reflection will indicate that the theory has its greatest value where long and wide upward and downward moves take place. . . . Regardless of its merit, the Dow theory as applied to the present-day market is of great importance from a historical point of view. The theory was the first systematic recognition of the fact that stock prices follow trends, and that a trend, once established, tends to remain in force. It is this principle that underlies a good deal, though by no means all, of technical work."*

Take a look at the Dow Jones charts in Figures 8 and 9. The first (Figure 8) shows what the Dow had to say in terms of figures during the years 1929–1930 — the period beginning the great depression — and then through 1971.

If you had been a Dow theorist when would you have sold your shares in those years?

Figure 9 is a chart showing the four recent serious market declines: 1957, 1962, 1966 and 1969–1970. Would the market have given you a warning?

All this may give you an inkling of why Mr. Dow will become such a regular part of your investing life. Often your stocks will rise and fall for no apparent reason, and not even in the same direction as the Dow, like the ripples that move on the surface of the water with a fascinating waywardness. At other times there might be specific reasons for your stocks to move by themselves. For example, if suddenly the president of a company in which you owned stock died, the price might drop because some investors might believe that a succeeding management would be less effective. Or if your company suddenly announced a new product, the price might rise suddenly, well above any proportionate rise in the Dow average. Or perhaps over a few months' period you and other investors decide you can do better by selling and investing in another company in the same industry. This might drop the shares of one stock and

---

*Mr. Tabell contributed an interesting chapter on forecasting stock prices in a book called *The Anatomy of Wall Street*, edited by Charles Rolo and George Nelson (New York: Lippincott, 1968).

Moody's Investors Service

Figure 8

Wright Investors Service

Figure 9. The Stock Market and the Economic Cycle

boost the shares of the other over an intermediate period, all out of proportion to any market trend.

Generally over the long term you will find that if all stocks are moving up in price yours will tend to do the same, and in a long decline all shares will tend to weaken in price including your issues, even though they may be hot-shot specials.

The best way to follow the action of the Dow is in its own "home" — the *Wall Street Journal*. Read it every day, or at least once a week, and the charts will soon be telling you their story of market trends.

However, don't become so enamored of the Dow that you forget the growing importance of some other averages. Perhaps one of the most valuable to be used in connection with the Dow is the Standard & Poor average of 500 stocks, a much larger and more representative group than the companies included in the Dow. Since the S&P 500 also includes many small, new companies, it gives an indication of how they are faring.

Thanks to the computer age, the New York Stock Exchange and the American Stock Exchange have begun to compile their own averages. They include virtually the entire list of stocks listed on the exchange at any given time. They do not have the seasoning of the Dow but they are fast gaining adherents. Eventually, I think, they will emerge as the most useful.

Generally speaking, the investor should be aware that three types of influences affect the market. They might be summarized this way: 1) world events; 2) economic trends in the U.S.; 3) conditions in the market.

Sometimes world events — such as political upheavals, devaluation of some currency, a threat of war — will dominate the market. At other times economic trends within the United States — the business cycle, tightness of money, consumer intentions, etc. — will be the top influence. Then again conditions in the market will be paramount, such as overspeculation, sharp changes in earnings, lack of investment money. These factors, like waves on the ocean, must be considered in the changing tides evidenced by the various averages.

In recent years several types of growth-stock averages have been introduced and investors in the future probably will follow them more closely as opportunities open up in new fields. Ask your broker, if you are interested in the more speculative type of stocks, which growth-stock average he suggests that you follow.

One important idea has been stressed in recent years; namely that the stock market is not always a good indicator of business conditions. Proof of that came in 1962 when a sharp drop in the booming speculative market (the so-called Kennedy market break) came at a time when business conditions were very prosperous. The reverse can be true, also — the stock market can lag even when business is recovering, such as happened just before World War II and just afterwards, and perhaps this can be attributed to mass emotion — investors reacting with the same pessimism.

Generally, however, the fact remains that the Dow and other averages have broken sharply at times of business declines, and usually have given a little forewarning.

Whether you consider yourself a fundamentalist or use a technical approach to the market, the Dow and some other leading averages belong in your thinking. What fascinates me about Mr. Dow is that probably no man connected with the investment world is so well known to so many millions of investors; certainly not the heads of the big brokerage firms or the president of the New York Stock Exchange, not famous analysts, not the head of the Securities and Exchange Commission. Furthermore, I cannot think of any other man whose surname is connected with an important theory and yet who did not actually propound the theory.

Mr. Dow expressed his ideas primarily in editorials, and at one point he made a statement which I think might predict the future: "It is not impossible that with better knowledge, greater wealth and wiser methods the extent of the advance and of the decline may be smaller, but until human nature changes materially there is not likely to be abandonment of the law of expansion and contraction in business and discontinuance of its effects on the prices of stocks."

Happily, if he is right there will always be good swings in the market up and down, offering stockholders opportunities. In future years, however, my guess is that the swings may not be as vigorous as the ones in 1962 and 1969.

10 | The Feeling Isn't Mutual

In the past five years or so two trends have become apparent in Wall Street. Many brokerage firms, harassed by rising costs and bookkeeping snarls, definitely have lost interest in the small investor. Their clerical staffs cannot keep abreast of the sea of paperwork generated by ever-rising trading volume.

Consider the figures for trading on the New York Stock Exchange and the American Stock Exchange (see Table 9). Not included are 500,000,000 or so traded on smaller exchanges and the millions of shares of over-the-counter stocks traded each year — a vast number which has never been counted.

With such volume to keep them busy, no wonder that brokers have been less interested in cultivating the small investor. All of this presents a paradox because the army of investors has grown from perhaps 2,000,000 in the early nineteen forties to about 32,000,000 in 1972, mostly due to the "be-kind-to-the-small-investor" policy of many firms in earlier years.

At the same time mutual funds have multiplied in number and grown large in size, offering their shares to small investors. Brokers have helped this growth partly because they receive higher commissions for handling mutual fund sales than they do trading shares for a small investor, who buys odd lots or maybe a round lot of 100 shares occasionally. Furthermore, by putting the small investor into mutual funds the brokerage firm puts no strain on its own research department and lightens its bookkeeping load.

So you can expect that your broker might try to talk you into a good mutual fund. He will, of course, attempt to find out what type of mutual fund will suit your personality — a go-go growth fund, an old liner, or a fund that specializes in certain types of stocks, like science-oriented companies. This is supposed to give you the feeling that you are investing in a fund tailored to your needs or aims.

	NYSE	*ASE*
1950	655,300,000	114,900,000
1955	820,500,000	243,900,000
1960	958,300,000	300,600,000
1965	1,809,400,000	582,200,000
1968	3,298,700,000	1,435,765,000
1969	2,850,784,000	1,240,742,000
1970	2,937,359,000	843,116,000
1971	3,891,317,000	1,070,924,000

Table 9

Frankly, I do not like mutual funds except for the lazy investor who doesn't want to make the effort to do her own searching, or for the frightened investor inhibited about approaching the stock market on her own.

Anyone who wants the challenge of investing tends to avoid mutual funds for several good reasons.

Buying into a mutual fund — buying its shares — usually costs about 8 percent in fees, called the "loading" charge. Some funds have a little lower price tag than that, while some charge more. Generally funds cost quite a bit more than investment in stock. This you can see by comparing this 8 percent figure with the commission tables (Figure 16) for stock purchases on pages 268–269.

True, you are placing your money in expert hands in a fund, but for this handling each year you also pay a fee. The operating cost is high, to start with. The president, vice-presidents, the analysts, the bookkeeper, the transfer agent (usually a bank) receive high salaries. The fund must have an office, usually an impressive one which means high rent. It also employs experts such as accountants, lawyers, perhaps even a public relations firm. This overhead comes out of the profits or income from securities in which it invests your money and many other people's money.

In other words, with a fund you place a relatively expensive third party between you and your investments. It's like buying prepared potatoes au gratin in a package instead of peeling your own potatoes, cooking them, adding cheese and baking them in the oven.

With this in mind, let's define exactly what a mutual fund is. It's an investment company, regulated under the Investment Company Act. Generally speaking there are two types of investment companies: the open-end, or mutual fund type; and the closed-end, another species.

The mutual fund is the open-end variety because it issues an unlimited number of shares to meet the demands of buyers. If you, your best friend and exactly 1,000,000 other people each buy a share in the same mutual fund, the fund will have 1,000,002 shares outstanding. If half the people sell their shares then the mutual fund shares drop back to 500,001. In that sense, the mutual fund creates its shares on demand. Instant creativity, you might say.

The financial sections of major newspapers usually carry a brief listing of the best known of the mutual funds, but there are many others available whose prices can be learned through your broker.

One of the oldest and most prestigious funds is Boston based — Massachusetts Investors Trust, which operates several types of funds under its aegis. On a particular day you might find a listing like this for MIT (its nickname):

MIT   12   13

This range means that the fund will sell its shares that day at a price of $13 a share and will buy them at 12. The purchase price includes the 8 percent "loading charge"; there is no further charge when the shares are sold. A mutual fund by law must be ready to buy its shares back from a shareholder on demand.

The prices quoted change at least once a day for all funds, and some funds price their assets more often. The prices are based on the value of the underlying securities in the portfolio on that day.

The fund takes your money and invests it in securities; generally common stocks, though there are also bond funds. However, a fund always keeps a certain amount of money in the form of cash in the bank or in quickly negotiable government or corporate issues such as commercial paper.*

The mutual fund tends to keep only enough cash on hand to meet required redemption needs or to take advantage of sudden opportunities in the stock market. It likes to keep well invested in common stocks either for fast appreciation, or for high yield, or a combination of quality and growth, depending on the aims of the particular fund as outlined in the prospectus it issues.

The mutual fund shareholders receive notices that detail just what the dividend payment (usually paid quarterly) involves in the way of actual dividend income or capital gains, or both.

There are a small group of funds, about which your broker will not be apt to tell you — the so-called "no load" funds. These funds sell directly to the public from their offices, and not through brokers or mutual fund salesmen. Hence they do not charge the usual 8 percent loading fee, but you can join their ranks as a shareholder, usually without any fee. Naturally, like the load funds, they have overhead expenses which must be paid out of revenues received from their investments, so there is an operational cost involved.

Here are the names of seven well-known "no loaders" that might be worth investigation: De Vegh Fund; Drexel Funds; Loomis-Sayles Funds; One William Street Fund; Rowe Funds;

*Commercial paper are short-term issues sold to raise working capital by well-known companies such as General Motors, Standard Oil, CIT Financial. See Chapter 18.

LISTED	SYMBOL	INDICATED DIV.	RECENT PRICE	PRICE RANGE (1972)	YIELD
NYSE	TY	$0.89	30	33 - 28	3.0%

CAPITALIZATION: (12/31/71)

	(000)	(%)
($2.50)pfd.	$ 37,637	5.3
Com. & Surp.	b 675,027	94.7
Total	$712,664	100.0%

Shs. ($0.50)-(3/31/72)-18,991,627

NET ASSET VALUE PER SHARE:

	3/31	6/30	9/30	12/31
69	33.95	33.45	32.67	33.67
70	30.32	24.33	27.88	30.66
71	32.74	33.81	33.97	35.54
72	36.31	37.45		

DIVIDENDS:	RECORD	PAYABLE
0.19	9/24/71	10/1/71
0.21	12/21	12/30
1.52C.G.	1/21/72	2/28/72
0.18	3/24	4/1
0.18	6/23	7/1

Figure 10. Tri-Continental Corporation

LISTED	SYMBOL	INDICATED DIV.	RECENT PRICE	PRICE RANGE (1972)	YIELD
OTC	---	$0.42	12.46	15.56 - 12.46	3.4%

CAPITALIZATION: (6/30/72)

Com. & Surp. $2,019,579,432

Ctfs. ($0.333)-160,421,255

NET ASSET VALUE PER SHARE:

	3/31	6/30	9/30	12/31
69	16.16	15.73	15.18	14.82
70	14.49	11.68	13.37	13.46
71	14.54	14.32	14.06	12.52
72	13.12	12.59		

DIVIDENDS:	RECORD	PAYABLE
0.11	9/30/71	10/22/71
0.112	11/30	12/17
1.71 C.G.	12/31	2/11/72
0.097	3/30/72	4/28
0.097	6/30	7/28

Figure 11. Massachusetts Investors Trust

Stein, Roe & Farnham Funds; Scudder Stevens & Clark Funds. Your broker won't tell you about them because he wants to sell a fund that will pay him a commission to sell you shares.

The second major variety of investment companies consists of the so-called "closed-end" investment trusts. These companies issue stocks just like the regular corporations on the Big Board, and thus they are called closed-end.

One of the largest is Tri-Continental Corporation, listed on the exchange. The shares are bought through brokers just like the stock in any other company listed. Figures 10 and 11 show what kind of a record Tri-Continental had during the past ten years compared with MIT, a famous growth-type mutual fund, but not a go-go fund.

The investment trust, either closed- or open-end, thus offers you the strength of diversity— spreading your investment risk — along with expert handling of your investment expertise. The point is that you are paying quite a high price for this convenience — and in some cases too high a price.

That is why many brokers believe you can do better in the stock market using sound recommendations from a good brokerage firm. One such exponent is Donald Regan, president of Merrill Lynch, Pierce, Fenner & Smith, the nation's largest brokerage firm, which has grown large by catering to small investors.

"I think the small investor can do better by himself than he can investing in mutual funds. I think also he can outdo the S&P index of 500 stocks," Mr. Regan told me recently in an interview, in response to a question about mutual funds and his firm. For years Merrill Lynch studiously avoided selling mutual funds because the firm's founder, the late Charles E. Merrill, disliked them and believed his brokerage firm could do better for the small investor. He emphasized a large research department offering its services — facts and recommendations and portfolio reviews — free of charge.

In September 1969, Merrill Lynch finally began to sell funds to its customers; but as Mr. Regan's statement indicates it made the move with a certain lack of enthusiasm, a kind of "if you can't beat them, join them" philosophy.

Today mutual funds have increased their assets to well over $50 billion, and they have millions of shareholders. Naturally when a fund buys a block of stock as an investment through a brokerage firm the commissions are large — a business that brokerage firms don't like to do without. Initially Merrill Lynch offered about a dozen selected funds, watched over (interestingly enough) by a woman analyst in the research department.

One suggestion for the woman investor is this: take a small amount of your capital and buy a few shares of a mutual fund or a few shares of a closed-end investment company like Tri-Continental. Keep the shares for at least two years, while meanwhile you buy shares of some individual stocks with the remainder of your money. Then see if you agree with Donald Regan that the small investor can do better by himself than with the funds. In measuring results, remember to deduct the commissions on the stock and the loading charge for the fund shares.

These days the snowballing rate of inflation has caught up with so many investors that the average family faces the chilling thought that the value of its insurance policies has dropped sharply in terms of today's dollars. The man who felt secure with $50,000 of life insurance a few years ago realizes that the sum would hardly provide a living income for his wife and children, even supplemented by the social security payments they would receive. His wife obviously would have to use up the capital and might have to go to work.

This unhappy state of affairs has awakened many people to the need for regular investment — including the insurance companies.

The insurance industry has awakened slowly, however. When I wrote a few years ago that a man might do well to buy additional insurance through a term policy and invest the difference between that and the higher premium he would pay for ordinary insurance, the president of a large insurance company wrote me indignantly. He made it seem as if I were attacking motherhood by pointing out that insurance does not provide protection against the ravages of inflation. Enclosed with his letter was a brochure he had apparently written years ago citing the danger of investing and the possibility of another major depression. What a lot of nonsense!

As if to indicate that the more alert leaders of the insurance industry have become aware of inflation, most insurance companies are going into the mutual fund business. Some are starting their own funds; more are buying control of going funds or affiliating with them. This should be proof enough that the smooth-talking insurance salesmen realize that Americans know they cannot keep up with inflation just by buying insurance in additional amounts.

Today more and more insurance salesmen (as well as stockbrokers) will be talking to you about mutual funds. As a variation on the theme of combining insurance and mutual funds in a package deal, some companies have been formed to lend you the money — at high rates of interest — to set up long-term programs which you "pay" for monthly.

A much better way, I believe, is to make sure you have enough life insurance on your husband, and if you need more buy additional term insurance while you build up an investment program. But keep the two separate. In other words, first, make sure you have sufficient insurance coverage and second, invest regularly in stock—but bypass the mutual funds.

The new trend in Wall Street is for brokerage firms to sell life insurance as well as mutual funds and stocks. I suggest that you buy insurance from insurance companies and stocks from brokers, and not get involved in a package deal.

Furthermore, don't sign up for any contractual plans that tie you up for regular monthly payments, because they usually involve some sort of penalty if you cannot keep up with the program.

If you only have a small amount to invest, there is the New

York Stock Exchange's monthly investment plan. You can invest as little as you want (down to a minimum of about $40 every three months) and if you need to spend the money elsewhere there is no penalty.

If you still feel that you must buy a mutual fund, a point to remember is that insurance salesmen, since they have just recently begun to offer the funds, usually will not be able to give you a wide choice. And they will of course be biased in favor of the funds affiliated with the insurance company (or companies) which they represent. In contrast most big brokerage firms are prepared to handle a larger variety of funds. Also, since the brokerage firms' research departments have been studying funds for a much longer period than the insurance companies, they will have the edge in analysis (I believe) for a few years at least. Also, if you are interested in super growth-type funds, another point to consider is that insurance companies tend to be much more conservative in their investment outlook than do most brokerage firms. The go-go fund you might hear touted by your friends probably will not be handled by insurance salesmen.

Besides, for those persons who don't want the trouble or the excitement of investing for themselves, there is another way to relieve themselves of responsibility — a method known to many, many widows. Let a bank's trust department take over your affairs. It can be done by several methods.

Commercial banks offer investment-advisory services, combined if you wish with taking custody of your funds and sending you dividends, etc., from your investments. It's like the bus company slogan of "leave the driving to us."

Many large banks, starting with the big ones and more recently the medium-sized ones, have common trust funds. They will take sums of money such as $100,000 (and possibly as low as $50,000) and put the funds into stocks and other securities along with other trust funds. This master portfolio is managed continually by the bank's investment department. Some banks have several types of such funds — one for growth, another for investment safety through bonds, etc.

The idea of centralized investing of trust funds resulted from a desire of the banks to handle people's money with greater efficiency and offer them a broader basis of investment. The trend has been growing and within the next few years probably many small banks will make available common trust funds for relatively small sums of money. The fees for such funds generally are much lower than the loading charges of mutual funds.

Still another method of shifting investment responsibility is to hire an investment adviser. These advisers need not be as expensive as you might think: usually their service entails a small basic fee, plus a percentage of the capital gain achieved each year on your shares. The way such an arrangement ordinarily works is that you place your shares in the hands of your own brokerage firm, and your broker sells or buys the stocks recommended by the investment adviser. Thus you have the peace of mind of knowing your shares are held in safekeeping by the broker. If he thinks that the investment adviser is doing a bad job or trading you in and out too much he might warn you. On the other hand, since your adviser is paid partly on the results he obtains for you — the capital gains — he is not apt to trade merely for the sake of commissions, as a broker might do.

There are many well-known investment advisory services, such as John Magee, Inc. of Springfield, Mass., the Wright Investors Service, Standard & Poor's, and Moody's Investors Service. And all of these services offer another approach, as well as direct management of accounts: they publish regular advisory brochures, usually weekly, to which you can subscribe for a nominal amount each year. This might be a very helpful idea for the new investor.

Don't forget that subscriptions to investment advisory services as well as fees for managing accounts can be deducted from your taxable income. Thus if you are in the 30 percent tax bracket about one-third of the money spent is saved.

A final thought is this. It is foolish to expect miracles from any kind of investment management in a short space of time. If you do hire an adviser, turn your money over to a bank, or invest in mutual funds, be patient for at least two years before you judge the results.

11 | Togetherness Can Be an Answer

Investing can be — and should be — fun. It doesn't have to involve a grim, joyless, greedy pursuit of dollars. Nor do you have to go it alone.

A much more gratifying approach for women than mutual funds, I think, is to join an investment club. If you cannot find one in your neighborhood needing a new member, then consider forming one with a group of friends, associates in business, or women in your community whom you meet in group projects.

Indeed, intelligent, sophisticated women can obtain the benefits of mutual funds — diversification and experienced handling of money — and yet enjoy the excitement and achievement of investing individually by belonging to an investment club. In a sense, you can have your cake (with icing) and eat it too, because investment clubs entail none of the onerous costs of mutual funds — the 8 percent loading fees and the costs deducted for the fund's high-priced management.

In the last twenty years investment clubs have grown like wildflowers in unusual places, wherever there are a few enterprising people. In 1951, the year of its founding, the National Association of Investment Clubs — NAIC, for short — estimates there were about several hundred investment groups in the nation. As far as can be discovered the first progenitors of today's investment clubs began around 1900; the concept is not new even though you may not have known much about these clubs or heard much until the last few years. Today the total of investment clubs probably exceeds 20,000, and of this number about 13,000 clubs belong currently to the NAIC, with roughly 200,000 individuals in the member clubs. Clubs have sprouted in unlikely places all over the world: there is a group called the Polarettes in Alaska, and clubs exist in such places as Okinawa, India and West Africa.

As can be imagined investment clubs vary widely in membership and aims. Some clubs follow the "men only" rule; others consist of married couples, while a few have a mix of single men, single women and couples. Some have members mainly in the same age bracket; others welcome a variety of age groups from the young careerist to the person approaching retirement. Often clubs attract persons with more or less the same backgrounds, people who mingle socially with each other in clubs, business or churches. On the other hand, certain clubs take pride in the fact that their membership includes a group of persons with widely varying backgrounds who do not necessarily see or know each other in business or social life, but meet mainly at club meetings.

However, if you are a professional woman or a married woman whose husband cannot spare the time, or does not have the interest, to become associated with an investment club, perhaps the best type would be a woman's group.

When a logical woman first thinks in terms of a new interest or an avocation apart from her daily life she considers the drawbacks and the possible deterrents. "My husband would laugh about it," a woman might say when the subject of investment clubs is raised. Some men visualize women's investment groups as a kind of harem of voluble women, imbued with their husbands' ideas about investments and mouthing them while they meet to sip coffee and munch cake, in between discussing children and skirt lengths, with a few interpolated remarks about stocks based on tips from friends or rumors in newspapers. Then, after a quick telephone call to a broker but without research, the group votes to buy such and such shares and then adjourns. To save fuss, such a club keeps bookkeeping to a minimum, trusting to the smartest member of the group as far as figure sense goes to give a financial report from time to time. No doubt such investment clubs do exist, giving the husbands of the club members plenty to smile about.

Successful clubs with women members do not operate this way, and there is no need these days because good help is available at little cost.

In 1951, Thomas O'Hara, who had long been a member of a successful male investment club in Michigan, launched NAIC as a nonprofit organization dedicated to promoting economic education among members of investment clubs and providing organizational and advisory assistance to the groups.

His enthusiasm for investment clubs had a practical basis, because he was an early member of one of the most prosperous of them all. He joined the club in 1941, a few months after it was organized, and contributed $20 a month for a period of years, for a total of $3,820 (he skipped a few years when he had financial problems) and by the end of 1959 — almost eighteen years after its founding — the value of his holdings had reached $23,624. It has continued to prosper at a much faster pace in the years since.

Figure 12 shows the more up-to-date results of another club, with some wishful thinking evident in the "projected worth" column. Note how the club members have recovered from the 1971 drop in the market.

A typical club follows these four basic principles:

It invests a sum once a month in common stocks regardless of market conditions.

It reinvests dividends and capital gains immediately, for faster growth of money. Money begets money, especially when the fast compounding principle is at work.

It concentrates on buying growth stocks in companies whose sales appear to be increasing at a rate of at least 10 percent or more compounded yearly. The focus is on companies that

(Jan. 1) Year	Accumulated Amt. Dep. in Club	Projected Worth	Actual Worth
1961	$1,440	$ 2,000	$ 2,000
1962	1,680	2,440	2,450
1963	1,920	2,924	2,345
1964	2,160	3,456	3,000
1965	2,400	4,042	3,700
1966	2,640	4,686	5,550
1967	2,880	5,395	5,860
1968	3,120	6,175	8,400
1969	3,360	7,033	10,100
1970	3,600	7,976	8,470
1971	3,840	9,014	7,590
1972	4,080	10,155	8,870
1973	4,320	11,411	
1974	4,560	12,792	
1975	4,800	14,311	
1976	5,040	15,982	
1977	5,280	17,820	
1978	5,520	19,842	
1979	5,760	22,066	
1980	6,000	24,513	
1981	6,240	27,204	
1982	6,480	30,164	
1983	6,720	33,420	
1984	6,960	37,002	
1985	7,200	40,942	

Figure 12. Arab Investment Club Member Worth Projection

Assumed: $20.00/Month Investment ($240/Year), No Withdrawals. 10% Annual Growth, Compounded (3% Dividends, 7% Appreciation) could reasonably be expected to be financially stronger five years from the time of investment.

It follows the principle of diversification.

All this sounds good, but a woman might ask another question, "Well, suppose I don't like the women involved in an investment club?" An answer to this is that many clubs are composed of women — or men — not necessarily moving in the same social groups or sharing the same interests. Variety can add a great deal to a club.

A woman can be a demon athlete — an expert golfer or tennis player much of her life — but that need not prevent or deter her from associating with serious, intellectual types, or with social butterflies. After all, if she serves on committees in the local hospital, charities, or in her church, she rubs shoulders with all types. She may be antisocial and prefer the confines of her own home, but in a businesslike venture such as an investment club she could tolerate gregarious, talkative types with whom she might not feel comfortable socially. She might worry about some domineering types of women — the eager church worker who always heads the altar guild, or the PTA president who thrives on running meetings; but a well-organized investment club has rules to restrain the overzealous and stimulate the stragglers.

Most successful investment clubs operate by a strict set of rules providing that the "jobs" in the club are rotated regularly among members and that all must participate. When it comes to deciding on an investment after thorough research, the group votes, using majority rule.

"What about money?" a woman might ask. "Can I afford it?" "Can I trust the other members?" These are good questions. Many investment clubs provide that members can put in as little as $10 a month and usually there are top limits, perhaps a top of $30 a month so that the eager members can be limited and not dominate.

As for honesty, very few investment clubs, properly organized, have found defalcations. In the first place the money is put in the hands of a good brokerage firm — a transaction handled by the treasurer, usually with a check — and if cash is to be permitted to accumulate for later investment it usually goes into a savings account, with the usual provisions that only certain members can check it out.

Many clubs have bonded their members at a slight annual cost through insurance companies. Furthermore, membership in the NAIC, which costs $30 a year for the club and $1 for each member, includes a $25,000 bond covering any such difficulties.

"What about taxes?" a woman might ask, and this perhaps is the best question of all. Here again the NAIC has a manual ($3 a copy for nonmembers) which outlines the ways of organizing an investment club. The usual approach is through a partnership because of simplicity and certain tax advantages, unless the members of the club are in a very high tax bracket.

The law involving taxes on a partnership applies the conduit principle. The profits — whether from dividend or capital gains — flow through the club to the individual member, or "partner." She must report them on her income tax.

Here is the way a leading tax organization expresses the system: "Each member reports her proportionate share of dividend income (as if dividends were received by her) and capital gains or losses (as if they were her own capital gains or losses) after offsetting the club's expenses against such income. Once the club member reports her share of club income she is not taxed on it again. If it is not distributed by the club that year or in ensuing years she adds the reported gains to her cost basis of club membership."

Suppose that a member wants to resign from a club after a few years and take out her money. Generally the club has a provision for this, just the way a mutual fund does, based on the valuation of the club's investments at the time. The bylaws would contain a provision as to the actual procedure.

Let's take a look at a successful women's investment club called the Mobiles, in Royal Oak, Michigan, with thirteen members. It includes a group of women in various fields: a nurse, telephone company employee, a beauty shop manager, a substitute school teacher. Some are married and middle-aged while some are young, professional women.

The club operates on the theory that they are not in the market for frivolity but are working to attain some practical knowledge of investment while at the same time they endeavor to build up funds for later years. Their contributions amount to only $10 a month but in 1969, after about five years of investing a total of $9,160, the club had virtually doubled that amount. In fact, their average rate of return had been much better than many mutual funds — 26 percent a year. The years 1969–1971 brought a halt in progress, but now the pace has resumed.

The aim of the club as outlined in the bylaws is to concentrate on sound growth stocks they might want to hold for several years for price appreciation. Their target is to double their money on stocks every five years.

In researching a stock they consider the company's outlook and its management, not the condition of the stock market at the moment. Thus they use a method called *dollar cost averaging*. (This is generally what most people use when they invest through MIP — the New York Stock Exchange's monthly investment plan.) By this method the club invests the same amount of money periodically, usually every month, in the same stock it has been accumulating. When market values are high, the same amount of money, say $130 a month, buys fewer shares than a month later when stock prices have dropped 5 percent or so. However, over a period of time they believe that the market cost of their shares will average out well below the high point the stock reaches in price during a year.

Sally Janke, one of the members of the Mobiles, discussed this investment theory in an interview: "Generally what we do is to buy more shares of something we already hold and know is good. We like to accumulate a hundred shares of an issue." She was speaking in mid-1969 when the stock market had fallen quite sharply and many investors were dismayed. "It's hard," she added, explaining that club members often were assailed by doubts at a period when the stock market was low generally. "We even tend to lose faith in the stocks we own because they are falling, too."

However, since dollar cost averaging is the club's basic policy, it sticks to its intention. Individual investors often fare well with dollar cost averaging.

In fact, NAIC advocates such an approach to the market because over the long period it has paid with good results. In any event it urges each investment club to adopt and stick to a specific investment policy, or at least to set basic guidelines as to what it will buy and how it will act during inevitable periods of boom or recession.

Some pointers follow:

INVESTMENT IDEAS. Most investment clubs wisely eschew hot tips and rumors that periodically make the rounds via friends, business acquaintances, or in written materials. Women love to gossip but usually such tidbits should be avoided in the investment thinking of a club. Members on their own can pursue such will-o'-the-wisps, if they wish, but a club is advised to avoid them.

Clubs should regularly keep charts (see Chapter 14) because they can tell a story more effectively than mere figures or conversation about a company. One group of charts should be kept on the stocks already owned, showing the prices of the stock, perhaps on a weekly basis of highs and lows, and indicating annual sales volume and per share earnings. The second group of charts should be kept on stocks being considered by the club. From these charts the members can get a good idea of the past history of each company in terms of sales and profits and price action of the shares, which can be compared with other investments.

Where do investment clubs get ideas for securities? Their broker might turn over to the club recommendations of his firm's research department with the figures they want. Members of the club on the basis of their reading of newspapers, investment letters, and magazines will suggest ideas. Then there are the inevitable suggestions from friends and other outsiders.

CLUB SIZE. The NAIC recommends that clubs limit their membership to about ten and no more than fifteen persons and that contributions be a minimum of $10 a month.

If a club allows itself a bigger membership, even on the theory that some new members will drop out after the initial eagerness wanes, it runs into logistics problems. The average living room, in a house or apartment, would be overcrowded with more than fifteen persons, even allowing for an absence or two. And since most club hostesses serve coffee and cake or cookies during the monthly meeting, serving more people than fifteen could become expensive, even though the hostessing of the meetings is rotated each month.

At the same time clubs should remember that they face the prospect of attrition because sooner or later a few members will 1) move from the community; 2) become sick or even die; or 3) become disinterested and resign. It's a good idea for the club to anticipate this by asking occasional guests to the meetings with the idea of adding "new blood" to fill out the vacancies as they occur.

FINDING A BROKER. A club might have to do some serious searching — or even selling of itself — to arouse the interest of a good broker (see Chapter 7). Some clubs have tried to do this by inviting a friendly broker, man or woman, to join the club. However, most brokers probably will say they are too busy or already belong to such a group. In fact, I think it is preferable not to have a broker member because then the club might be overly swayed by his superior knowledge of the market. They might lean on him too much for ideas and not do enough of their own research.

A young broker, perhaps a little hungry to build up his roster of customers and contacts, often is a good person for an investment club to seek out. If the club's investments are successful the individual members probably will want to open their own accounts with a brokerage firm — a good source of business for the broker. Furthermore, most women club members have husbands or friends who could also bring business to the broker. This could be stressed by the club's committee assigned to pick out a broker.

Once a broker has been found, then the club should appoint one person (or two at the outside) to deal with him — calling him with orders to buy and sell, or asking for research material and recommendations. In other words, the other members of the club should not be permitted to bother the broker with vague questions or a scattering of inquiries.

In 1969 the NAIC reported that some clubs were turned down by brokers who claimed that small groups did not do enough business to merit the expense of opening and handling their accounts. Unfortunately, Wall Street and its member firms have been going through a period of discouraging the small investor. However, some of the big brokerage houses with many branch offices cannot — and dare not — take this attitude because they rely on volume. Try them if your group receives a cool reception.

ORGANIZATION. Every club, as well as every business, needs a table of organization, detailing the duties of various office holders. For example, one person in an investment club should be assigned the job of contact with the broker. Another might hold the office of treasurer for a year. Another member might have the task of charting the prices of stocks, along with sales and per share earnings of the portfolio investments, reporting each month on how the stocks are performing and if the investment goals are being achieved. A study group might be assigned to make recommendations for new shares to be purchased, backing their proposals with charts.

Other members might be assigned to give reports each month on various factors relating to investments. Often a club will find that they need not change their portfolio, and field reports can keep the group alert and interested when there is little to discuss about current investments. For example, reports could be made possibly every month or periodically on topics like these:

Economic trends

Emerging industries — the new growth areas that every club should follow

Overlooked stocks that might recover in price

Esoteric investments such as puts and calls, commodity futures, commercial paper — probably the club will not invest in these, but it can help educate members as to their role

Individual industry groups and their trends — banks and financial stocks, public utilities, railroads, steels and other metals, chemicals, autos, etc.

BOOKKEEPING. The clerical aspects of a club need not be boring, especially if the club follows a simple principle of limiting new investment to units of $10. Thus a member can invest each month a unit of $10, two units worth $20, etc., with some sort of maximum so that wealthy investors could not dominate the club by having a much larger investment stake than the average member.

MEETINGS. On the principle that there should be no "silent partners" in investment clubs, the club probably should adopt a rule that members must attend at least nine monthly meetings a year, or be asked to resign. Exceptions could be made in the case of long sicknesses or accidents, etc.

REINVESTMENT. The NAIC urges clubs to reinvest dividends and capital gains so that the fund can grow as fast as possible. However, there will always be members who need to take their dividends or gains out, possibly to help pay for children's college bills, hospital bills, etc. This should be allowed, provided a little advance notice is given so that the club can obtain the cash.

The point about steady reinvestment is that with a large amount of capital the club can take advantage of buying round lots of stock (100 shares) as well as attracting more active interest from the broker.

Remember the importance, too, of compound interest, something the average investor learns back in high school days and

The spectacle of modern investment markets has sometimes moved me towards the conclusion that to make the purchase of an investment permanent and indissoluble, like marriage, except by reason of death or other grave cause, might be a useful remedy for our contemporary evils. – John Maynard Keynes

Is anybody listening?

We all know of at least one club that's not. It's only 16 months old, and would you believe that in that time the club has sold twenty-six (26) issues? Would you also believe that the club's portfolio is now worth only about one-third of what the members have invested?

You can believe it. Since the first sentence is true (26 shares sold), it's practically automatic that the second is also true (two-thirds of investment lost).

On the other side of the coin, a member of NAIC who has owned Eastman Kodak for many of the nearly 85 years used in the table below has traced the company from its first public offering of stock in 1884 and given us a beautiful example of the value of compounding and long-term investment.

Although the longevity of this particular example is carrying things a little beyond the scope of our usual thinking, even the modern picture is significant.

The one share bought at $100 in 1884 would today have grown to 24,536.84 shares, and at a recent price of $105 would be worth considerably more than $2.5 million.

Here's a story you might tell about investing the next time conversation lags at a party- and don't forget to mention how being an Investment Club member can help one's investment program:

GROWTH OF KODAK COMMON STOCK

Year	Changes in Stock	Number of Shares
1884	Eastman Dry Plate and Film Company - First public offering of stock - at $100	1
1889	The Eastman Company- shares split 3 for 1	3
1892	Eastman Kodak Company (New York) - shares split 4 for 1	12
1898	Kodak Limited (England - shares exchanged 26 for 1	312
1901	Eastman Kodak Company (New Jersey) - $100 par value shares exchanged for pound sterling shares at approximately 1 for each 8.25 shares held	37.83
1902	Warrants issued to purchase 1 for each 4 shares held	*
1922	10 for 1 stock split	378.3
1929	Rights issued to purchase 1 for each 10 held	*
1939	Warrants issued to purchase 1 for each 10 held	*
1947	5 for 1 stock split	1891.5
1948	5% stock dividend declared (1 for 20)	1986.075
1949	5% stock dividend declared (1 for 20)	2085.38
1950	10% stock dividend declared (1 for 10)	2293.92
1951	10% stock dividend declared (1 for 10)	2523.31
1952	5% stock dividend declared (1 for 20)	2649.48
1954	5% stock dividend declared (1 for 20)	2781.95
1956	5% stock dividend declared (1 for 20)	2921.05
1959	1 for 1 stock distribution	5842.10
1963	5% stock dividend declared (1 for 20)	6134.21
1965	2 for 1 stock split	12,268.42
1968	2 for 1 stock split	24,536.84

*Assumes warrants and rights not exercised. If all warrants and rights had been exercised through investment of additional capital, present number of shares would be 37,113.96.

promptly forgets. Table 10 will remind you of the power of compounding.

The records of many investment clubs show that 10 percent and more return (dividends and capital gains) can be achieved without miracles over a period of years.

	$10,000 Invested		
Rate of Return	10 years	20 years	30 years
3%	$13,440	$18,060	$ 24,270
5	16,290	26,530	43,220
8	21,590	46,610	100,630
10	25,940	67,280	174,490

Table 10

PORTFOLIO MIX. A final interesting recommendation of NAIC is that a club's portfolio should be a mixture. About 25 percent of the club's monies should be in stocks of big companies in major industries, which show a pattern of regular growth. Another 25 percent should be allotted to stocks of smaller companies in somewhat riskier fields — the go-go–type growth stocks. The remainder should be put into companies ranging between these extremes.

A comment well worth noting, from the NAIC magazine *Better Investing,* is reproduced as Figure 13. It is interesting that early in 1972, brokers were still recommending Eastman Kodak.

12 | The Stuff of Dreams

Speculation is a heady thing, the stuff of which dreams are made. If you think about it, everyone is a speculator, but the degrees of risk-taking range widely. Yet, the word comes from the Latin *speculari,* which can be translated several ways: to spy, to explore, to reconnoiter, observe, watch for. All meanings indicate that the speculator is a careful, shrewd risk-taker.

For example, the National Safety Council tells us that every time you, a presumably safe driver, climb into a car and drive a few miles to the local supermarket you are putting your life at risk. More car accidents happen within twenty miles of a person's home than on the major highways where speed is dominant.

Risk belongs to daily living, even including the hopefully happy marriage that the bride undertakes. She may have married a Bluebeard, a Dr. Jekyll and Mr. Hyde, a Robin Hood, or a Casanova, or some other less-than-desirable type.

The point is that putting your money in the stock market can be risky, and for some people more speculation will be involved because they choose to take more risks than other persons. Yet, more than driving a car on dangerous highways, more than picking a husband, stocks can involve predeterminations and knowledgeable speculation. And they can be quickly sold; cars and husbands cannot be changed so readily.

In speaking about the stock market, brokers or news writers often talk this way: "Speculative buying pushed prices up today"; or "The government is worried about too much speculation; margin requirements may be raised." It sounds as if speculation was dangerous and slightly unsavory, or a darkly unrighteous act.

Speculators generally can be defined as large or small. The large ones have plenty of money to move in and out of the market and take risks. Since they have sufficient money and borrowing power they can afford losses. The small speculators operate with much more limited funds, are more apt to be hurt financially if prices drop sharply, are less sophisticated, react too much, even panic their way into losses.

Basically speculation involves one or more of these eight factors:

1. Taking risks
2. Quick trades
3. Stress on 10 percent or more
4. Stop orders
5. Borrowed money
6. Use of leverage
7. New areas, new issues
8. Systems, or determined approaches

TAKING RISKS. To speculate implies taking a certain amount of risk. An elderly conservative woman would take a risk if she kept virtually all her money in the shares of one company, though she might not realize it was risky.

Years ago my obstetrician, an elderly, brilliant, very successful New York doctor, often chatted with me about the stock market. He told me that he lived through the depression in 1929 and since then he had kept most of his money in bonds, corporate and government. In being so conservative he took a risk with his future because bond interest did not keep pace with inflation.

The father of a man I know was a professional writer, articulate, pleasant, never drank too much, didn't smoke, never lost jobs, made a good salary writing, didn't go out with other women besides his wife, but he had a glaring weakness — gambling.

He spent most of his salary each week betting on horses, football pools, anything. He couldn't resist a bet. As a result he lost his wife, his house, an inheritance, and everything except his job, even though the publisher threatened to fire him from time to time because of creditors on his heels. A psychiatrist couldn't help him. He was at the razor edge of risk-taking, where losses cut deeply.

A famous risk-taker and consummate salesman of ideas was real estate tycoon William Zeckendorf. His grandiose dream of building vast real estate complexes always involved a large amount of risk, glamour and borrowed money. He would have fared all right except he built on some "sand," and when a recession came along a few years ago his creditors forced his company into bankruptcy.

The point is that many people take risks unconsciously; others cannot resist risk-taking to the point of testing their fate. The wise risk-taker knows how much he can afford to risk (or lose) at a certain time and how much risk might be involved. He builds on realities or good possibilities, not just hopes or fear.

QUICK TRADES. A speculator pays little attention to dividends and current income. He stresses price appreciation. Of course, in calculating his overall return he does figure dividends plus appreciation. He hopes to turn over his money as many times a year as possible, so he is prepared psychologically to move quickly in and out of the market, without regard to the six months' holding period for establishing capital gains. However, if a situation does require half a year or more to work out, he willingly holds on.

This requires knowing the commission rates and figuring how much of a rise — a point, two points or more — is needed for a quick, worthwhile profit after commissions and income taxes.

Let's see how a quick trade might work out. There has been a rumor that Photo Corporation (imaginary company) plans to introduce a new type of camera. You buy 100 shares of the stock after investigating the company (you find out it has a good earnings record, etc.). The broker gets you the stock for a price of $10 a share. A round trip commission (the total of the commissions charged when you buy and when you sell) will require about $50, plus state transfer taxes of a few cents a share when you sell (see list of typical commission rates in Chapter 18). This means that your hundred shares of the stock must move up half a point to cover these costs alone. You are in the 30 percent tax bracket, meaning that Uncle Sam takes that percentage of any profit you make above your cost. If the stock goes up to 11½, you figure you will make about $100 above the commission and you can keep about $70 of this (the remaining $30 goes to Uncle Sam). So you tell your broker to sell at this point — 11½ — on the theory that you will be content with making $70 for an in-and-out trade. The trade is completed and you are happy at the result even though the stock jumps higher before a reaction sets in.

STRESS ON HIGH PERCENTAGE RETURN. A smart trader does not wait until the last moment to sell; he is content with a quick, tidy profit. In the example cited, if he only makes one such successful trade per month he has made 12 times $70, or $840 a year on his $1,000, or a very high return after taxes. A good speculator turns his money even faster than that in a favorable market.

Sometimes speculators who trade in and out spend part of the day either watching the board in their broker's office or they consult with him frequently over the telephone. Quite often they are chart traders, which means that when a certain formation appears on the charts they keep of price movement for favorite stocks, they will act. They tell their broker to buy at a certain price and sell at a certain price, with the use of stop orders placed slightly below their purchase price; they will automatically be sold out if prices run counter to their thinking. Speculators classed as successful do not let emotion or ego keep them in a stock whose price is moving against them.

STOP ORDERS. Typically, a speculator makes more use of stop orders than most investors, resorting to them both as downside protection and upside profit assurance.

The smart speculator doesn't grab for a stock. He approaches it with the caution of a man approaching a cobra — quietly, determinedly and patiently. This is a "thing" the speculator wants but on his own terms.

For example, many speculators will place a buy order — GTC — until they get a stock at their price. The price might be a few points below the level around which the market for the stock has been jumping for a few days or weeks. Speculators know from experience that day-to-day movements usually range widely enough over a period of time so that their orders often can be filled at the price they want.

Once the shares have been bought the speculator keeps in close contact with his stock, a basic difference between him and an investor. The investor relaxes and waits; the speculator watches his stock day-by-day, jots down price changes, probably charts them for a better view.

He isn't bothered by the day-by-day changes necessarily but he wants to detect and follow trends. He has set for himself a target price for the stock — not a greedy one, if he is wise. He might expect it to rise 10 percent. Once it has achieved this he would sell. A stop order would be in the market on the upside to automatically take him out at that point.

Naturally, if the market for the shares was booming, perhaps along with the trend in stocks generally, he might raise his upside stop order from time to time. At the same time he would protect himself from downswings by stop orders under the current market price. Thus if he bought a stock at 50 originally he might place a stop below this level at 47, figuring if he was so wrong in his estimate of the stock's potential a $3 loss per share (minus commissions) would at least free him from a bad situation.

If the stock proceeded to move up to 53 he would move up his downside stop order as well, perhaps to 50. At that point his new stop price matches his original price for the shares, meaning if he was sold out at that level there would be no loss except the commission. Suppose the stock rises to 54, and his stop has been upped to 51. Now he has covered the price of the round trip commission; and if he sells above this level he will have a profit. Also, he raises his topside limit to 58.

Let's assume the stock rises to 58, a price about 16 percent above his purchase price. This is the point at which he placed his upside stop order and the stock is sold.

Psychologically, I have a feeling that if a speculator places a stop order at the time he first buys the shares it can have a good effect. The order to sell at 58 shows up on the specialist's book on the floor, along with the order to sell around a point or two below the market level. If a specialist has a large amount of sell orders well above the current price for the shares, it might reinforce his thinking about the stock. The specialist with his feel for the market often judges his own position by what appears in his books.

The problem is that the average investor and broker don't know what the specialist has on his books in the way of buy and sell orders.

BORROWED MONEY. Many speculators have margin accounts with a brokerage firm. Buying on margin is a method of trading stocks with the use of borrowed money.

First of all, it requires the opening of a margin account with a brokerage firm. Unfortunately, perhaps, many brokerage firms will not permit women to open margin accounts. If they do, often they require a husband's written permission. I think this is a form of discrimination, but apparently it arises from some unfortunate experiences brokerage firms have had with women customers. Like tigers, apparently the females are more dangerous than the males of the human species, when disappointed in stocks, if not in love. It's probably better for most women not to think of a margin account and not to bother searching for brokerage firms that will permit a woman to have such an account.

A margin account can be dangerous in this respect: the Federal Reserve system, the nation's central banker, sets the so-called margin rate on a percentage basis (see page 88). When speculation tends to increase sharply, the Fed often raises the margin requirement. On the other hand, when market prices are in the doldrums, the Fed might decrease its margin requirement to encourage more purchases of securities.

Let's suppose the margin rate is 75 percent. That means that you must put up in cash in your margin account or have securities available in the account to provide enough loanable value to be the equivalent of 75 percent of the purchase price of a stock. The broker will lend you the remaining 25 percent, for which he will charge you the current rate of interest. In the past ten years (1962-1972) the margin rate on such trades has ranged from 50 to 80 percent.

If the margin in your account runs below the requirement because of a decline in the price of your stock your broker will notify you immediately, by telephone or telegram, that you must provide more cash or collateral. Some brokerage firms, to give themselves added protection, require more margin than the basic Federal Reserve regulations.

Remember if a margin call goes out to you one day, it must be answered the next. If not, the broker can sell out the stock, and you have no legal recourse against him even if the stock gains 10 points the next day. The responsibility rests upon you.

The tumbling prices of stock in 1929 when many investors used margin accounts were accelerated by the forced sale of stock owned by people who couldn't raise the cash to save their positions. In those days, before the advent of much government control, speculators often bought stocks for 100 percent margin. They were buying dreams and mortgaging their souls for them.

The woman speculator who believes that she needs to obtain more money for her ventures can do it by a method a little safer than buying on margin. She can first purchase 100 shares of a sound stock — the kind that ordinarily doesn't show much price volatility — and take these shares to her local bank. There she can ask for and generally easily obtain a collateral loan.

For example, a woman might invest in 100 shares of AT&T selling around 55, for a total of $5,500, on which a bank might lend her 75 percent of the amount, or roughly $4,000 in cash.

Then she could use the $4,000 to speculate. Meanwhile the AT&T shares would pay a dividend each year, and if the bank asked her to reduce the loan from time to time she could use the AT&T dividends to help do this. I consider this method much less dangerous than using a margin account; yet it provides what can be called the leverage of more money.

Naturally she will have to pay the loan off at the bank someday, but if the basic shares are sound the bank probably will let her loan remain on its books for a long time. She will have to pay interest quarterly at whatever the current rates are.

USE OF LEVERAGE. Investors often hear the word "leverage" used, just as above it was applied to borrowed money that gives an investor more funds for trading. There are other forms of leverage, too.

Brokers and speculators speak knowingly about "leveraged" situations. These are stocks that for various reasons can show high price swings. They offer speculators good chances for fast profits.

A typical leverage situation might be this, involving a company we will call Super Electronics. Let's say that this is a well-established company in a growth industry, which has a bond issue requiring $100,000 in interest payments yearly, preferred dividends that take another $100,000, plus 100,000 shares of common stock.

In 1970 the company earns $300,000, and to a stockholder its status looks like this:

$100,000 for bond interest
100,000 for preferred dividends
100,000 remaining for stockholders, or $1 a share

Now let's suppose that in 1971 Super Electronics has completed a big order for a new product sold to the government, and earnings increase sharply to $500,000.

$100,000 for bond interest
100,000 for preferred dividends
300,000 remaining for stockholders, or $3 a share

In other words, operating earnings (for simplicity's sake we haven't considered taxes) have increased by about 66 percent or $200,000, but for holders of shares of common stock this has resulted in an earnings increase of three times $1, or $3, triple their money.

Naturally, the mere fact that earnings have increased sharply does not mean the company will necessarily pay out the additional net income to stockholders: most growth-type companies, especially small ones, conserve their cash for reinvestment in more plants and equipment. But speculators in a leveraged situation like this count on one or two things happening.

The shares purchased at, say, $25 a share when earnings were $1 might rise in price to $50 a share in 1971 when they are earning $3. Furthermore, even if the company didn't increase its cash dividend it might issue some stock dividends. As mentioned before, stock dividends in a growth company tend to reflect the higher price hopes of investors.

Speculators gravitate to situations where leverage like this can occur. Often they can find it when a company has senior securities such as bonds and preferreds ahead of the common.

NEW AREAS, NEW ISSUES. When they can buy them, speculators like new issues. As mentioned before, your broker probably will not be able to fill orders from you to buy shares in companies offering their stock publicly for the first time — the so-called new issue market — unless 1) you happen to be a large, important customer; 2) you are one of his relatives; 3) the new issue is a large one like Comsat*; or 4) it is one that has failed to arouse the public appetite.

However, you might be able to pick up new issues at reasonable prices a few days after they have reached the market. Sometimes, a short time after the new issue is sold publicly

---

*Comsat, formally called Communications Satellite Corporation, operates the commercial communications satellite system — those marvelous pictures televised of the 1972 Olympic Games, for example!

Congress formed Comsat by law in 1963 as a private corporation, with stock outstanding. It's traded on the New York Stock Exchange.

the speculators who were able to buy shares dump them, and the price of the stock drops sharply in reaction.

Before you buy a new issue your broker is required by law to provide you with a prospectus — a brochure which must be filed first with the Securities and Exchange Commission. It gives you basic, unvarnished facts about the company, and the aim of the SEC is to make sure that the truth is told in an unvarnished way. Naturally, the lawyers who file the prospectus with the SEC try to say as little as possible, but the SEC can insist that they revise it, often half-a-dozen times. For instance:

A cement company in Oklahoma had to explain that it had no plant in operation at the time of the stock offering and was going to operate in a largely agricultural community. Oddly enough, it turned out to be a very good investment. Its name: Oklahoma Cement Company.

A fried chicken company had to state that its most important asset was the name of the company, which had been "rented" from a leading singer, Minnie Pearl. She would receive a certain amount of money each year for the use of her name. Said the prospectus: "If Mrs. Cannon (whose stage name is Minnie Pearl) should die or become physically disabled the loss to the company of her continued promotion could have a materially adverse effect on the success of the company." The company did not fare well after a few years.

An "act of God" takes on significance in the case of one company — the Real Eight Company, a treasure-hunting salvage business. In its prospectus the lawyers wrote: "A violent hurricane or other act of God could possibly shift the present sunken valuables where the company is conducting salvage operations . . . or could bury these valuables under a substantial amount of sand." Furthermore, the state of Florida must share any of the company's treasure findings, with its "take" put at 25 percent of the market value.

(The reader of the prospectus for this fascinating venture also learns that "the diving operations do not require professional deep sea divers and it generally employs qualified scuba divers who are frequently college students." Obviously, this is not a prospectus that a woman should pass on to her son, if she wants him to settle down after college into a nice, easy desk job.)

Sometimes, as in the case of another company called Monroe Combining Company, which provides laminating service to fabric converters and apparel manufacturers, the prospectus reveals deficits. That company had a working capital deficit as of December 31, 1967, placed at $61,166. Also, the prospectus noted that the underwriter's commission was quite high.

Don't ever consider buying a new stock without reading the prospectus, word by word. Not only do prospectuses make fascinating reading, but they also can change your thinking. As mentioned before, the prospectus is the one time when a company has to "let down its hair" and tell the truth, at least in so far as the Securities and Exchange Commission's lawyers can make them mention some of the possible difficulties, drawbacks, competition, etc., the company faces.

Sometimes reading a prospectus is enough to warn an investor away from a certain issue. Then if he buys the stock and it turns out badly he has no one except himself to blame. While the Securities and Exchange Commission makes a company reveal essential negative facts, it does not in any way endorse or not endorse the issue. It is a watchdog, not a judge.

The investor stands alone when he judges a new issue, and even his broker does not have responsibility beyond providing the prospectus and recommending against the stock, if the issue appears to be too far out, or speculative. Brokerage firms do not like to underwrite or put their customers into situations that turn sour, if they are reputable firms. As you gain experience you will learn which firms are more reputable than others in the underwritings they handle or stocks they recommend. And even good brokerage firms, with the best of intentions, can make mistakes about new issues — especially during a period of intense speculation.

The speculator, or indeed any smart investor, must be on the alert constantly for new areas of investment or for overlooked ones. Perhaps the overlooked industry of today will produce the growth stocks of tomorrow: it seems to me that the number of actual new industries will be limited by the already fast pace of economic growth.

Few people these growth-conscious days pay much attention to the dear old steel stocks, like Bethlehem Steel and U.S. Steel, corporate bastions both and important to basic industry. True, there has been much talk about competitive steel being imported cheaply from overseas and competing products like aluminum and plastics stealing some of the traditional market away from steel. However, at low prices of 1971 the steel industry appears to be out of fashion and often overlooked by investors. This kind of neglect occurs in any typical business cycle when investors are distracted by more glamorous industries. Yet, financially, an underpriced stock can offer the same lure of appreciation and perhaps even more than an overpriced growth stock.

Another neglected situation, for example, appeared several years ago when savings and loan association shares were low priced because of a lull in the construction market. A stock like Financial Federation could have been picked up in 1966 for $8 a share and in 1968 it sold as high as $40, a good increase for an investment held about two years. (In 1970 it dropped to $9 and since then has sold at about $22.)

Who bought Financial Federation at its low point in 1966? Speculators who believed that an upturn in building would soon follow, as it did, and that savings and loan companies would participate, as they did. It was a worthwhile speculation combining the best elements of an industry in a depressed cycle of activity with inherent growth in demand for its product — money to build houses. The nation needs additional housing to meet the needs generated by a rapidly expanding population and by rising aspirations of dwellers in substandard buildings. In fact, the person who reasons out an investment opportunity like this can consider himself more of an astute investor than a hit-and-run speculator.

Naturally new growth situations also capture speculators'

attention, and they can be more risky by nature. The interest in them often is cyclical, with a few alert stock traders nibbling at attractive growth stocks, then other "fish" joining them and finally a rush for the bait by the speculative public. By this time some of the big fish are already moving out of the stock into others, taking their profits. Typically such a speculative boom collapses. Thus the smart speculator tries to get in early, or not at all. Selling out *before* the stock attracts large public support is important.

An example of a speculative boom bursting came in 1962; still another less significant downturn came in 1966 and then there followed the serious one of 1969–1970.

A list of some important growth areas since World War II provides an interesting chart of speculators' interest:

GROUP I

Photography	Electronics
Textbook publishing	Savings and Loan Associations
Boating	Computers
Uranium	Bowling

In the group above each industry mentioned has been the object of a speculative boom followed by a sharp decline after some second thinking by investors. The correction of speculative excess is a fact of life, usually resulting with the "bandwagon" investors getting hurt. Later, some of the industries reasserted themselves, such as textbook publishing, which is now a solid investment field.

Group II includes some more recent speculative industries:

GROUP II

Lasers	Nursing homes
Fried chicken	Ski resorts
Oceanography	Auto clinics
Silver refining	or repair shops
Hospital equipment	Motels

Let's take bowling from Group I as a typical example of speculation that proved successful for agile investors and tragic for the less sophisticated ones.

Back in 1960 two major companies, both listed on the New York Stock Exchange, spearheaded the growth of popularity of bowling as a sport for the entire family. Many companies, as you may remember, formed employees' bowling teams for weekly exercise and fun. Bowling tournaments were televised, mute testimony to the widespread interest in the sport. Many ex-baseball or football stars permitted their names to be linked with bowling alleys. High schools had bowling teams and so did some colleges. It was an "in" sport.

Two companies dominated the field, primarily because modern bowling requires complex "spotters" which have replaced pinboys who used to set up the pins. Their names were American Machine and Foundry Company (now called AMF, Inc.), maker of several lines of complicated equipment such as bread-making machines; and Brunswick Corporation, better known for sports equipment such as billiard tables.

AMF developed its automated pinsetter somewhat ahead of Brunswick. At first AMF rented its equipment, while Brunswick sold its line. To promote the sport both companies spent large sums of money for contests and prizes, and helped finance alleys.

Unfortunately, like so many fads, the business got out of hand, in that 1) too many bowling alleys opened in relation to the amount of actual business in some areas; 2) some operators entered business without experience and with too heavy borrowings; 3) some parents didn't like the type of people hanging around bowling alleys; and 4) as in all sports fads, public interest eventually turned elsewhere.

As business revenues in the alleys dropped sharply, the two companies found themselves as creditors with some bankrupt bowling properties on their hands and public interest declining. At the same time some smaller bowling companies, not as diversified or as well managed as AMF and Brunswick, went into bankruptcy. And many of these fringe companies had raised capital by selling stock to unwary speculators.

Brunswick, with its earnings badly hurt, decided to diversify further. Today bowling supplies, which once accounted for a major part of company sales, now constitute less than 15 percent. Here are the price ranges of Brunswick stock before, during and after its glamour period.

1958	$4–9
1960	21–50
1961 peak price	74
1967	7–17
1972	37–55

Same company in 1958 as in 1972, yes, but earnings and prospects far different. There isn't much to say, unhappily, to speculators who bought at the price of 74. Even if they haven't sold already and taken their losses they probably will wait a long time to recoup. *Sic transit gloria,* temporarily. However in mid-1972 the range was 37–55. The company has diversified widely in boats, golf equipment, ski equipment, and more.

On the other hand, the speculators who bought at between 4 and 9 a share in 1958 and sold later at a much higher price can well recall Brunswick as a sound investment.

The prices for AMF show much the same pattern in the years 1958–1967. Today, however, the company receives only about 8 percent of its revenues from rental of its pinsetter and has many new prosperous lines. Note the early 1972 price range.

1958	$ 8–15
1960	24–46
1961 peak	63
1967	14–25
1972	47–63

The interested woman speculator should persistently seek from her broker and elsewhere lists of growth areas. Sometimes she can glean ideas of where growth will occur from her own experience as an observer of fads as well as from her reading. At the same time she should keep in mind those industries which have recently gone through declines — and a shake-out — but yet offer renewed growth possibilities, like textbook publishing, teaching machines, cycle issues like steel shares or building materials suppliers, makers of sports equipment, etc.

She should remember what is here today in this fast-moving world can be jaded and played out tomorrow — at least temporarily. Think in terms of those round- or square-toed shoes for women popular about a decade ago that became the fashion once again in 1969 and 1970; then faded away during 1971. Speculation requires speed, imagination, and lack of sentimentality. Good speculators are willing to change their investments with as little emotion and as quickly as they would change a shirt, or in the case of a woman, a blouse.

SYSTEMS, OR DETERMINED APPROACHES. Speculators in the course of history have adopted some unusual techniques. In fact, often the successful ones will smile and say vaguely, "I have a system."

Probably the most successful speculators are those who buy growth stocks and then trade by using charts (see Chapter 14), buying and selling as their charts indicate. But I have heard, and you will, too, of many unusual approaches.

One elderly retired broker I know has the greatest admiration for the business acumen of two Texans called the Murchison brothers, who built a fortune investing. For a period of years they bought shares in many small insurance companies. Sometimes they merged the companies. This broker bought shares in the same insurance company everytime he read that the Murchisons had made a purchase. By doing so over a period of years, he made a good profit. Perhaps other small speculators can capitalize on following the actions of the big boys, if they can find out who the big boys are and what they're doing.

An elderly woman I know disapproved of drinking, smoking

and chewing gum, and she frowned on speculation. However, she knew that many other people — the great mass of the public — did these things, so she invested much of her money in liquor, tobacco and shares of American Chicle Company (now part of Warner-Lambert). Her investments fared well.

There's a rabbi in Chicago who has made money for years trading in pork bellies, a commodity future (see pages 247–252), on the theory that "I can't eat it, but I can try to make money on it." Millions of people love bacon which is the product that results from pork bellies. With prosperity on the rise the bacon market grows continually.

Dancer Nicholas Darva used an odd approach to the market, studying stock quotations and picking stocks that seemed to have unusually large price increases in a rising market. After watching them increase for a while, he would buy shares and then place a stop order a few points below the purchase price. As the stock rose he increased the price of the stop order. Adoption of this method fitted his itinerant life because he gave dance recitals in many unusual parts of the world, often being far removed from stock market quotations. Using cables or telegrams he could keep his broker informed; through stop orders he protected his positions.

In the chapter on investment clubs (Chapter 11) it was mentioned that many clubs utilize dollar cost averaging, picking a growth stock and buying a certain number of shares at regular intervals. When market prices are up they pay more and thus get fewer shares; when the stock's price is down, the same amount of money buys more shares. They work on the theory that the average price over a period of time will be favorable if they have picked a good, growing company.

Contrarians, led by an investment analyst and adviser, Humphrey Neill, and his associate James L. Frazer, use a theory called the contrary-opinion theory. They like to do the opposite of what most people are thinking. When most people are pessimistic and out of the market, the contrarians often take the plunge into the cold water. When the public takes a swim, and especially a long bath, they are sunning on the shores waiting to plunge again. It is a worthwhile attitude and you can read more about it in Mr. Neill's books.

13 | How to Be a Bear without a Growl

Hope springs eternal, as the saying goes, and nowhere is that fact more evident than in the stock market.

Americans have always had faith that time would better all things, that stocks would go up and therefore much would be well with the world. Oddly enough, over the last two hundred years or so the bulls in America have been right — the population has grown steadily, industrial production has surged, gross national product (the total of all goods and services in terms of dollars) has increased almost steadily year after year, and the standard of living has improved. Except for occasional setbacks, stock prices have shown a rising tendency.

Yet some interesting facts can be cited to show that there is always room for the pessimist, and especially for the pessimist with a sense of timing.

The National Bureau of Economic Research made a detailed study of recessions for the hundred-year period stretching from 1854 to 1954. From this perspective it found that the one hundred years encompassed 24 business cycles. On the average the economy expanded for 29.9 months in the typical cycle and then it contracted for 19.9 months.

Generally, a booming economy has brought with it a booming stock market, the enthusiasm for one probably inspiring zest for the other. These upswings have then been followed by recessions or depressions, usually causing much lower stock prices.

As might be guessed, the longest and sharpest of the contracting periods came following the 1929 stock market crash, and it lasted for forty-three months.

The 1929 crash and ensuing depression proved so devastating that it brought profound changes in the government's whole attitude toward the economy. Since then the government has played a more active role in the economy, providing social security benefits, unemployment compensation, make-work projects, deficit spending to encourage business expansion. Furthermore, the Federal Reserve system has refined and sharpened its techniques of operating in the money market, so that it can encourage economic growth — or slow down an overheated economy. It can effectively change interest rates and raise or lower margin requirements on securities trading.

Americans have become imbued with the idea that never again can this country suffer a depression like the 1929–1933 crash. They probably are right in this assumption. But that hardly limits the opportunities for an investor to act and think like a bear, if he knows how. The opportunities still remain.

Table 11 gives a list of declines in the Dow Jones industrial average since 1957, giving the duration of the decline and the months it required for prices to recover.

Each of these recent setbacks offered a bear the chance to make money.

Yet the typical investor, always the optimist, did not look at declines as opportunities to conserve profits already made or to take aggressive action to make money by acting like a bear. Instead, he placed more reliance in the growth figures, such as the fact that the Dow Jones industrial average has progressed upwards from as low as 161 back in the period after World War II to just below 1,000 in 1966, and it moved above 1,000 late in 1972.

Since recessions in the economy and the stock market are a fact of life, then why don't more investors, especially intelligent ones, try to learn how to protect themselves?

HOW TO BE A BEAR WITHOUT A GROWL

Books on the stock market by the hundreds tell the investor how to buy common stocks for their growth potential. But very few books, possibly a handful, tell him how to profit from an inevitable bear market. The irony is that back in the early nineteen sixties the growth-stock psychology so gripped the imagination of the investing public, brokers and writers that books on the stock market did not even mention short selling or the use of "puts" or other methods of protection. Instead, books tried to vindicate the payment of prices astronomical in terms of current earnings, carrying out the thesis of growth, growth and more growth to carry prices inevitably upwards. The 1962 denouement changed opinion somewhat, but still there were few books that told the story of profits from bear operations.

Year	Decline in DJIA	Length in Months	Recovery in Months
1957	19% to 419	3	11
1960	17 to 566	9	5
1962	27 to 535	6	15
1965	10 to 840	1	3
1966	25 to 750	10	28
1969–1970	35 to 630	8	12

Table 11

The reasons apparently belong to the fuzzy area of psychological trauma in the minds of many stock market writers. No one likes bad news, especially brokers who find it hard to persuade customers to act bearishly. Today few young brokers can even remember the 1929 depression. The thinking among many brokers is that the activities of bears should be the prerogative of professional traders and speculators. Operating as a bear can be risky, a fact that is all too often pointed out. "Don't sell America short" has become kind of a brokers' fishing line. And in fact it's hard to discourage the investor, who has bought some shares with the idea that they will go up steadily. Hence investors tend to hang on, or if they do sell, they tend to panic and dump shares at the wrong time.

Books that do mention methods of acting like a bear, such as selling short, hasten to warn the reader that many famous bears have died in bankruptcy. Daniel Drew usually heads the list, although the books don't usually add that his once good friend Jay Gould tricked him into his downfall. Jacob Little is another bear cited as dying a poor man.

Some books even go to the extent of quoting that elder statesman Bernard Baruch as saying, "Bears don't live on Park Avenue." Yet Mr. Baruch made a large amount of money as a very young man taking a bear position in a famous so-called "growth stock" of the early nineteen hundreds — Amalgamated Copper. But more about that later.

In fact, the American psychology of eternal optimism runs counter to bearish thinking to such an extent that a stock market iconoclast can suffer in his personal relations if he is unwise enough to discuss his pessimism. For example, it's pleasant enough to say to a friend who works for AT&T something like this:"You're with a great company. I have some of the stock and have owned it for years. I'm sure it will keep going up. It's the kind of stock people ought not to sell — ever." For this the speaker will receive, no doubt, an appreciative smile, not mentioning nodding acquiescence. Most employees tend to be faithful to their company's stock.

On the contrary there's nothing simple or even socially acceptable about saying to the same man, "Your stock is going up too fast. It's headed for a fall. Suppose the government investigates rates. You ought to sell." The result: a cold look and instant argument, possibly even the end of a friendship.

By nature, the bear must be a lonely man, able and willing to keep his pessimism to himself unless he can find a few others thinking along similar lines. Even if he proves temporarily right and makes money, or at least preserves his money, he remains suspect.

The case of AT&T in 1962 and again in 1966, a stock long considered the widow's friend, provides a good example.

Naturally there will always be telephones and an increasing population to use more of them. Furthermore, AT&T, once primarily a public utility, has firmly established its diversification as an electronics age company.

Yet, despite its stability and its roster of long-term stockholders, AT&T took a bad tumble in 1962 in the generally declining market, which dropped it from 68 to 49.

In 1966, AT&T's tumble came for a very different reason. It became the subject of a government investigation into its rates and practices. Giving impetus to its decline from 70 in late 1965 to 49 in 1966 was a drop also in the stock market.

From these two sharp drops in a sound stock, the average investor can glean two important points:

1. Even the soundest stock, like AT&T with its record earnings, will be hurt in a bear stock market, as happened in 1962. Declining prices won't leave it untouched anymore than they will some fly-by-night stock in which speculators have had a run for their money. True, the drop may not be as sharp as in more volatile stocks, but there will be one.

2. Even such dominant companies as AT&T can be hurt by the prospect of a government investigation — an influence that will be translated into lower stock prices. What other impacts can hurt a big company? Copper companies lost some of their market when a sharp price increase in the metal led consumers to use substitutes. The poor showing made by General Motors during Ralph Nader's first big auto safety investigation undoubtedly hurt the company's image and the price of its stock. A major lawsuit against a company can have a devastating effect on stock prices; so can a sudden unexpected upheaval in management. A new development such as Crest toothpaste and its endorsement by a dental group helped one major toothpaste maker at the expense of others in the business.

Perhaps what today's investor sorely needs is a better sense of history. For this there are several good sources. In *Extraordi-*

nary Popular Delusions and the Madness of Crowds, Charles Mackay explores one of the momentous stock price breaks in history — the "South Sea bubble," which occurred in the eighteenth century. His book was written about a hundred years ago but it still remains pertinent for today's investor. Anyone who reads it will never look at the stock market with rose-tinted glasses again. For the 1929 break, economist John K. Galbraith has written a fine study called *The Great Crash, 1929.*

History is with the bull; economic growth is with the bull; psychology is with the bull; and books on the stock market cater to the bull. Where does that leave a bear? In a very comfortable position, *if* he has the right approach. He must be a loner and an individualist and coolly analytical, willing to act contrary to the crowd or the herd of bulls. If he is right more times than wrong he can achieve the satisfaction of knowing he stands out among the group.

How then can the investor know when a market nears its peak and when he should act like a bear? No one can pick the top exactly, but as the market reaches new heights there are some guideposts. A few stock market analysts become restive. There are certain well-known ones who tend to act more bearish than others. Subtle warnings will be sounded. Perhaps these will be limited at first to suggestions that the outlook is hazy and that the investor should begin to build up some cash to take advantage of opportunities later, coupled with a warning to eliminate weak sisters in a portfolio.

There may be talk of large investors taking money out of the market and putting it in the bank, or in bonds, or in hedge stocks like utilities. The term "large investors" includes not only wealthy individuals but the mutual funds, insurance companies, and other such organizations.

Analysts have a sense of the market — a closeness that other investors often lack. They soon learn when some of their firm's large institutional customers are moving out of stocks and building up cash.

Then, too, there are basic economic questions the investor

hoping to be an active bear will ask. Is unemployment rising? Are industrial orders falling? Are machine tool orders falling? What about corporate profits? Are they falling or are profit margins narrowing? What about sales of autos, a key industry? What about inflation? Is consumer income dropping or being cut by taxes or higher living costs? Are stocks priced too far in the future in relation to current earnings, as happened in 1962?

If the bear is concentrating on a certain stock, rather than the market, he will focus on its special weakness. Often a bear can find a deteriorating situation in a single stock at a time when he has no particular worries about the stock market as a whole. In this case he will be asking such questions as: Is management poor? Is the company losing its share of the market? Has it been outpointed in technology by another company? Have its growth prospects slowed?

Both types of bears — the one watching the market as a whole and the one following a single stock — should keep their eyes on the *short interest* figures, published each month by the New York Stock Exchange (the American Stock Exchange also issues short interest figures). A copy of this release can be obtained from the exchanges, but an easier method is to read the major New York newspapers, such as the *New York Times* or the *Wall Street Journal,* which usually carry a story and data each month on the short interest figures for leading companies.

A short interest situation arises when a person sells stock he does not own, by borrowing stock temporarily with the idea of returning the stock later, on the assumption he can buy it back then at a lower price. A large short interest position in a stock indicates that a great many people believe the price may drop.

However, a point to remember is that every short position must ultimately be covered. So if shares drop the shorts — the speculators who sold short — must enter the market and buy an amount of stock equivalent to the amount sold short. Some of the short sales, of course, could be against stock already owned that could be delivered.

Some analysts follow these figures with interest, but their interpretations vary. However, the short interest amounts to a relatively small part of total sales of stock, never more than 5 percent even in depression 1931.

There are four basic ways of translating a bearish outlook into action:

1. SELLING OUT AND PUTTING THE CASH INTO SAVINGS ACCOUNTS. When stock prices are at unusually high levels and the market is dominated by speculative activity, the government is likely to take corrective measures, such as increasing margin rates and raising the discount rate. An increase in the discount rate — the charge banks must pay when they borrow from the Federal Reserve system — tends to raise interest rates along the line: the prime rate banks charge their good customers, the rates on personal loans, the interest on mortgages. As interest rates rise, deposits in savings banks, savings and loan organizations and such institutions look more attractive. Thus investors are assured of a good return on the money they take out of the stock market, probably higher than the dividend yield on many common stocks.

Bonds, too, offer an inviting haven for money taken out of equities. In a period of high interest rates bonds sell at depressed prices, and therefore offer not only a good yield but some capital gains possibilities. When the business cycle has turned upward again and the Federal Reserve system has once again lowered the discount rate, the prices of bonds rise again.

2. SHORT SELLING. There is little real difference between selling a stock short and buying it long as a process; but most investors, though they may be perfectly willing to risk their money buying expensive stocks of speculative appeal, can't think in terms of selling short.

A short sale arises when a customer asks his broker to sell, say, 100 shares short for him; and to do this the broker "borrows" the stock, from another customer who leaves the shares in the broker's hands, or from shares that the firm owns, or from another brokerage firm. Then the broker sells the shares as he would handle any other selling order. The money received from the sale goes into an account held by the broker in the short seller's name.

The short seller must eventually buy back from the market the borrowed shares and close out the position. (If the price should happen to move against him — go up instead of down — he will be required to put up cash to meet margin requirements.) When he closes out the position, if he buys lower than he "sold," his profit will be the difference between the sum in the brokerage account received from the sale of the borrowed stock and the amount it costs to buy back the 100 shares of stock to be returned to the lender. The profit will be minus commissions, taxes, etc.

Short selling has long been popular among professionals and sophisticated individuals. However, it must be pointed out that there is an upside risk. A stock owned can go down sharply in price but it can go no lower than zero — the point at which no one will pay a cent for it. But in the case of a short position the upside price is unlimited theoretically. A stock could zoom from $5, to $50, to $500, and even higher. But while the warning is worth considering, the rules of the stock exchanges these days prevent squeezes such as existed in the case of Northern Pacific. Also, most short sellers help protect their positions on the upside with a judicious use of stop orders, so that if a sudden rise should send up the price too high, too fast, they will automatically close their position by purchasing shares. This cuts the risk.

3. SELLING AGAINST THE BOX. Many investors are understandably reluctant — possibly for tax reasons, possibly for sentimental reasons — to sell stocks they have bought or inherited at a very much lower price. Or, perhaps they are unwilling to sell because they own shares of the company in which they work. To protect themselves and yet avoid liquidating their positions (and avoid stiff capital gains taxes) they can sell short, against the box, a variation on the short sale.

Visualize, for example, an investor who owns 100 shares of

General Motors priced around $100 as the market begins to make highs. He becomes worried about the outlook, expecting a decline in prices. So he asks his broker to sell 100 shares of GM short. If, as he expects, the market falls, dragging GM to 85 he can buy 100 shares in the market and make delivery to close his short position.

He still owns his 100 original shares, and though they are down to $85 at current market levels, he has made a 15-point profit on his short sale (minus the brokerage expenses involved). In essence, he has protected his investment at around the $100 level. If, contrary to his judgment, the market moves up, he would have a profit on his own original shares, but a loss on his short position. Either way, he has an "insurance policy" fixing his price at the $100 point minus expenses.

4. OPTIONS NAMED "PUTS" (see also pages 245–247). While this has been less widely used, the system appeals to some bears because it gives them leverage — a large position relative to the money put up — and a known exact amount of dollar risk at a given time.

Perhaps the least complex way of thinking about options is to relate them to a house a person thinks he may buy. Suppose the person doesn't want to buy immediately, because he lacks the cash or can't move for six months. He asks the owner of the house to give him an option to buy the house within a certain number of months, and for this privilege he pays a few hundred dollars. He can either exercise his option and buy the house or change his mind and let the contract lapse.

In terms of the stock market, such an option to buy would be described as a *call*. A call gives an investor the right to buy 100 shares of stock within a certain period, often three months, sometimes six months, occasionally a year. For this he pays a fee. Any time within the period he can exercise the option, or he can let it lapse. The choice remains his. Naturally, he would only buy a call option on a stock if he thought the price would ultimately rise sufficiently above the costs involved to assure him a profit.

A *put* is merely the opposite action. In this case it could be related to a person who owns a house and believes he might want to sell within three months or so. For the privilege of selling to someone he pays that person a fee and receives what can be called a "put." Within the stated period he is guaranteed the right to sell the house. The choice is his.

In terms of stock a put gives the holder of such an option the privilege of selling 100 shares of a stock. He need not own the stock to buy a put. All he has to do is make delivery by buying the stock in the open market and handing it over to whomever has sold him the put.

Naturally, if the price of the underlying stock goes down enough he will exercise the put by asking his broker to purchase 100 shares and make delivery. If the stock does not recede in price enough to make delivery worthwhile, he does nothing. The put lapses. All he has lost, or risked, is the fee involved in buying the put, usually $137.50 on a three-month put, possibly more.

Puts and calls are sold through dealers who are members of the Put and Call Brokers and Dealers Association. The put and call contracts are guaranteed by member firms of the New York Stock Exchange. Thus the underlying shares bought or sold to fulfill the contracts, when exercised, are handled by brokerage firms. Anyone can buy a put through his own brokerage firm. Large New York newspapers regularly carry advertisements placed by put and call dealers, indicating what stocks are being offered as either puts or calls and the premiums involved.

In one sense, the use of puts involves more technical knowledge than short selling. Furthermore, many account executives of brokerage firms, long accustomed to short sales, do not have much experience with puts.

Another sound approach for the bear with a large portfolio of stocks might be the writing of options. For every put or call issued, there must be someone who stands on the other side of the contracts — namely an option writer.

Suppose that an investor becomes discouraged about the outlook of the market. For example: he owns Delta Airlines, in which he has a good profit. Believing the stock still shows a rising tendency, but satisfied with his own capital gain, he decides to write a call on his stock. This obligates him to deliver 100 shares of Delta to someone who has bought his call. For writing the option he receives the premium of several hundred dollars, minus the broker's fee. When the call is exercised, as he expected it would be, he delivers his own 100 shares of stock. He has closed out his position and earned a few dollars while doing so.

A variation on this idea is the writing of options covering both sides — a put and a call. In the trade this is called a straddle. Generally only one side would be exercised, and in this Delta case it would be the call. However, the option writer would have received two premiums — one for writing the call and one for writing the put.*

One of the most impressive bears of all time was none other than Bernard Baruch, who tells the story of his own winning venture selling short Amalgamated Copper many years ago.

Without putting up a penny of their own money, a group of businessmen decided to launch a company called Amalgamated Copper Company, which acquired Anaconda Copper and some other properties in exchange for a bank check made out for $39,000,000, not to be cashed for a while.

Then the organizers sold $75,000,000 of securities in the new company at $100 a share, with plenty of fanfare. Once this money was in hand, the owner of Anaconda who had agreed to sell the properties was told he could cash the $39,000,000 check.

Then the fun began. Men with prestigious names became directors or sponsors of Amalgamated. Their aim was to form a trust that would control much of the world's copper supply and thus keep prices of the metal high. Those were the days

---

*A person with a good-sized portfolio could earn possibly 15 percent a year by writing straddles on his shares.

when industrial trusts were popular and the government had as yet made few attempts to break them up.

The price of Amalgamated moved up quite steadily to 130, within a few months of the offering date of the shares.

Bernard Baruch had watched the formation of the company, including its obvious overcapitalization, and he was convinced that the price of the share was much too high. More than that, he reasoned that the current high prices of copper would eventually curtail demand and then the market would become glutted with unsold supplies of the metal.

At this point he sold Amalgamated short. As it does in Wall Street, the news got around that Baruch was selling short, and some important business friends warned him not to antagonize "the big fellows."

"I was also being told how wicked it was to be short of the market, and to tear down a constructive enterprise. All this is nonsense, of course. If the Amalgamated organizers had not overcapitalized and then blown the stock up, it would never have risen to such heights or descended to the depths it afterwards did. What was dropping the copper shares was the irresistible force of economic gravitation seeking its proper level," he recalled in his memoirs.

Amalgamated soon cut its dividends from $8 to $6 a share, and the news of that forced the stock's price further downward. Eventually it dropped to 60. Mr. Baruch, who was only thirty-one at the time, reported that his profits on his short transaction in Amalgamated amounted to $700,000.

In the spring of 1962 a modern bear named Jeb Wofford made a small fortune in the stock market while many people were losing large fortunes. A midwesterner best known as a member of the 1952 Olympic equestrian team, Jeb Wofford (unlike Mr. Baruch) had no experience on Wall Street. In fact, aside from the rigorous discipline required to train for championship riding, he had few qualifications for any kind of business.

Late in 1961 he had become seriously worried about the handling of his family's money, much of which was held in trust by a large midwestern bank. The bank officers refused to sell out the common stock holdings, pointing out that the investments were in high quality companies like American Telephone and Telegraph and International Business Machines. Where could they find sounder investments? And what about the capital gains taxes that would have to be paid? Such stocks, they insisted, would ride out any economic downturn. Besides, they doubted that any drastic market break would occur.

Mr. Wofford, believing that the market was heading toward serious trouble, disputed this kind of thinking. He reasoned there must be effective ways to operate as a bear — that is, one who expects stocks to decline — and thus protect one's capital in a market downturn. He began to read everything he could find about business cycles, and he subscribed to numerous market letters and advisory services. Having carefully studied the basic ways of operating as a bear and the costs involved, he began to try his luck in the market around the beginning of 1962.

By April, Jeb Wofford had begun to make substantial sums of money. A stockbroker brought Wofford to the attention of the *New York Times,* and an article was written about him which was published eventually in June. By then there was no doubt about it: Mr. Wofford had profited greatly from his operations as a bear prior to and during the second biggest stock market break in history, during which the Dow Jones industrial average dropped about 26 percent. His profits were estimated at several hundred thousands of dollars by his broker.

There was no skulduggery involved. Jeb Wofford, thanks to his own determination, disciplined judgment, and shrewdness, succeeded as a novice where many more experienced men had failed.

What he did any other investor can, and possibly should do — at least to some extent — if he believes that a market has moved up so far that it stands in danger of a sharp reversal.

He devoted himself and a limited amount of capital — $30,000 — to buying puts. He centered much attention on

IBM puts, owning more than 20 of them at one time. On each he made a profit. The prices of IBM the first six months of 1962 show that he could not lose:

January 2	572
February 1	554
March 1	543
April 2	525
May 1	462
May 28*	361
June 1	385
June 14	300

Do bears follow fundamentals or do they use the technical approach? Among professional traders, there are many and perhaps a majority who follow a strictly technical approach, selling short when their charts, usually kept daily, indicate that price levels have been broken on the downside. If they are faithful chart followers then they must sell.

However, many individual bears tend to watch the fundamentals. For example, Bernard Baruch took the short position in Amalgamated Copper because of his faith in facts — namely that the metal had become overpriced and that sales must decline. A chart in this instance probably would have indicated a bullish outlook because of the artificial support given the stock by promoters. The promoters attracted unwary investors who through lack of information about the copper price situation and the overcapitalization of the company bought the stock at high prices on hopes.

Jeb Wofford also followed the fundamentals, believing that overspeculation in the stock market would correct itself. However, he applied a technical approach in keeping with his own interest in statistics. He kept voluminous price records of the companies in which he held puts.

It can be argued with irrefutable logic that a bear *in the long run* must surely lose because of the steady growth of the economy

*Day of big break; a drop of 37 points from previous day.

of this country and of the world. To convince yourself of the truth of this argument turn back to the chart in Figure 9 showing the trend of the Dow Jones industrial average over a long period of years. Bears like Bernard Baruch and Jeb Wofford knew this as well as any bull, but they believed that quick short-term profits could be made with a bear approach, and they were right.

Thus the important idea for every sophisticated investor to grasp is that it pays to be a bear at times, but not all the time. However, as indicated before, there are times when it pays an investor to be bearish in a specific stock even though you are not pessimistic about the trend in the market as a whole.

In the case of a technological breakthrough, one classic example is the introduction of Crest toothpaste and its endorsement by the American Dental Association. The ADA endorsement "bulled" the shares of Crest's maker, Procter & Gamble, and hurt the prospects of rival toothpaste makers, such as Colgate-Palmolive.

To summarize, the smart woman investor can — and should — act like a bear at times, even when her old reliable stocks are involved. She can do it in three ways, depending on her acumen.

1. She can sell her shares and sit out a recession with cash or short-term government securities, or enter the bond market.

2. She can sell short, either stocks that she thinks will be hurt by a recession or a setback in its own industry. She can, of course, sell short against her own holdings, the device known as "selling against the box." By doing this she "nails down" the paper profits she has in her position.

3. For the sophisticated person who wants to be an active bear, the purchase of puts provides a way of doing this while knowing the exact cost, if wrong about the trend of the stocks.

14 | Desirable Bottoms, Dangerous Tops

Your broker, speaking for the investment analysts from whom he gets his information, may talk impressively sometimes of "fundamentals" versus "technicalities" influencing your stocks, as mentioned briefly in Chapter 13. To put it differently, he might speak of fundamental research as contrasted to technical research, or the fundamentalists versus the technicians. Don't let the high-flown language ruffle your poise.

It's not so difficult to understand. In Chapter 8 on the work of the analyst, the stress was on some of the practical methods he uses to arrive at his conclusions, such as sales and earnings trends, competitive factors, price earnings trends, economic cycles. In applying these he uses what your broker calls fundamental research. He remains largely disinterested in the so-called technical factors ever present in the market.

Generally speaking, most of the research that reaches you — the investor — is of the fundamental variety: advice to buy or sell based on basic information plus some educated judgments of managerial skills and competitive factors.

However, most analysts also keep some sort of charts which give them a "picture" of the way a stock's price is acting — in relation to earnings, in relation to general stock movements, and in relation to changes in the economy. In the same way the analyst watches charts of price trends of the so-called stock market averages. These are a tool to help his thinking just as a slide rule or a computer is.

Some analysts go further than this and live or work almost wholly by charts. In other words, they call themselves technicians and they plot the course of stocks on their charts just as a navigator charts a ship's course, jotting down price changes sometimes hour by hour, day by day, week by week. Often they use complex interpretations.

These technical analysts take themselves very seriously and sometimes to the average investor their talk sounds like riddles. They approach the market with a dramatic flair. From my observation they usually are the type of person who thrives on modern art because they can weave their own messages into it, and use technical jargon to interpret what they mean. True technicians ignore fundamentals: they trade stocks strictly by their charts. Their followers tend to be the more sophisticated type of in-and-out traders.

The formations made by their charts in relation to the volume of shares traded at the same time tell them a story. They can give an opinion, for example, as to when a stock is under accumulation and thus is rising in price because of the impact of large buy orders. On the other hand, they can "read" from their charts when a stock is being sold in volume, forcing down the price. At a time when institutional buyers, namely the mutual funds, pension funds, college endowment funds and big trusts, account for about fifty percent of the trading volume, such information is important.

The charts can tell them when a stock rises to the point where "resistance" sets in and enough sales can be expected to come into the picture to force it down. Or, conversely, they can figure when a stock sells at a low enough price to attract enough orders on the buy side to firm its price once more.

It stands to reason if every investor, and hence all investment analysts, bought or sold only on the basis of similar interpretations of what charts say, there would be a rush to buy (or sell) the same stock at the same time. Like a hopeless traffic jam, traffic in the shares would have to stop or slow down.

Luckily it doesn't work out that way. There are so many

DESIRABLE BOTTOMS, DANGEROUS TOPS

investors, individual and institutional, in the market at any time that some may be buying and some selling the same stock at the same time, and all for very logical reasons.

Obviously, if hundreds of thousands of investors are watching a stock for technical indicators to either buy or sell, it is valuable for an investor to be aware of how such charting is done.

As you become more skilled in investing you may want to keep charts yourself. Furthermore, you probably will be curious about the technical aspects.

Perhaps the best books on the subject have been written by John Magee — a doubleheader, boxed together, called *Semantics of Wall Street* and *Technical Analysis of Stock Trends,* in which he covers the various important formations that can be seen on charts.

In a sense, a chartist can be described as a man who wants to follow the crowd — of fellow sophisticates, that is. As you remember from Chapter 5 on how the stock market operates, the specialists who "run the books" for particular stocks on the floor of the exchange, keep little books. In them they write down orders to buy and sell shares that cannot be exercised currently because the prices are "away" from the orders.

Obviously when quite suddenly a large number of the orders on their books are exercised, then the spate of orders for such stocks will show up on the tape and will have an effect on the market. Charted, these price swings under the impact of buy and sell orders at various levels constitute the "food" the chartists digest hungrily.

This information might come to you in capsuled form like this from your broker, "Well, Polaroid has just made a triple bottom. It looks like a buy."

What would this mean in terms of a chart? It means that over a period of time the stock has dropped, say to a price of 50; then buying, perhaps from a batch of orders listed in the specialist's book, has suddenly been activated and pushed the price ahead. Perhaps the price continues up again for a while and then drops once more to about 50 with the result that another group of orders enters. Once again the price moves up quite sharply. After a further decline to the 50 level, the price might once again take off for an even higher level than the two upswings before. To a technician the triple bottom might indicate a stock ready to take a sustained flight, if not into the wild blue yonder at least up high enough to satisfy some traders' desire for capital gains.

Perhaps at such a point in time you should buy, too. Your broker, if he has faith in the technical analysis done by his firm, might suggest that you do so.

A triple top, on the other hand, acts like a red flag for some analysts. It can indicate that a stock is having trouble rising above a certain level. Let's say in this instance the price of the stock moves up to 70 at which time selling enters and slaps it down smartly like a naughty child. Once again it dares rise to the same level and once again it gets put down by a large number of selling orders. Perhaps quite a few owners of the shares have good profits and want "out" at 70. Once again after the decline the stock thrusts its head upwards to the 70 point, then declines. About that time a technician might advise that the stock should be sold, or at least not bought, because it has been unable to move above the 70 level.

No wonder that brokers and analysts are excessively interested in tops and bottoms — and not yours or any other woman's — during the working day. A top means the point or level at which the stock apparently cannot move higher — a time to be cautious and possibly sell. A bottom indicates a point or level at which a stock's price probably cannot go lower but which could indicate a recovery.

Since brokers are much more savvy about bottoms than tops — about urging you to go into a market rather than to get out of it — they will talk to you more often about bottoms.

When a stock is falling fast and steadily no one can tell the prices at which a turn will come. Perhaps the person with the best idea, if he's alert, is the specialist on the floor of the stock exchange. He can take a look at his book and know how many buy orders he has at various prices. True, the stock buyer can change his mind overnight or a few hours after he has placed an order, but still the weight of orders must give the specialist a good idea of the market. The trouble is that only the specialist is supposed to know what is on his books.

However, chartists, by keeping their noses close to their charts (many of them are serious, bespectacled types) and their slide rules handy, think they can figure the turn about the time it comes, if not the exact price.

One of their most useful configurations is called "the head and shoulders formation." It looks very much like just that, and with a little imagination you see the left shoulder, looking at it from your direction as a reader, then the price rise that forms the so-called "head," and the price decline which is followed by another little rise that takes the right shoulder no higher than the left, and then drops even more sharply as if to form an arm.

A technician following the chart in Figure 14 might advise a sale around the time (and price) that the right shoulder fails to go much higher than the left — that is, around October 23. Of course, a little shrug might alter his opinion.

On the chart in Figure 14, from October 16 to November 27 you see the almost exact reverse involving the shoulders and the head. The technician would note that the left shoulder facing you droops, steadies, then droops to a much lower head, followed by an upswing and a leveling which evens the process.

All of this signals to the avid chartist a bullish outlook for the stock. Its declines apparently brought in enough buying orders at such lower levels to bring an upswing. Hence the technician might be writing reports urging the firm's customer to buy, buy. With this he would include a few fundamental facts such as prices, dividends, and perhaps targets to which he thinks the price might rise based on the earnings outlook. In this case there was an upswing.

Figure 14
Broker's Comment

SYS SYSTRON-DONNER. Scientific Instrumentation 1,680,000 Shares Common. Hi & Lo: 1971-72, 24 3/4, 9 3/4; 1970, 28 5/8, 7 7/8. There would be those who would say that "SYS" has "broken the up trend" and is therefore weak. We don't exactly agree. We see no real weakness here at this time. We see a stock that has moved generally up in a steady trend. And would not split hairs about the failue of "SYS" to "bounce" off the long-term trendline. We would be considering also the volume action; and the various support levels. Notice that every time this stock has reacted it has retreated only to a previous support level; a previous top or series of tops. We see nothing wrong here.

Recommended: To buy SYS SYSTRON-DONNER at the market. Closing Limit 20.

Generally, even the most technical of the chartists, who maintains that he lives by charts alone, does include a few fundamentals in his analysis, though he probably won't admit it.

On the contrary, the fundamentalist who claims he hates charts uses them at least to give him a picture of the movement of a stock he is discussing.

Should you keep a chart of your pet stocks — those you already own and those in which you are interested enough to consider buying? Yes, it can be a very rewarding experience to follow the course of your stocks on paper, especially if you plan to hold them for a relatively long period of time, such as long enough to establish capital gains.

Suppose that you have acquired a portfolio of half-a-dozen stocks, including some pivotal ones and a couple of go-go growth types, with the idea that you will hang on to all of them until they have given you a 15 percent increase in price, in each case.

Of course, not being a completely blind or a foolhardy investor you will sell before you reach these targets if your broker advises you to get out of a stock for a specific reason such as a change in the company's earnings outlook, or if your own research gives you a solid reason for selling. A belief that the economy is headed into a recession or that the stock market will reel backward under the impact of credit restrictions because of the fight by the government against inflation could be a good reason — a sound reason for getting out of the market altogether.

You decide that you will chart your stocks regularly, picking a weekly schedule. For simplicity's sake let's say that you decide to take the range for the week and the final price each Friday. You need six pieces of graph paper, quite large, a pencil and a Sunday newspaper that carries the high-low range for the week and the closing price in its stock quotations.

Most every school student can provide a parent with graph paper, and it's a good way to induce your child subtly to take an interest in the stock market, too. Mark out a long horizontal line on a piece of this paper and a long vertical one that meets it at right angles. The horizontal, or base, line should be notched by your pencil into 52 parts, with the printed lines of the graph paper giving you a vertical sweep. In this way your chart can cover a full year.

On the penciled vertical line you can notch off the price levels for your stock.

In essence your chart consists of simple little vertical lines with two or three "ticks" on each:

Obviously, the week's high price is the top tick made with your pencil, and the low is the bottom one. The middle tick, in this case is the closing quote. It might, of course, be the same price as the high or low. Ignore the fractional prices, raising them to the nearest full price if more than half a cent, and cutting them to the next lower price, if less than half a cent, unless you are a stickler for more accuracy. Whichever way you approach your charts, at least be consistent.

A second important part of your charting (and now you become a fundamentalist) is to note major news events on your chart, such as a report by your company of much higher quarterly earnings, or news of peace in Vietnam. You have to use your sense of logic. For example, a worsening of the Mideast crisis often alarms politicians and makes front-page headlines, but particular stocks may be insulated against such reports. A cosmetic stock probably would not react, unless of course the whole market swings up or down.

If there is a definite market movement on news, then you should note this on your chart.

In making your charts you might find that prices also drop when the company pays a stock dividend. The date and the amount of the stock payment should be noted on your chart. Generally, you will notice that the stock dividend is soon absorbed and the stock moves on without much change.

However, if the dividend happens to be of the size called a stock split then you will have to revise your chart accordingly. For example, if a stock selling for $100 is split two for one, the price probably drops to the $50 level for a while and then, hopefully, edges upwards in price. The reason is that often stocks that are split belong to companies that have rising earnings — the kind attractive to eager buyers like you.

If the stock split is two-for-one or three-for-one your charting doesn't become that much harder because you can think in terms of halves, or thirds. You can rechart the year's prices, or you can simply double (or triple) the prices in the newspaper after the split becomes effective and continue your chart through the year.

Now for the neat, clean Grecian touch of bar graphs at the bottom of your price charts:

They will tell you the trading volume in your stock each week. For a chartist this volume is important because by means of it she notes, for example, that when the price falls to a certain level a large amount of volume enters, apparently pushing the price upwards again.

Another helpful addition to your chart keeping that need not take you more than a few minutes now and then is a series of sales and earnings graphs for your company. These could be bar graphs:

```
              Sales
         |‾‾‾‾|
   1969  | net|
         |5½% |_____
         |____|_____|

   1970  | 6% |_____
         |____|_____|

   1971  | 8% |_____
         |____|_____|
```

If your company is growing it should be increasing sales each year and earnings, too. If it can increase the percentage of net income to sales, so much the better.

As a stockholder, you need to follow these important relationships because if sales falter you want to know why. It might be a time to sell. Also, if earnings do not rise as fast as sales, that also gives you something to ponder about.

Once you have become accustomed — and enthusiastic — about keeping charts, then you might want to add more sophisticated variations. Frankly, I prefer the simple approach to charting outlined in this chapter.

15 | The Care and Feeding of Securities

Your stocks deserve personal attention much the same as you give your children. You should be enthusiastic, determined, persistent, analytical, and the more objective the better. You cannot sit back relaxed, saying, "They can take care of themselves." Even if you have held a stock twenty-one happy years or more it still needs watching.

The most important aspect of a stock, like a child, is how it turns out. Its behavior takes close watching.

DIVIDENDS. The first thing to know about your company, once you have become a stockholder, is its dividend policy, which often can be figured from prior years.

When you bought the stock your broker probably said something like this during the discussion, "The stock pays $4 a year." Perhaps you had obtained some data on the company from reference manuals or from brokerage firms' analysis.

From his remarks you might assume that every three months you could expect $1 a share, but you could be wrong. Some companies do have a "regular" common dividend rate, which they would not miss despite earthquakes, wars, etc.* Others might lower their dividends or skip them if earnings become bad, but otherwise stick to a regular schedule.

---

*The Pennsylvania Railroad (which became the Penn Central) regularly paid dividends every year from 1848 to 1969, even in years when it had losses. Then in 1970 it was derailed into bankruptcy. The Singer Company is a well-known persistent dividend payer, starting with 1863; it is still going strong. *Vive la différence!*

Suppose you are entitled to a dividend and it fails to arrive. Wait about ten days after the payment date and then check with the company. Remember mails are slow and inefficient these days. In writing the company write directly to the secretary, at the head office. However, if you have been a stockholder for a while you probably have noticed the name of the bank on which the dividend check is drawn. For faster service you can write directly to the bank. The name of the bank or "transfer agent" handling dividends should be written in your notebook.

Most companies report that very few dividend checks are lost. On notification, the bank will stop payment of the check and issue you a new one, after making sure that your mailing address is correct — a source of some lost checks. There will be no charge to you, but don't confound the problem by cashing the same dividend checks twice, or you will cause much trouble.

Losing a stock certificate is a much more serious matter, and it can be costly to you in money and trouble, not to mention worry.

Since stock certificates can become lost, especially when they are owned by elderly, absentminded or much traveled investors, the better part of wisdom is to have the shares registered in your name (meaning the dividends and annual reports will come to your home) but held by your broker. Then the certificates themselves are his responsibility. Regularly you will receive a statement from the brokerage firm indicating what shares it holds in your account. If you happen to be in Pakistan or Alaska and suddenly decide to sell you can notify your broker, and he has the shares on hand.

STOCK DIVIDENDS. Many companies pay dividends in the form of shares of stock, or a mixture of cash and stock, especially in the case of growth-type companies that want to conserve cash and funnel it back into the company.

Stockholders often relish stock dividends on the theory that they generally receive something worth money. In truth, they don't. If you pause to think for a moment, you can liken a stock dividend situation to a pie that is sliced a little thinner.

Suppose a company has 1,000,000 shares outstanding, and you own 100 shares or 1/10,000 of the company. Now let's assume that the company suddenly announces a stock split of two for one. It now has 2,000,000 shares outstanding, and it sends you a certificate for 100 additional shares, giving you a total of 200 shares. Now figure out your proportionate interest, which is still 1/10,000 part of the company. Your slice of the company is just the same, although it really is two slices of the pie. It has been cut into smaller pieces just as you might do if you suddenly expected more guests for dinner.

However, a shareholder in a growth company likes these splits because generally they are issued only by companies whose earnings are growing, and thus when the stock is split two for one, the price doesn't quite drop to one-half the former price. If it does, it soon moves proportionately higher.

Stock splits are mentioned ahead of dividends in stock because they are easier to understand, and easier to follow in terms of price trends. Actually, splits and stock dividends are close relatives, both indicating that the same company is cutting the pie — the same pie. The rule of thumb of the New York Stock Exchange is that a split is anything amounting to more than 20 percent, while anything less, such as a 5 percent payment in stock would be called a dividend. A 20 percent payment could be dubbed a one-for-five stock split — namely one new share for each five owned.

Suppose that a company declares a 15 percent stock dividend, and you own 100 shares. You would receive a certificate for 15 additional shares. If you owned only 10 shares, a 15 percent stock dividend would mean 1½ shares. The company might mail you one new share and the cash equivalent of the fractional shares. The cash amount would be based on the average price of the stock at a certain date, such as the date the declaration of a dividend was made.

IBM has been mentioned endlessly by financial writers as the classic example of a company that has grown fast and done well for its stockholders by conserving cash and paying stock dividends and stock splits. IBM's progress illustrates the case of a company whose stockholders share a pie that grows more valuable with persistent regularity. However, there may be other reasons for a company to split its shares. If the stock over a period of time has risen to a high price level — for example, $100 or $150 a share or more — the company might split the shares two for one, three for one or even five for one, to lower the price and hence make it more accessible to small stockholders.

Still another reason is that a company might want its shares lower priced so that it could help ward off a takeover by having the shares more widely held by a large number of stockholders, assuming that more investors would buy the stock. Naturally, it would cost more for a group interested in taking over a company if they had to reach many thousands of stockholders, compared with just a thousand or so.

Often when the stock is split, the company raises its dividend rate. Thus a $50 stock (current market value) that paid a $2-a-share dividend might be split into two shares, worth $25 each after the split, but paying a $1.10 dividend each.

A company quite often splits its shares and raises its dividend at a time when it fears a proxy fight, a psychological move to please stockholders with the possibility that the split shares might eventually rise in value proportionately higher than before the split, nudged upwards by the higher dividend in cash.

PROXY FIGHTS. A proxy fight is a battle usually waged to get control of or otherwise change the management of a company by an outside group. Of course, in some closely owned companies proxy fights have been waged by unhappy members of the family owning control of the company. At the other extreme, occasionally a proxy battle is begun by one small stockholder in a large corporation.

In any event, the dissident group appeals to other stockholders for approval, asking them to vote in favor of a new slate or a few new members to the board of directors. Directors play a key role in a company because a corporation is ostensibly run by its directors.

However, there are boards and boards. In some companies the board is nothing more than a rubber stamp group that smiles at the chairman and/or president and votes whatever they suggest. Other boards work hard, argue hard, and voice opinions.

For years the nation's big oil companies generally had "inside" boards, composed almost entirely of company officials and the companies' legal counsel. The oil companies used positions on the boards to reward retired or elderly officers and as a training ground for executives who hadn't yet reached the top of the ladder but might soon. The theory was that the oil business needed, not outside blood, but an infusion of executive talents within the company because of the specialized nature of the business.

The theory for outside boards, especially in consumer-type industries, is that a group of leading men from many fields can contribute new and varied ideas.

In either case, since the board of directors at least nominally runs the company, it remains the focus of interest in proxy fights.

PREEMPTIVE RIGHTS. One of the valuable rights made available to you as a stockholder in some companies, notably American Telephone and Telegraph and Consolidated Edison, for example, is called preemptive rights. It means the right of the stockholder to buy shares, usually at a favorable discount, ahead of the public. Sometimes the rights offering involves an offer of debentures or preferred stock.

The company will mail you a letter outlining the rights offering and giving you a chance to exercise the rights. Don't ever throw away the letter containing the rights in the offering because most always it has some money value for you. In Chapter 18 you can find more details about rights offerings and how to figure by a formula what the rights should be worth in cash.

THE ANNUAL REPORT. Once you become a stockholder you will begin to receive quarterly reports. Not all companies mail them to stockholders, because they are expensive, but the typical large listed company does. Some are quite elaborate, such as the quarterly reports of General Motors, picturing a new model car on the cover. Others are a simple sheet of paper or a two-page folder. The quarterly statements usually include sales, earnings, net income per share, and a simplified balance sheet for the recent quarter.

Sometime after the end of the company's fiscal year but some weeks before the annual meeting, the shareholder receives the annual report. These too range widely from fifty-page color jobs to a two-page folder. Some have a short message from the president or chairman; some a lengthy one which discusses not only the company's operations, the industries in which it operates, but also comments about the state of the economy (and occasionally even the world).

Reports, especially some of the British corporate statements, have a fascination all their own. Large companies with worldwide operations must have a grip on local events in various parts of the world. An annual report can provide some interesting insights. I have often thought that a good historian should read annual reports of major industrial corporations over a period of years to give him an interesting new course of study for economic history.

Be sure that before you go to your company's annual meeting you read the proxy statement. It will tell you about any proposals that will come before the meeting. Such proposals can run an unusual gamut. I remember one in which it was mentioned that the company intended to buy the president's house for $200,000, certainly a subject that could be bitterly debated at the annual meeting. Still others contain proposals on changing the bylaws to make it harder for outsiders to take over the company by merger. For example, in 1969 Tiffany & Company stockholders were asked to vote in favor of such a plan. The company, relatively small as corporations go, has been worried about eager outsiders who would love to gain control of it and possibly add the big jewelry and silverware maker to their conglomerate business. Tiffany, of course, has a certain prestige which has not been lost on some of the fast-moving merger masters.

The proxy statement will also contain the names of directors to be voted at the meeting, or by mail. Be sure to mail in your signed proxy, voting for directors and the proposals, or against them as you see fit. Better yet, go to the annual meeting in person. It will be worth the effort in broadening your investment IQ.

The annual meeting is conducted according to an agenda. At some efficiently run meetings, the stockholders receive a copy of the agenda, carefully indicating at what points they can speak. Other times the chairman or president, whichever one presides, will announce the procedures, indicating when stockholders can make motions or ask questions, and when the voting for directors will begin.

Obviously, it is much fairer for the questions by stockholders to be raised before the voting of directors, so don't sit idly if a management pushes through the voting, walking over such an obvious right.

What are some of the questions that a stockholder might want to raise?

Mergers — these days many companies have become merger-minded. Some mergers work out well for a company; others cost too much in terms of the stock or cash that must be paid for the company acquired.

Managements differ widely in their attitude about mergers, and it is a subject that should be aired with the stockholders. For example, some companies acquire only those firms that make sense — that fit into their corporate structure neatly. Warner Lambert, a pharmaceutical company, acquired American Optical, a maker of scientific instruments. The two scientifically oriented companies fit together. Gulf & Western Industries is a conglomerate that doesn't make much "sense," since it has spread itself over fields as widely varied as motion pictures, cigars, agricultural products, auto parts and zinc. How a stockholder can analyze the prospects of a company like that, I cannot understand.

Products — successful and not so successful — should be a subject for discussion. Sometimes stockholders can give management hints or ideas about products. Every company, sooner or later, has a product failure, and stockholders have a right to know why.

Management turnover — sometimes if many top people in a company's management are leaving, it can spell trouble ahead.

There's usually a reason. For example, vice-presidents came and went at Revlon some years ago like people going through a revolving door. The president was hard to deal with. It took a while for the situation to be smoothed over; meanwhile, the stock jittered in price. Sewell Avery, when he headed Montgomery Ward, fired vice-presidents by the dozen; so much so that stockholders became alarmed at the direction the company was taking.

Labor costs, ever rising, are a point of discussion at many meetings. Does the management expect a long strike in a particular year? How can increasing wages be offset by more automation?

The annual meeting is the one time of year when a stockholder can ask questions freely — and expect answers. Furthermore, other stockholders listening to the answers or in some cases the lack of answers from management can get ideas about the investment quality of the stock. Often at the meeting the chairman or president will volunteer a prediction about the outlook for the year, or look even farther into the future. This is not necessarily information that he puts into the annual or interim reports. It may come in reply to searching stockholder questions.

Unfortunately, I have attended some annual meetings as a financial reporter during which no stockholder asked about future earnings, and the president offered no prediction. I cannot imagine a stockholder not wanting to know this information, and yet the opportunity slipped by.

Don't be shy. Get on your feet and ask what the outlook is. The head of your company has the job of ordering his experts to plan ahead, budgeting both costs and reinvestment of capital, along with scheduling new products. He knows what the company plans to spend on plants, machinery; he knows how sales are going currently and he has, possibly in his pocket, projections made by his sales managers for the ensuing months. He knows also the level of expenses; his labor relations director probably has alerted him to the higher cost of wages, especially if a new contract is about to be negotiated. A strike or other crisis can always occur and change the best-laid plans; but often a company president even has a pretty good idea whether this will happen. In the company's laboratories, there are often unpublicized new products ready for the production line, and the president has a pretty good idea of their potential too. Naturally a large number of new products, more than the investor realizes, fail each year for lack of enough advertising, inability to get consumer acceptance or other reasons. Still, a company president has a good idea of what new products can do to help earnings and their chances of success.

If he doesn't know all this then he might not be a good president. As a stockholder you have a right to ask questions along these lines. In some cases you will receive straightforward answers; sometimes the replies will be devious. The more stockholders ask, generally the better the meeting is and the better answers they receive.

Naturally, stockholders also want information about dividends, and a president has some good ideas about this, too. He will often field the question by saying that only the directors can declare dividends — an obvious remark. However, a persistent stockholder might point out that directors usually act on dividends in accordance with the suggestions of the company's president. Many presidents are quite willing to tell the annual meeting what they plan to recommend.

The range is wide among companies in their thinking about

dividends. Growth-type companies like to pay little or nothing, relying on stock dividends or the fast price growth in the shares to keep stockholders happy. Other companies regularly allot about 50 percent of earnings to dividends; still others pay out up to 90 percent.

At many annual meetings you will see in action some of the so-called gadfly stockholders — a group epitomized by people like Lewis Gilbert, his brother John, and Mrs. Wilma Soss. You may not like them, either their personalities or their persistent questioning of management at meetings, but they have been crusaders, making major gains for the small taxpayers, just as Ralph Nader has won safety features in cars from a recalcitrant auto industry.

Years ago in the nineteen thirties as a young man, Lewis Gilbert went to the Bethlehem Steel Corporation annual meeting. He rose up and demanded to know why the management was paying a retired corporate official, Charles Schwab, then in his eighties, a pension of $250,000 a year. True, the official in question had helped develop the company, and there was no doubt that Bethlehem Steel was a wealthy organization. But Mr. Gilbert challenged the right of management to pay what even nowadays would be regarded as a huge pension and bonus.

It is unfortunate that many successful business leaders develop an ego complex so advanced that they think it should be measured in terms of millions of dollars payable to them by their companies. In this case the pension would have been the highest ever paid to a corporate official, at least as far as anyone could find out at the time. Remember, those were depression years.

Mr. Gilbert, a bustling, determined man, who can be sarcastic when necessary, astounded the meeting with his protest. How much is a man worth?

In those days it never occurred to the stouthearted, dignified, high-handed leaders of major companies that the high pensions and salaries they voted officials — usually a rubber-stamp vote — would be questioned by humble stockholders, especially ones that owned only a few shares.

In the case of Bethlehem, Mr. Gilbert won the battle ultimately and the company did not pay the high pension it had intended, cutting it to $180,000.*

Often even today corporate officials deride Mr. Gilbert, his brother, and Mrs. Soss for their persistent questions. Fellow stockholders sometimes shout "Sit down, shut up," and worse, at them. Still their various crusades have highlighted one significant point — the fact that an owner of one share has just as many rights as the owner of a million shares. He can question, criticize, suggest at the annual meeting. The so-called gadfly stockholders have stung many managements into improvements that might not have occurred except for them.

The awful truth is that most stockholders are not willing to fight for their inherent rights and they tend to sit quietly, or limply sell their shares if the management fails to move in the right directions. Sometimes they are so limp that they watch the company go slowly down the drain — without even plugging their own losses on the shares by selling.

It takes a feisty, determined, vociferous, embarrassment-proof stockholder to stand up year after year and demand improvements in the midst of arrogant corporate officials and antagonistic stockholders.

To their credit the Gilberts and Mrs. Soss have scored some advances: 1) companies like Bethlehem Steel have become more sensitive about paying huge pensions and bonuses; 2) companies now provide more data in annual reports and also (in many cases) issue interim reports and post annual meeting reports; 3) reports break down more items like sales and earnings by divisions and foreign operations; 4) meetings are being rotated to other cities from the company's corporate headquarters, so that wider groups of stockholders can attend; 5) some companies have adopted cumulative voting for shareholders.† The gadflys have insisted

---

*Mr. Gilbert commented: "I was satisfied at the reduction, especially since Schwab told me he was hard up."

†Cumulative voting permits stockholders to lump their votes for directors, so that minority directors have more chance of getting elected.

on company auditors being present at meetings for questioning by stockholders — a good idea at a time when some companies have had accounting problems.

For example, a few years ago there was the Billie Sol Estes case, which involved several large finance companies holding, the gadflys thought, collateral in the form of fertilizer which did not exist. Or the famous "salad oil" swindle involving a subsidiary of American Express Company because of vegetable oil that did not exist. In this case some major banks holding warehouse receipts for the oil were caught without any oil to back the receipts; a brokerage firm failed as a result of the swindle and another was forced into a merger.

Such cases were not by any means uncovered by small investors, but the fact that the Gilberts and Sosses stand ready to ask questions does keep management more alert — running scared sometimes.

Stockholders' own worst enemies these days are themselves. If a few more would rise and ask questions at annual meetings they would 1) get more answers, and 2) be treated better.

For example, in 1969 a small woman stockholder (owner of a few shares) rose at the Engelhard Industries annual meeting in Newark and asked why the company had so many vice-presidents, all obviously highly paid officials. One logical answer to the question could have been that the company had recently gone through a merger and thus acquired quite a few officers who were vice-presidents. A second reply could have been that the company, which deals in precious metals, is basically a selling business which requires skilled experts to head each of its many types of selling operations. But management, apparently surprised by the question, did not have a good answer but floundered quite badly. Those of us who attended the meeting got the feeling that the management will think a long time before it creates new vice-presidents.

Women stockholders, especially, appear to be either lazy, unsure of themselves or shy at annual meetings. It's sad because they, more than most men, have the time and energy actually to attend meetings. And one stockholder voice crying in the corporate wilderness can — and in fact has — brought worthwhile changes.

Many years ago there was a famous engineer-inventor working for General Motors called Charles Kettering, who became fascinated by the prospects of a new kind of engine which had been invented by a German named Diesel. For some years Kettering tinkered with a Diesel engine in a boat he owned; then he convinced the GM management that Diesel engines could be used successfully in railroad locomotives. The nation's two leading builders of steam locomotives scoffed at the idea, convinced that the Diesel could never replace or perform as well as the modern steam engine. While Kettering tried desperately to find a railroad president adventurous enough to buy and try one of his Diesels, the two companies, American Locomotive and Baldwin Locomotive Works, apparently ignored his efforts.

Finally, Kettering found a man named Budd, the president of the Chicago, Burlington & Quincy Railroad, who took a chance and tried out the first GM passenger locomotive Diesel. It succeeded so well that gradually other railroads began to buy Diesels, but still the two old-line steam engine builders lagged behind.

The result was amazing for U.S. industry. GM, the large automobile builder, won the market for Diesel locomotives. Baldwin went into bankruptcy; American Locomotive experienced some lean years.

Stockholders of those days, if they had been alert, could have predicted the outcome — and sold their stock in the steam engine builders who lost a multimillion dollar market.

Probably much the same action — to sell out — would have been taken by truly attentive stockholders present at Merritt, Chapman and Scott annual meetings in recent years. The management was led by Louis Wolfson, who often failed to attend the meetings; or if he did come, he sat quietly ignoring most stockholder questions, with a supercilious smile on his darkly handsome face.

Mr. Wolfson was a "raider." In the nineteen fifties and sixties there were any number of fast-moving men like him, empire builders, raiders, organizers of conglomerates, who took control of various Big Board companies. When names of men who are known as raiders appear on the board of directors of your company, make sure you go to the annual meeting. It can be revealing. It can be a warning signal for you to consider selling your shares. Is the raider interested in building up the company? Or did he obtain control to sell it out, dissolve it, or just to put his relatives into lucrative jobs? These are questions you might consider.

You cannot gain a real impression of a company just by reading the annual report. You can often get a real insight by going to the annual meeting. For example, you can look over the directors and principal officers. Are they the kind of men you would trust with your cash? There is more and more talk these days about the Mafia gaining control of some companies either as a cover-up for illegal activities or with the idea of milking the company.

Recently I went to an annual meeting during which a stockholder asked a good question: Why had the president put his son on the payroll as the advertising manager? The president, on the defensive, immediately justified the appointment by claiming the son was the person best suited for the job. Perhaps, but I wouldn't buy a share in that company. Nepotism is an ugly word in a company trying to build up good relations with stockholders. Naturally, if it's a small, family-dominated company, that is another matter. There the stockholder usually goes into the investment with his eyes open.

Let me put it more bluntly in a way that you as a woman probably can understand better than most men. As a newspaper reporter, I have covered hundreds of annual meetings. If I look at the board of directors of a company and say to myself, "I wouldn't want to marry any of them or have my daughters marry them either," then you can be sure that I would never invest a cent in that company, even if it was the fastest growing one

I could find. Such a company comes to mind, not because of the annual meeting, but because the president told me once he spent a large amount of the corporate money on art. As a stockholder I wouldn't like that, although I enjoy good art.

Just reaching conclusions about the character and attitude of the company's officers and directors on various occasions has saved me more money than I have lost, by not putting it into such a company's stock. It is an application, I suppose, of that characteristic called "woman's intuition" — something that most men would deride but that for some reason works much of the time.

The role of the small stockholder, I think, will widen dramatically in coming years, especially in the light of recent narrowing of profit margins and real slowing of corporate growth, which has eliminated some of the phony growth that comes from inflation.

Don't forget that small stockholders have waged some long and dramatic — and successful — corporate battles. Perhaps the most colorful in modern history involved a man named Walter Meyer, a lawyer in New York. He was a common stockholder for years in a railroad called the St. Louis Southwestern, more familiarly called the Cotton Belt, since it operated in the large cotton-growing area of Texas.

The Cotton Belt was a "bridge" line which stretched from the city in its name — St. Louis — south to cities like Houston, Texas, and Little Rock, Arkansas. It carried a large amount of agricultural produce such as cotton and rice from the Southwest. Southern Pacific, a much bigger railroad that owned large amounts of Cotton Belt's bonds, took more than a paternal interest in the smaller railroad because it linked SP lines with others in the area.

During the depression the Cotton Belt, like other southern carriers, flopped into bankruptcy. As the creditor (owner of all those bonds), the Southern Pacific was only too happy to have the Cotton Belt go through the bankruptcy wringer, because in the process the stockholders would be eliminated. And as the major bondholder SP would end up as virtual owner of a railroad with a new, streamlined capitalization. However, SP's lawyers reckoned without Mr. Meyer, who proved a very formidable small stockholder. He jockeyed the case through the courts for a very simple reason: he had the foresight to believe that the Cotton Belt, formerly a good, sound earner, was only temporarily embarrassed financially. He also guessed that the South would grow industrially (which it did, especially after World War II), owing to new businesses in the area. He also believed it was unfair for the SP to eliminate any chance for the common shareholders to participate in what could be a bright future.

He turned out to be right. The railroad soon began operating at a profit because of World War II; and after the war it continued to fare well. Yet still the SP insisted on its rights as bondholder to take over the railroad. The case moved slowly and ponderously, as most lawsuits do, through the courts up to the Supreme Court.

By the time it reached the apex — the Supreme Court — the truth had become embarrassingly obvious to the SP, to the government and to the public: the Cotton Belt had not only recovered from the effects of the depression but had become one of the most prosperous railroads in the nation. Yet still it was technically in bankruptcy. Finally, Mr. Meyer won his case.

The Cotton Belt emerged from bankruptcy, probably the only railroad in history that could make such a claim. Its stockholders fared well, all because of Mr. Meyer's bitter, tedious fight.

Another outstanding corporate battle won with the help of small stockholders involved the late Robert R. Young. In those days I worked as a financial writer for the brokerage firm Merrill Lynch. One day my editor said, "I noticed a little item in the *New York Times* about Alleghany Corporation receiving about $10,000,000 in cash from sale of an investment. Go interview Robert R. Young and find out what he is planning to do with the cash."

I made an appointment to see Mr. Young, head of Alleghany, who greeted me with southern gallantry, leaping up from his chair and sitting me down near his desk. He said, "I can spare only fifteen minutes." An hour later I left in a slightly dazed condition.

After some preliminary questions I had thought out ahead of time, I posed the $10 dollar — or $10,000,000 dollar — one. He thought for a moment and then said with a little smile, "Oh, I might use it to take over the New York Central." I could hear a gasp from his public relations director, Thomas Deegan, sitting nearby on a couch.

Back at the office, no one believed my report that Mr. Young had made such a statement about the N.Y. Central. For one thing, the railroad was dominated by the Vanderbilt and Morgan interests. Furthermore, it had vast assets compared with Alleghany Corporation. It sounded like a very small corporate flea trying to irritate a very large dog.

Disbelief prevailed to such an extent that I had to telephone Newport, R.I., with a Merrill Lynch vice-president listening, to have Mr. Young repeat from his summer home his plan about the N.Y. Central. The brokerage firm had a scoop which it sent over its wires and gave to the news services such as Associated and United Press.

Mr. Young was a brilliant man, and in the back of his mind he knew that he needed small investors to help him win control of the N.Y. Central. So he gave the scoop to my brokerage firm, the largest one in the country, and one that had long posed as the small investor's friend. His proxy fight, with the help of small investors, proved successful and he did take over the N.Y. Central in one of the most colorful fights in history.

Proxy fights can be profitable for the small investor. As the battle approaches a climax, she will find herself approached by both sides wanting votes. In such a case, the small investor should consult her broker. As the battle reaches a climax, the price of the shares probably will rise. Whether she should keep them and what side she should favor are the questions she must decide.

In conclusion, as a stockholder don't underestimate your

power as a small investor. Don't overestimate the quality of the management of your company. You have a right to view them critically, without rose-colored glasses.

Don't ever get caught, as many small stockholders did some years ago, in a company such as U.S. Hoffman Machinery. It was badly hurt financially by its chairman named Harold Roth, later sentenced to jail. For years he had borrowed money from the company, at the same time he received a salary of about $50,000 a year. As a result of his financial downfall due to overspeculation, Mr. Roth established an unusual claim to corporate fame. As far as I know, he was the only chairman who ever appeared on a corporate balance sheet as a liability because of the money he owed the company. Each year for a long period the company deducted a certain sum from his salary to pay off the loan. He shouldn't have been kept on the payroll, but he was — despite shareholders' objections.

And what about the shareholders? At one time the shares sold as high as 22⅛; today the company is out of business.

16 | Your Demanding Uncle

Uncle Sam is a very nice man who has given women lots of opportunities to make money, but unfortunately he has a very shrewish mistress who scares some people too much. Her name is Taxes. At present, not unlike Madame Pompadour of centuries ago, she has the upper hand in government.

Government officials and congressmen and state legislators say weakly, "We can't do much about stopping the rise in taxes." They can, of course, by cutting back spending and waste; but consumers don't make their wishes known forcefully, nor as loudly as the government spenders do. At local levels, however, voters have been rejecting more and more bond proposals for new schools and other public endeavors.

Like inflation, taxes are something the investor has to learn to live with and understand.

Sometimes men and women say rather grandly, "I have such a large capital gains in that stock that I can't afford to sell it." What they are saying — foolishly I believe — is that they are scared to take their profits and pay taxes on the gains. But in reality there's *no* gain, no profit, until it is nailed down in cash, especially these days when stocks move up and down quickly in price and fashions in investments change.

The point to digest is: take your capital gains at appropriate times. Don't be scared about the high tax you might have to pay.

How do taxes work?

In the first place, in terms of your personal income, the federal government applies two types of taxation: regular income tax depending on your income level after exemptions and deductions, and a second form called capital gains taxation levied on profits you have made in property like stocks, your house, paintings, etc. This applies only when the specific property is sold.

Table 12 gives some of the current percentages applicable to various income groups after exemptions, charitable and other deductions.

Tax Bracket	Individual Return	Joint Return (man and wife)
25%	$ 8,000	$12,000
32	15,000	20,000
36	18,000	24,000
42	23,000	32,000
45	26,000	36,000
50	32,000	44,000

Table 12

Generally speaking, your family fares better if you can file a joint income tax, a method available to married couples. A widow or single person with dependents can file as head of household, which is more favorable usually than filing as a single person.

As you know, there are certain exemptions allowed such as $750 a person for 1972 and a similar amount for any dependents; also a 15 percent, or $2,000 maximum deduction for standard items like charities, medical expenses, etc., unless a long form is filed for itemized deductions.

Dividends that you receive from any company in which you have stock is included as regular income. However, the first $100 in dividends can be excluded by a husband and $100 by a wife, if she owns shares, too. Often, if a husband owns all the shares in the family, it's a good idea for him to give his wife some of the stock (he could give her up to $3,000 worth a year free of gift tax) so that she will have enough dividend income to take this $100 exclusion, too. Or, they can get up to $200 dividend exclusion if they own shares jointly.

Interest you receive from bonds, or that is credited to your account in savings banks or comes to you from a credit union (this is often called a "dividend" but is classed as "interest" payment for tax purposes) must be listed as income. Interest does not qualify for the $100 deductible as do dividends from stock.

If you buy a security such as a bond or stock and sell it within six months then you have what is called a short-term capital gain. You must add any profit you made on the transaction to your regular income to be taxed at the rate applicable to your tax bracket. Naturally you can deduct the cost of commissions, transfer tax, etc. before you arrive at the figure for the profit. The simplest way to figure this is to take the purchase price and add to it the fees paid when you bought and paid when you sold it, and subtract this total from the price at which you sold the shares.

However, if you have kept the bond or stock more than six months, the profit becomes subject to a much more favorable rate. You have what is called a long-term capital gain, and this is subject to only one-half the regular tax rate. To put it another way, you add only 50 percent of the gain to your taxable income unless you have a gain over $50,000 or are in a very high tax bracket, at which point the rules are different.

In case you have a potpourri of short-term and long-term gains, here are the general rules that apply:

1. All long-term gains and all long-term losses should be added up separately. The difference between them will be either a net long-term gain or a net long-term loss.

2. In the same way, the taxpayer should add up short-term gains and losses, to determine whether she has either a net short-term gain or a net short-term loss.

3. If the taxpayer finds that he has a net short-term loss, the

total can be used to offset up to $1,000 of ordinary income. Furthermore, the Internal Revenue Service permits individuals to carry over unused losses for additional years. When carried over they retain their "character" as either short- or long-term losses.

Under the new tax law, only 50% of a net long-term loss may be taken against ordinary income. Thus, it takes $2,000 of net long-term losses to produce a $1,000 deduction.

4. If the taxpayer has more net long-term gain than net short-term loss, she offsets and treats the result as net long-term gain.

5. If the net short-term gain runs larger than the net long-term loss, the difference can be handled as net short-term gain.

Be wary of something the IRS frowns upon — "wash sales." It is a trap into which a sentimental woman shareholder might easily fall. Often unwitting investors think they will sell a stock to take a loss on it, but then they want to buy it back. An example might be a dear old favorite like AT&T, which falls quite sharply sometimes and then attracts more interest again.

However, the IRS will not permit the taxpayer the loss if she buys back substantially identical stock within thirty days before or after the sale of original holding. The advice, if you want to buy back such a stock, is to wait at least thirty-one days, or invest your money in a company in a similar industry. But note that the "wash sale" rule applies only to losses and not to gains. Thus you can sell a stock and nail down the profit and buy shares in the same company shortly afterwards, without fearing the application of "wash sale" rule.

A good question is when should you sell as a calendar year is about to end. You should think about it shortly after Labor Day, because sophisticated investors are doing just that — pondering their portfolios. Some brokers believe that the well-heeled, well-schooled investors sell well before the year-end to establish either capital gains or losses because they have no psychological block about clinging to stocks, especially those in which they might have losses. They want to make a clean sweep and be ready for a new year of trading.

The smaller, less sophisticated investor tends to wait to take his gains or losses until almost the last moment. Often prices of stocks in November and December move lower under the impact of such selling. This last-minute gains or loss taker often gets lower prices late in December and then finds it might cost him more to invest again after the new year begins.

With the help of your broker — and his tax brochures — plan your strategy.

The tax break for long-term capital gains explains why so many investors speak of them favorably, especially if they are in high income tax brackets. Suppose that you and your husband are in the 32 percent tax bracket (meaning an income after exemptions and deductions of about $20,000), and you have a gain of $1,000 that year on stock. You will pay about $320 of it to Uncle Sam if you sell before six months, but wait that one day after six months and your tax liability drops in half to $160. Worth waiting?

Remember the actual day you buy a security and the day you sell is important. The Internal Revenue Service measures the six months' holding period this way:

The holding period must be six months, plus one day, for a gain to qualify as long-term. The holding period does not begin until the day after the purchase date, *but* it does include the day of sale. Example: stock bought January 15 would qualify if sold on or after July 16. Or property bought April 30 would become long term if sold November 1 or after.

Taxes have various complexities as you probably know. Since many women do not fill out their own tax forms, relying instead on their husbands, trust officers or lawyers, they generally know little about some important and helpful gimmicks. In fact, once they digest the fact that capital gains are tastier than straight income, they neglect the rest of the menu served up by Uncle Sam.

In that small, ever-present stock notebook it's a good idea to keep track as you buy and sell shares of your profits and losses, whether they are long term or short. You can get the facts easily each month when the broker sends you a statement about your account. As the year-end approaches you will have an idea of your tax position. Then you can consult your broker about what you should do.

Your comment might be like this: "I have $1,500 in long-term gains, and about $150 in short-term gains, on paper. What shall I do? Is it a good time to sell?"

Before each year-end there comes a period, usually in October and lasting partly into November, when brokers begin to talk about tax selling. The firm will probably bombard you with written material about tax selling and switches for tax purposes. Read carefully even if you don't understand at first. At this time you can be sure the sophisticated investors — the big boys — are busy selling to establish losses or gains, as they want, in relation to their own tax position. It is as if brokers come alive in the fall, suddenly remembering your existence and hoping they can persuade you to make some trades, too.

Is it better for you to spread gains over two years — gains you have on paper? It might be wiser not to sell all your stocks and take profits if you expect your income to be the same next year as it is this year. In other words, by selling only half you can balance your tax liability better between the two years. Remember the whole point is to keep your tax bracket as low as possible. If this is the case, your approach might be to sell part of your investments towards the end of the year and sell the others that have gains early the following year. Remember your tax year, although you file an income tax every April 15, runs from January through December 31 of the prior year. In other words taxes for the year 1971 were paid, or the final return filed, by April 15, 1972.*

Does it appear that next year your income might fall sharply? Perhaps your husband plans to retire and live on his pension,

---

*Naturally, most people who work pay a large part of their taxes each year through withholding by their employer. Also, many people file and pay quarterly taxes on income not subject to withholding.

or there may be other reasons. Then you might want to postpone the selling of any stocks this year until next year.

Does your husband expect a large increase in salary next year, or will you inherit some money? Then take the gains this year if it is more favorable.

The point to remember with regard to taxes is threefold:

If possible keep stocks six months and more to achieve the more favorable capital gains rates. But keep in mind that it would be foolish to hang on to stock for six months if the market is going against you, just to achieve such gains.

Don't hang on to a stock forever just because you are afraid to pay capital gains. That's being penny wise, pound foolish. Or as one broker I know says, "It's penny-ante thinking."

Try to think in terms of relating your income in a particular year to potential gains (or losses), so that you can schedule in your mind the best time to take such gains — or such losses. Unfortunately, many small investors overlook this idea of scheduling, because they don't realize they can save taxes or they think saving a few dollars is not worthwhile. A few dollars saved each year over a period of years adds up. Even $50 saved in taxes can be worthwhile, if it can be achieved by a little forethought in planning when you will take your gains.

Getting Off Tax Free

For years, as mentioned in Chapter 2, there has been one form of security exempt from federal income taxation. Unfortunately it is now being eyed by legislators and government officials as a form that must yield to their impatient needs for higher taxes. Municipal bonds have been excluded from federal income taxation as well sometimes as taxation by the state in which they are issued, because of a man only remembered by his name, Hugh McCulloch. Ironically, he was a government official.

It seems that the state of Maryland much preferred its own

Joint Return	$8 to $12	$12 to $16	$16 to $20	$20 to $24	$24 to $28	$28 to $32	$32 to $36	$36 to $40	$40 to $44	$44 to $52
% Tax Bracket	22	25	28	32	36	39	42	45	48	50
2.50%	3.21	3.33	3.47	3.68	3.91	4.10	4.31	4.55	4.81	5.00
2.60	3.33	3.47	3.61	3.82	4.06	4.26	4.48	4.73	5.00	5.20
2.75	3.53	3.67	3.82	4.04	4.30	4.51	4.74	5.00	5.29	5.50
2.80	3.59	3.73	3.89	4.12	4.38	4.59	4.83	5.09	5.38	5.60
2.90	3.72	3.87	4.03	4.26	4.53	4.75	5.00	5.27	5.58	5.80
3.00	3.85	4.00	4.17	4.41	4.69	4.92	5.17	5.45	5.77	6.00
3.10	3.97	4.13	4.31	4.56	4.84	5.08	5.34	5.64	5.96	6.20
3.15	4.04	4.20	4.38	4.63	4.92	5.16	5.43	5.73	6.06	6.30
3.20	4.10	4.27	4.44	4.71	5.00	5.25	5.52	5.82	6.15	6.40
3.25	4.17	4.33	4.51	4.78	5.08	5.33	5.60	5.91	6.25	6.50
3.30	4.23	4.40	4.58	4.85	5.16	5.41	5.69	6.00	6.35	6.60
3.35	4.29	4.47	4.65	4.93	5.23	5.49	5.78	6.09	6.44	6.70
3.40	4.36	4.53	4.72	5.00	5.31	5.57	5.86	6.18	6.54	6.80
3.45	4.42	4.60	4.79	5.07	5.39	5.66	5.95	6.27	6.63	6.90
3.50	4.49	4.67	4.86	5.15	5.47	5.74	6.03	6.36	6.73	7.00
3.55	4.55	4.73	4.93	5.22	5.55	5.82	6.12	6.45	6.83	7.10
3.60	4.62	4.80	5.00	5.29	5.63	5.90	6.21	6.55	6.92	7.20
3.65	4.68	4.87	5.07	5.37	5.70	5.98	6.29	6.64	7.02	7.30
3.70	4.74	4.93	5.14	5.44	5.78	6.07	6.38	6.73	7.12	7.40
3.75	4.81	5.00	5.21	5.51	5.86	6.15	6.47	6.82	7.21	7.50
3.80	4.87	5.07	5.28	5.59	5.94	6.23	6.55	6.91	7.31	7.60
3.85	4.94	5.13	5.35	5.66	6.02	6.31	6.64	7.00	7.40	7.70
3.90	5.00	5.20	5.42	5.74	6.09	6.39	6.72	7.09	7.50	7.80
3.95	5.06	5.27	5.49	5.81	6.17	6.48	6.81	7.18	7.60	7.90
4.00	5.13	5.33	5.56	5.88	6.25	6.56	6.90	7.27	7.69	8.00
4.10	5.26	5.47	5.69	6.03	6.41	6.72	7.07	7.45	7.88	8.20
4.25	5.45	5.67	5.90	6.25	6.64	6.97	7.33	7.73	8.17	8.50
4.40	5.64	5.87	6.11	6.47	6.88	7.21	7.59	8.00	8.46	8.80
4.50	5.77	6.00	6.25	6.62	7.03	7.38	7.76	8.18	8.65	9.00
4.60	5.90	6.13	6.39	6.76	7.19	7.54	7.93	8.36	8.85	9.20
4.75	6.09	6.33	6.60	6.99	7.42	7.79	8.19	8.64	9.13	9.50
4.80	6.15	6.40	6.67	7.06	7.50	7.87	8.28	8.73	9.23	9.60
4.90	6.28	6.53	6.81	7.21	7.66	8.03	8.45	8.91	9.42	9.80
5.00	6.41	6.67	6.94	7.35	7.81	8.20	8.62	9.09	9.62	10.00
5.10	6.54	6.80	7.08	7.50	7.97	8.36	8.79	9.27	9.81	10.20
5.25	6.73	7.00	7.29	7.72	8.20	8.61	9.05	9.55	10.10	10.50
5.40	6.92	7.20	7.50	7.94	8.44	8.85	9.31	9.82	10.38	10.80
5.50	7.05	7.33	7.64	8.09	8.59	9.02	9.48	10.00	10.58	11.00
5.75	7.37	7.67	7.99	8.46	8.98	9.43	9.91	10.45	11.06	11.50
6.00	7.69	8.00	8.33	8.82	9.38	9.84	10.34	10.91	11.54	12.00

The tabulations above emphasize the fact that the tax-exempt income means More $32,000 net taxable income bracket must find a taxable investment with a return of

Table 13. Tax-Exempt *vs.* Taxable Income

$52 to $64	$64 to $76	$76 to $88	$88 to $100	$100 to $120	$120 to $140	$140 to $160	$160 to $180	$180 to $200	Over $200	
53	55	58	60	62	64	66	68	69	70	
5.32	5.56	5.95	6.25	6.58	6.94	7.35	7.81	8.06	8.33	2.50%
5.53	5.78	6.19	6.50	6.84	7.22	7.65	8.13	8.39	8.67	2.60
5.85	6.11	6.55	6.88	7.24	7.64	8.09	8.59	8.87	9.17	2.75
5.96	6.22	6.67	7.00	7.37	7.78	8.24	8.75	9.03	9.33	2.80
6.17	6.44	6.90	7.25	7.63	8.06	8.53	9.06	9.35	9.67	2.90
6.38	6.67	7.14	7.50	7.89	8.33	8.82	9.38	9.68	10.00	3.00
6.60	6.89	7.38	7.75	8.16	8.61	9.12	9.69	10.00	10.33	3.10
6.70	7.00	7.50	7.88	8.29	8.75	9.26	9.84	10.16	10.50	3.15
6.81	7.11	7.62	8.00	8.42	8.89	9.41	10.00	10.32	10.67	3.20
6.91	7.22	7.74	8.13	8.55	9.03	9.56	10.16	10.48	10.83	3.25
7.02	7.33	7.86	8.25	8.68	9.17	9.71	10.31	10.65	11.00	3.30
7.13	7.44	7.98	8.38	8.82	9.31	9.85	10.47	10.81	11.17	3.35
7.23	7.56	8.10	8.50	8.95	9.44	10.00	10.63	10.97	11.33	3.40
7.34	7.67	8.21	8.63	9.08	9.58	10.15	10.78	11.13	11.50	3.45
7.45	7.78	8.33	8.75	9.21	9.72	10.29	10.94	11.29	11.67	3.50
7.55	7.89	8.45	8.88	9.34	9.86	10.44	11.09	11.45	11.83	3.55
7.66	8.00	8.57	9.00	9.47	10.00	10.59	11.25	11.61	12.00	3.60
7.77	8.11	8.69	9.13	9.61	10.14	10.74	11.41	11.77	12.17	3.65
7.87	8.22	8.81	9.25	9.74	10.28	10.88	11.56	11.94	12.33	3.70
7.98	8.33	8.93	9.38	9.87	10.42	11.03	11.72	12.10	12.50	3.75
8.09	8.44	9.05	9.50	10.00	10.56	11.18	11.88	12.26	12.67	3.80
8.19	8.56	9.17	9.63	10.13	10.69	11.32	12.03	12.42	12.83	3.85
8.30	8.67	9.29	9.75	10.26	10.83	11.47	12.19	12.58	13.00	3.90
8.40	8.78	9.40	9.88	10.39	10.97	11.62	12.34	12.74	13.17	3.95
8.51	8.89	9.52	10.00	10.53	11.11	11.76	12.50	12.90	13.33	4.00
8.72	9.11	9.76	10.25	10.79	11.39	12.06	12.81	13.23	13.67	4.10
9.04	9.44	10.12	10.63	11.18	11.81	12.50	13.28	13.71	14.17	4.25
9.36	9.78	10.48	11.00	11.58	12.22	12.94	13.75	14.19	14.67	4.40
9.57	10.00	10.71	11.25	11.84	12.50	13.24	14.06	14.52	15.00	4.50
9.79	10.22	10.95	11.50	12.11	12.78	13.53	14.38	14.84	15.33	4.60
10.11	10.56	11.31	11.88	12.50	13.19	13.97	14.84	15.32	15.83	4.75
10.21	10.67	11.43	12.00	12.63	13.33	14.12	15.00	15.48	16.00	4.80
10.43	10.89	11.67	12.25	12.89	13.61	14.41	15.31	15.81	16.33	4.90
10.64	11.11	11.90	12.50	13.16	13.89	14.71	15.63	16.13	16.67	5.00
10.85	11.33	12.14	12.75	13.42	14.17	15.00	15.94	16.45	17.00	5.10
11.17	11.67	12.50	13.13	13.82	14.58	15.44	16.41	16.94	17.50	5.25
11.49	12.00	12.86	13.50	14.21	15.00	15.88	16.88	17.42	18.00	5.40
11.70	12.22	13.10	13.75	14.47	15.28	16.18	17.19	17.74	18.33	5.50
12.23	12.78	13.69	14.38	15.13	15.97	16.91	17.97	18.55	19.17	5.75
12.77	13.33	14.29	15.00	15.79	16.67	17.65	18.75	19.35	20.00	6.00

Keeping Dollars. For example: A couple filing a joint return in the $28,000 to 6.56 percent to equal a tax-exempt security with a return of 4.00 percent.

banks to the bank called the Bank of the United States, which had been organized by the federal government; a brainchild, in fact, of that capable financial planner Alexander Hamilton. Banks in those days (the early eighteen hundreds) had a fondness for issuing money — and sometimes it could be described as printing-press money, because there were few assets behind it. As long as the banks kept it busily circulating it couldn't come home to roost for redemption into gold, of which there was a great shortage.

The federal government wanted a more solid basis for the banking system — an organization that would issue money and control the amount in circulation. Hamilton's thinking about a sound currency proved too advanced for his time. In Maryland, a clique in the legislature passed a law taxing the money issued by the branch of the Bank of the United States in Baltimore, with the idea of hurting the bank's business. A government official named Hugh McCulloch sued the state of Maryland on behalf of the government to prevent the severe penalty tax. The case called *McCulloch* v. *Maryland* went to the Supreme Court, which rendered a decision that has stood through this day.

Mentioning the theory that the power to tax is the power to destroy, the judges ruled that Maryland could not tax the issues of the federal bank; and therefore by implication that the federal government could not tax the issues of the states.

Ordinarily this case would not be important for the average investor, but it has made headlines in recent months because of charges that many wealthy persons can escape all or virtually all federal taxation by investing in municipal bonds.

Municipalities, states, counties, school districts, sewer authorities, and such have financed billions of dollars in improvements by issuing the securities called municipals because they can be issued at relatively low rates of interest to entice investors interested in the sweetener — tax exemption.

Naturally taxpayers in the municipalities like it because otherwise their taxes would rise to cover the interest on higher interest-bearing issues. Investors like it, especially those in the 30 percent tax bracket and above. Table 13 shows the tax effect on taxpayers in various brackets of an investment in tax free municipals and taxable issues.

Many observers do not believe that Congress can hurdle the protective fence around municipals erected by the old Supreme Court decision in *McCulloch* v. *Maryland* and some subsequent decisions. Also, it is doubtful whether the municipalities will give up without a fight. The nontax feature enables any little community to offer such bonds and find ready buyers in the highly competitive bond market.

However, the government is whittling away at the fence. President Nixon has won a minimum tax on wealthy investors who receive income from preference sources such as municipal bonds. Another approach has been to have the government underwrite some municipal issues when a city or town has been willing to give up the tax-exempt feature.

For the moderate and high income investor the subject of tax-free municipal income remains worthwhile to pursue, especially since each year with the rise in the cost of living taxpayers tend to move into higher tax brackets through compensatory salary and wage increases.

Gifts and Taxes

If you are a mother (or a grandmother) there is one aspect of investment planning you should consider. You can reduce your own taxes by giving stock or the money to buy the stock to children under twenty-one.

For example, at present the government permits you to turn over up to $3,000 a year to as many individuals of any age as you want. You do not pay a gift tax on this and they do not pay any income tax upon receiving it. If you had a hundred grandchildren, cousins or friends you could give them $3,000 each, or a total of $300,000 that year. You can do the same every year.

If you join with your husband in the gift giving, together you can turn over a total of $6,000 a year per recipient to as many individuals as you want, cousins, friends, parents. It's a valuable aspect of taxation to consider even if you are in a moderate income tax bracket.

For example, suppose you have saved up $21,000 for your son's college, you could turn it over to him at the rate of $3,000 each year. Then if the money were invested in stocks he would receive the $1,000 or so in dividends to be used for his expenses. You would save because your income would be reduced by $1,000, on which otherwise you would be paying taxes. A short-term trust could also be used to do a similar job for you — getting income away from you in your high tax bracket to a child who is in a low or no-tax bracket. Naturally, you need help from a trust officer, lawyer, or accountant in setting up such a plan.

Also, you can hand out a total of $30,000 once, over and above these $3,000 annual gifts. It's called the lifetime exemptions. Suppose you have a favorite grandchild. You could give him $3,000 each year for as many years as you wished. You could also hand him a total of $30,000 once ($60,000 if your husband joins). But remember the $30,000 tax-free gift is a total, a one-of-a-kind donation. It doesn't have to be handed in a lump sum or go to one person or be divided equally among many, but it is a total.

To summarize: It may be beneficial for you to give away $3,000 annually to one or more people throughout your life, thus reducing your tax liability. Beyond this, don't forget the $30,000 lifetime exemption.

One exception to the rule is that a gift made in contemplation of death can be challenged by the Internal Revenue Service. In such an instance the government applies a three-year rule. If the donor lives three years after the gift is made, all is well. If he dies within the three-year period the government might try to tax the amount involved at estate tax rates, which are higher than gift tax rates. The IRS will claim the gifts were made in contemplation of death, often hard to disprove. The giving habits of the donor would be a factor. Did he make gifts regularly? Or did he wait until after he had a heart attack or was very old?

A classic case was decided in 1972 involving Mrs. Hilda Beecher Stowe (related by marriage to Harriet Beecher Stowe).

Mrs. Stowe gave her sons large gifts of money and stock several years ago, but died within the three-year period. The IRS claimed the gifts should be part of the estate, thus taxable at higher rates. No, said the court. In its decision the court stressed the fact that Mrs. Stowe had danced at the St. Regis Hotel, in New York, until 3 A.M. one night at her birthday party, an indication of her liveliness despite her old age. She was in her eighties when she died.

The moral for families with elderly relatives is twofold:

Keep them dancing (playing golf, swimming, traveling, etc.).

Fight the IRS in court, where judges are looking sympathetically these days at elderly people who make gifts and then die within the three-year period.

GIFTS OF STOCK. Gifts of stock offer another advantage besides getting income away from the donor. There may be capital gains involved and thus the giver avoids paying the gains. At the time of the transfer the price of the stock becomes the price at which the child, or whoever receives the gift, will price it.

Most all investors face charitable demands each year. Some charities, like the Red Cross, Salvation Army, Community Chest, Girl Scout cookie sales usually are given amounts of money in cash. Investors might well consider giving their church (to which they make an annual pledge) or their college (for annual giving) a gift in the form of stock. The reason is a simple one with two facets:

1. A gift to charity can be deducted from regular income in reporting taxes to a large extent.

2. A gift of stock in which there are taxable gains means

that the giver escapes the gains tax and yet gets much of the market value of the gift as a reduction. The new law is complex.

Suppose you own Union Carbide stock bought at 40 and now selling for 50. You want to give your church $500.

You can take cash out of the bank in that amount. You could sell 10 shares of the stock and turn the resulting $500 over to the church, but you would have to pay capital gains on it, as well as your brokerage commission. The third way is merely to give 10 shares of the stock to the church.

It may sound complicated to you now, but when you are thinking of making a large contribution to a church or college, think in terms of giving stocks to save on taxes.

GIFTS TO CHILDREN. The New York Stock Exchange campaigned for years — and finally succeeded — in making it easier to give gifts of stock to children. Uniform rules now apply in most all of the states, replacing a hodgepodge of laws that made such giving difficult.

In buying shares for children you must tell your broker to have them registered with you (or anyone you choose) as custodian. The face of the stock certificate might read like this: "Elizabeth Jones custodian for Robert Jones a minor under Uniform Gifts to Minors Act New York."

It is wiser to have a third person — not the donor — act as custodian because of the three-year contemplation of death rule.

In such a case the stock probably should be invested in growth-type securities. The father of the child can still take his $750 exemption for the child on his income tax no matter how much income the child receives from dividends, as long as the child is under eighteen or in college and receives more than half of his support from the father (or mother, if a widow).

If you are interested in gifts of securities for children, your broker can supply a booklet describing the general rules that apply. One significant one is that the law requires that you hand over the securities to the child when he reaches twenty-one and you have to make an accounting if he requires it, so it behooves a donor to keep good records and invest the money wisely.

Furthermore, in line with changing the voting age to 18, many states now require that the securities be turned over at that age in the case of new custody accounts.

17 | Investments with Unusual Personalities

Like people, securities have varying characteristics. Some rather little-known ones can exert a very powerful influence on your thinking; or if not that, they can affect your life indirectly.

Some of these more esoteric forms of investment will remain on the periphery of your life. You may never own them but as a knowledgeable investor you should know what they are and what kind of help or investment function they perform. For example, there are bonds called "flower bonds" that could be useful for any woman with a dying husband or father. If you don't have cash on hand now there is still a way of buying cheaply 100 shares of that stock you are convinced will double in a year. If in 1973 or 1974 you believe that the price of silver is going to rise sharply, there's a method of buying the metal and keeping it stashed safely in a big New York bank called Irving Trust Company. Each involves a different type of investment.

Remember that wherever a few businessmen or government officials gather together with the idea of raising money for various ventures, they will think in terms of issuing some type of security to help finance or provide working capital for the operation.

Here is a list of some of the securities or types of investment about which you should know a little:

1. Municipal bonds
2. U.S. Government issues
   Savings bonds
   Treasury bills
   Certificates
   Treasury notes
   Long-term bonds
   Fannie Maes
   "Flower bonds"
3. Commercial paper
4. Federal funds
5. Equipment trusts
6. Puts and calls
7. Commodity futures

MUNICIPAL BONDS. With their traditional tax-exempt feature, municipals have long been called the "rich man's investment." Yet ironically they can help those of us in much lower income tax brackets today. The reason is that over the last decade salaries have risen sharply, pushing many people into higher tax brackets — although perhaps they don't feel much wealthier because inflation has taken such a toll.

The point to remember is that today even persons in the 30 percent tax bracket might find municipals advantageous. For more information on them — and the changes that might come in this investment area — read Chapter 16. Then ask your broker about municipals, especially requesting that he supply you with a brochure about them. In fact, even if you are not interested in them ask anyway. He probably will be impressed at the question, all of which can be part of your ploy to rouse his interest in your investment future.

U.S. GOVERNMENT ISSUES. To finance this multi-billion dollar government of ours takes continuing amounts of money. Sometimes, of course, the Treasury does not need as much money as at other times — around income tax payment dates, for example, when large sums of money flow out of our bank accounts into the government's hands. Almost every week, however, the Treasury is in "the market" — meaning the money market — to raise money. Naturally, like any shrewd businessman the Treasury would like to "sell" its securities at the lowest possible cost in terms of interest.

Look at it this way. If the government has to raise $1 billion to pay salaries, feed troops abroad, pay its light, heat and other bills for a while, it would like to do it as cheaply as possible.

The cost of $1 billion at 2 percent interest (and years ago during World War II the government did pay such a low rate for money) would run only $20,000,000; at 4 percent interest the cost would be $40,000,000; and this year the government has been paying 6 percent and more for money. When you think in terms of billions of dollars you can see the difference.

Generally the government offers two basic types of securities: the marketable and the nonmarketable.

The nonmarketable are the types that in all probability you know best — the *savings bonds* of various issues. During World War II they were called war bonds, and later defense bonds, and now they are advertised as savings bonds. As a safe place for money, they are all right; most Americans probably own some. Children often receive them from doting godmothers or grandparents to be put away for ten years or so and collect interest until maturity — the date at which the bond comes due.

They are called nonmarketable in that you can't go out and sell them to someone else; but you can turn them in at any time to the government. Your bank will do the work for you, and you will receive a certain amount, usually listed on the bond's indenture (the back of the crinkly certificate), plus the accrued interest to date of turning in the bond.

Don't buy savings bonds if you are interested in investing for good return and growth. Such bonds usually carry a low rate of interest, less sometimes than the amount you would receive from a savings bank account. They are a safe storage place for money, but *not* a sound investment in a period of rapid inflation. Occasionally the government tries to encourage additional sales of the savings bonds by raising the interest rate. But again, stay away from them as an investor.

The marketable types of government securities are much more interesting for investors these days because 1) they can be sold readily to other investors; 2) they respond to changes in interest rates — to changes, in other words, in the cost of money.

Among the marketable types of bonds about which you should

know are the so-called short-term, medium-term and long-term issues. As mentioned before, the Treasury tries to operate in the money market shrewdly. If the cost of money is high or rising as it was during 1969, the Treasury tends to concentrate on selling short-term issues, in the hopes that later it can "borrow" its money more cheaply after interest rates fall. In a period when interest rates are low the Treasury might stress the sale of long-term bonds, as it did in the nineteen forties, keeping its costs of borrowing low.

Treasury bills: virtually every week the Treasury sells bills, securities which are offered on a discount basis. This means that when you turn to the financial page of a newspaper you will find the Treasury bills quoted in terms of the percentage they yield if kept for a year, unlike bonds which (as mentioned on page 21) are quoted in terms of 100, 98, 87, etc. (meaning $1,000; $980, or $870).

Table 14 gives some selected quotations for Treasury bills that appeared in the *Wall Street Journal* in March 1972.

Date of Maturity	Bid	Ask
6–30	3.91%	3.63%
12–31	4.50	4.30

Table 14

Translated into written English this means if you want to buy $1,000 in Treasury bills (they come in denominations ranging from that small to $1,000,000) you would receive interest equivalent to 3.63 percent, if held to maturity, which is June 30, 1972. Remember that your return on a $1,000 bill wouldn't be a full $36.30 because interest is calculated on an annual basis; you will only own the bill from March through June. For convenience's sake the bills are quoted on this discount basis. This means that you would pay somewhat less than $1,000 for the bill when you bought it and if you keep it until maturity the Treasury will send you $1,000. Your interest lies in the difference between the price you pay and the $1,000.

Remember back in school, your mathematics teacher stressed the importance of figuring interest on a discount basis. Just in case you don't remember, Table 15 does the job for you, based on the use of 360 days to the year:

A = days to maturity	60	Formula	
E = discount basis	3.63	$F = \dfrac{E}{360} \times A$	
F = full discount	??		
G = dollar price	$1,000 - F		

Table 15

Let's say you will be holding the bill for two months or 60 days. It works out this way:

$$F = \frac{3.63}{360} \times 60$$

$$F = \frac{3.63}{6}$$

F = .605; or 60½ cents on $100, or $6.05 on a $1,000 bond
G = $1,000 − $6.05; or $993.95

The actual investment yield, down to the penny, on a Treasury bill is generally at a slightly higher rate than the discount basis. These are technicalities and needn't bother you unless you plan to do a great deal of investing in bills. The important thing is to realize that such short-term investments exist and might be useful, especially during periods of high interest rates. In 1969, for example, you could obtain a much better rate of return on such bills than from savings accounts, such as 6½ percent, and more.

Treasury bills, like many other government securities, are in bearer form, meaning your name does not appear on the certificate. Thus they can be transferred easily; on the other hand, they can also be stolen easily. Therefore if you do buy such bills do it through your bank or broker, and leave them in his safekeeping, or stow them immediately in your safe deposit box.

One point to remember is that the IRS considers the difference between the purchase price and the maturity value ($1,000) or the sales price an ordinary gain or loss — not the more favorable (to you) capital gain or loss, even if kept over six months in the case of a longer term bill.

Naturally, if you don't want to hold a bill to maturity you can sell it anytime in the market at a price equivalent to the bid price mentioned in Table 14 and quoted in terms of 3.91 percent.

Treasury bills generally are issued for ninety days, six months, or even a year maturity by the Treasury — but the big buyers of bills, such as banks, big trust funds, corporations, etc., often hold them only a few days or weeks, depending on their needs for cash. In other words they are readily marketable, with buyers always ready to purchase them or the government paying them off at maturity.

Another significant aspect to Treasury bills is the role of the Federal Reserve System. As mentioned earlier, the Fed can influence the trends in interest rates by buying and selling government securities. Every working day it is in the market, somehow. One of its most useful methods of influencing the cost of money is through buying and selling Treasury bills. If it sells millions of dollars' worth of Treasury bills, the interest rates obtainable on them will tend to go down, under the force of the law of supply and demand. If it buys them by the millions they can become scarce and the interest (or cost of them) will rise.

Certificates. In recent years the Treasury has lengthened the maturities of its bills so that nowadays some bills are as long in duration as some certificates used to be. Generally, certificates have been considered a longer term investment, maturing in about one year from date of issue. They haven't been used much in recent years.

Treasury notes come next on the list of securities for possible use in that they offer a medium length for investment — generally one year to five years' maturity. Banks and other institutions like them to help space out their portfolios; and conceivably they might be useful to large investors for such reasons, especially at times when they offer a chance to obtain high interest rates, as they did in 1969 and 1970, if the investors expect that interest rates might drop.

As for the Treasury, it often likes to lengthen its debt when it can favorably do so, in order not to be under much pressure to raise tremendous new sums of money when big issues of its securities come due. This middle-type security called notes permits the government to operate over longer spaces of time than by means of bills, and yet not tie up its credit on long-term bonds at unfavorable periods, such as very high interest-rate years like 1969 and 1970.

Notes can be obtained in denominations ranging from $1,000 on up to $5,000,000. In newspapers you will find them quoted in terms of $100 like bonds, with a bid and ask price. Next to this price range you will usually find a yield mentioned, which indicates the yield you would receive on your money if held to maturity, a date also mentioned. Besides this is the amount of actual interest the coupon bears. Here is the way the *Wall Street Journal* quotes such notes as of March 1972:

RATE	MAT.	BID	ASKED	YLD.
6%	11–78	99.13	99.17	6.08

In other words, if you buy a $1,000 note, you would pay 10 times $99.17, or $991.70 for the bond, bearing a 6.08 percent interest. You would receive $1,000 at maturity, plus interest.

Long-term bonds. Generally, the marketable Treasury bonds have been issued with a maturity of more than five years. They are available in both bearer and registered form, which makes them useful for various portfolio reasons. Like other marketable government issues they can be easily sold. Like the Treasury notes they are quoted in the newspapers with bid, ask, yield, interest rate and maturity date.

Perhaps the aspect of them that might puzzle you at first glance is why if the credit of the United States government is considered A-one do some of its bonds (and notes) sell well below 100 (or $1,000). The answer you know if you think for a moment.

Since interest rates are so high nowadays — 7 and 8 percent — for borrowing money from banks and taking out mortgages, then prices of bonds issued years ago when interest rates were much lower must reflect this, or no one in her right mind would buy a bond.

You will notice in the following listing of Treasury bonds (see Figure 15) that a 4 percent bond,* due to mature in August 1973 sells (early in 1972) at an ask price of 98.23, to yield 4.97 percent. On the same day a 3 percent bond due to mature in 1995 has an asking price of 77.14 percent, to yield 4.61 percent.

In the first instance, the Treasury will pay you $40 a year on its 4 percent bonds, but you are buying it for below the $1,000 price at $982.30, so your actual profit is quite a bit more than the 4 percent.

For the 3 percent bond, you are paying $771.40 for something that someday, if you hold it long enough, will pay you back $1,000.

Fannie Maes. Perhaps you will hear brokers or other knowledgeable businessmen talk of Fannie Maes. It's a nickname (Wall Streeters love nicknames for securities) for a very popular issue of government bonds, issued by a government organized agency called the Federal National Mortgage Association. The FNMA helps finance home building by buying and selling mortgages from and to banks, savings and loan companies, real estate groups, etc., who handle mortgages. When a bank wants more

---

*In the jargon of bondmen 4s of '85 would mean 4 percent bonds maturing in 1985 or 6s of '75 would mean a 6 percent bond maturing in 1975.

money to lend to you and other people interested in buying houses, it can sell mortgages from its portfolio to FNMA, and thus receive cash.

In turn, Fannie Mae raises money to handle its operations by selling obligations, usually called notes or debentures, to the public. These come in bearer form with denominations ranging from $1,000 to $100,000 and in various maturities.

Other government agency issues are also available from such issuers as the Federal Land Banks, the Federal Home Loan Banks, and many others.

You, as an investor, probably will never own such securities unless your trust officer or investment adviser puts some of your money in these markets temporarily for their desirable yields or maturities, or for their easy marketability.

"FLOWER BONDS" is a cheerful name for a useful type of government issue that might be a wise investment on the part of a woman about to become a widow or the child of a parent who is dying. If you face such a situation ask your broker about "flower bonds" — certain government bonds that can be tendered at full face value for payment of taxes owed by a decedent, providing they are actually owned by him at death.

The advantage, especially in a high rate of interest period like 1972, is that such bonds have been available at fat discounts under the face value. Thus if a relative is about to die and the estate he would leave might face a large inheritance tax, it could be favorable for you to persuade the dying person to buy (or have his trustee buy in his name) "flower bonds." For example, suppose the dying person could buy $10,000 worth of such bonds for a price of $8,500. At death they would be credited against estate taxes at a full $10,000, no matter when that person died, even if well before maturity date.

Because of this advantage, these bonds generally carry very low rates of interest in terms of yield to the owner, and thus they are not a good investment under normal circumstances. One point to remember is that they must be owned *by the decedent* — in his or her name — at time of death.

Government, Agency and Miscellaneous Securities

Friday, Mar 24, 1972
Over-the-Counter Quotations: Source on request.
Decimals in bid-and-asked and bid changes represent 32nds (101.1 means 101 1-32). a-Plus 1-64. b-Yield to call date. d-Minus 1-64.

Treasury Bonds

			Bid	Asked		
2½s,	1967-72	Jun	99.28	100.0	−.1	2.48
4s,	1972	Aug	99.31	100.3	−.1	3.74
2½s,	1967-72	Sep	99.2	99.6	−.1	4.38
2½s,	1967-72	Dec	98.20	98.24	−.3	4.29
4s,	1973	Aug	98.15	98.23	−.5	4.97
4⅛s,	1973	Nov	98.6	98.14	−.3	5.14
4⅛s,	1974	Feb	97.22	97.30	−.5	5.28
4¼s,	1974	May	97.20	97.28	−.4	5.31
3⅞s,	1974	Nov	95.28	96.4	−.4	5.47
4s,	1980	Feb	86.24	87.8	−.2	6.06
3½s,	1980	Nov	83.30	84.6	−.2	5.86
7s,	1981	Aug	105.28	106.12	−.2	6.10
6⅜s,	1982	Feb	100.20	100.28	−.7	6.29
3¼s,	1978-83	Jun	77.0	78.0	−.2	5.97
3¼s,	1985	May	76.20	77.20	−.4	5.69
4¼s,	1975-85	May	82.8	83.8		6.12
6⅛s,	1986	Nov	98.24	100.0	−.2	6.23
3½s,	1990	Feb	76.16	77.16	−.2	5.49
4¼s,	1987-92	Aug	77.24	78.24	−.4	6.08
4s,	1988-93	Feb	77.16	78.16	−.4	5.79
4⅛s,	1989-94	May	77.6	78.6	−.2	5.90
3s,	1995	Feb	76.14	77.14	−.2	4.61
3½s,	1998	Nov	76.22	77.22	−.2	5.03

U.S. Treas. Notes

Rate	Mat	Bid	Asked	Yld
4¾	5-72	100.8	100.12	1.86
6¼	5-72	100.17	100.21	1.72
5	8-72	100.9	100.13	3.91
6	11-72	100.28	101.0	4.38
4⅞	2-73	100.2	100.6	4.66
6½	2-73	101.14	101.18	4.68
7¾	5-73	102.30	103.6	4.82
8⅛	8-73	103.29	104.5	4.99
7¾	2-74	104.0	104.8	5.35
7¼	5-74	103.16	103.24	5.37
5⅝	8-74	100.4	100.12	5.46
5¾	11-74	100.9	100.17	5.53
5¾	2-75	100.5	100.13	5.60
5⅞	2-75	100.10	100.18	5.66
6	5-75	100.20	100.28	5.69
5⅞	8-75	100.8	100.16	5.71
7	11-75	103.28	104.4	5.73
6¼	2-76	101.14	101.22	5.76
5¾	5-76	99.17	99.21	5.84
6½	5-76	102.11	102.19	5.78
7½	8-76	105.30	106.6	5.88
6¼	11-76	101.8	101.16	5.87
8	2-77	108.13	108.29	5.88
7¾	8-77	107.29	108.13	5.91
6¼	2-78	100.19	101.3	6.02
6	11-78	99.13	99.17	6.08

U.S. Treas. Bills

Mat	Bid	Ask	Mat	Bid	Ask
	Discount			Discount	
3-30	3.86	3.14	7- 6	4.03	3.85
3-31	3.71	3.09	7-13	4.04	3.86
4- 6	3.42	3.06	7-20	3.98	3.84
4-13	3.50	3.08	7-27	4.06	3.90
4-20	3.48	3.16	7-31	4.06	3.90
4-21	3.41	3.21	8- 3	4.18	4.06
4-27	3.54	3.26	8-10	4.19	4.07
4-30	3.57	3.27	8-17	4.29	4.13
5- 4	3.61	3.39	8-24	4.30	4.18
5-11	3.63	3.43	8-31	4.31	4.17
5-18	3.65	3.47	9- 7	4.39	4.27
5-25	3.68	3.50	9-14	4.40	4.30
5-31	3.69	3.49	9-21	4.38	4.31
6- 1	3.77	3.63	9-30	4.31	4.15
6- 8	3.78	3.66	10-31	4.36	4.22
6-15	3.80	3.66	11-30	4.44	4.36
6-21	3.77	3.69	12-31	4.50	4.30
6-22	3.80	3.74	1-31	4.55	4.43
6-29	3.88	3.74	2-28	4.57	4.52
6-30	3.91	3.63			

Figure 15

If you do consider such bonds make sure that the purchase of them is timed and handled correctly so they meet the requirements of the Treasury. If your broker doesn't understand the use of such bonds, go to your bank. Trust departments of banks often use them in the individual trusts they handle, especially in handling the investments of very wealthy, very elderly individuals.

COMMERCIAL PAPER. This is the term used for another type of security that you will hear mentioned often, in newspaper articles and perhaps by brokers. You might sometime in your career have reason to invest in such "paper." Like short-term government bills mentioned earlier in the chapter, commercial paper is an investment for a relatively short period.

Commercial paper, however, is issued by corporations, usually well-known ones with prestigious names. These might include at any particular time General Electric, General Motors Acceptance Corporation, and other important firms like CIT Financial.

If you don't recognize the name General Motors Acceptance Corporation, you can probably at least guess (and correctly) that it is a part of General Motors Corporation. As a matter of fact, you may have done business with it if you have ever bought a General Motors car. GMAC is the part of General Motors that finances car purchases, not only the dealers who need money to carry all those cars in their showrooms but also individual car buyers who borrow to finance their cars. To handle the huge business it does with thousands of car owners. GMAC must constantly borrow money, often on a short-term basis, and to do this it issues this type of security called commercial paper — a promise to pay the stated amount at a certain date.

While some wealthy individuals do buy commercial paper, much of it is bought by financial institutions needing short-term investments.

Since the market tends to be a rather technical one in which the appeal is to a small group of investors, you will not find quotations for commercial paper easily available in newspapers.

FEDERAL FUNDS. This is one security that you should know about but which you will never be able to buy. Yet the interest rates these securities carry do play an important part directly in the life of your local banker and thus indirectly in your own. A bank has to keep a certain amount of money as reserves, but from day to day its excess reserves will rise and fall above the required level, depending on the flow of money into it from its depositors.

Suppose that you are a small depositor in a medium-sized bank, and your Aunt Minnie's executor suddenly alerts you that she has left you $1,000,000 to be deposited on a certain day in your bank account. Your first reaction might be to open a bottle of champagne; your second probably would be how to invest that money quickly after it arrives. For this you might select Treasury bills, those short-term securities mentioned earlier; or you might ask your banker to put the money in certificates of deposits, much like putting it in a savings account. Many banks issue their own certificates of deposit on which a good rate of interest is paid.

However, it could be that the bank might have the money on hand for a day before you make up your mind how to invest it. If it does have the use of such a sum, it would find itself possibly with some excess reserves that day. The bank can sell the use of these reserves in the market to other banks that temporarily lack reserves because of a sudden outflow of money.

Every day banks figure out their reserves and then they "buy or sell" the federal funds. In other words federal funds arise out of the excess reserves of banks. Every day some banks will need additional reserves while other banks will have too much money. It's usually a temporary situation on both sides.

But it underscores the point a good investor must remember, namely that money always has a price in the market and that money should be kept busy for that reason. The wise investor does not keep more than necessary in a checking account, because it bears no interest. She funnels her money into 1) short-term obligations or 2) into savings accounts, both of which give her a return on her money, whether it is to accumulate for a few days or weeks or months. Then when it has accumulated the idea is to put it into favorable long-term investments.

Just the way a bank keeps its excess reserves constantly in the market earning interest, the individual should learn to act with as much agility on a short-term basis, if she wants to permit her money to make as much as possible. Don't let money lie fallow, untended, uncultivated.

EQUIPMENT TRUSTS. These are yet another form of investment with which the public does not usually come into direct contact. While no individual can deal in federal funds for his own benefit, equipment trusts can be bought by anyone, but probably are not used by individual investors very often.

Next time you take a ride on a train look at the side of the Diesel locomotive or the shiny new passenger car and you might see a plaque indicating who owns the equipment — usually a bank.

Railroads and other forms of transportation need constant additions of new rolling stock — engines, passenger cars, etc. They finance these through equipment trusts. For example, a railroad will order some equipment; a bank will lend the railroad a certain amount of money with which to pay for the equipment and then it will own the equipment in trust until the railroad finally pays for it on an installment basis. In turn, the bank issues equipment trust certificates which can be bought publicly. While the bank as trustee stands technically as the owner, the actual owners are the buyers of the trust certificates.

Despite the long years of ups and downs — including many bankruptcies — equipment trust certificates have proved one of the safest forms of investment, for an obvious reason. A railroad cannot operate without equipment. Even if it goes into bankruptcy and its first mortgage bonds are worth very little, it still cannot stay in business without engines and cars. If the railroad did renege on paying the interest on equipment trusts, then the bank as trustee would repossess the equipment and would be able to sell or lease it elsewhere.

Furthermore, equipment trusts occupy a position ahead of first mortgage bondholders because of their claim on this moving equipment.

In the financial history of the United States, it is believed that only one issue of equipment trusts ever failed to pay off at face value, and that was an issue of Florida East Coast Railway equipment trusts, which ultimately did return their holders about 90 cents or more on each dollar of investment. In other words, the record of equipment trusts through depressions, wars, and the competitive downfall of railroads in their fight with planes and trucks and buses has been exemplary.

The second half of this chapter is devoted to two much more speculative types of "places" — not even deserving the name of securities — in which your money can be placed.

For sophisticated investors these places for money need not be purely speculative, and both types to be discussed can provide you with fancy profits if they are well handled.

The two esoterics that many investors do utilize are called *puts and calls* and *commodity futures*.

PUTS AND CALLS. Most brokerage firms avoid enlightening their customers about puts and calls because they are considered speculative. Another reason, quite frankly, is that many brokers know little about them. However, it is my belief that in the future more information will be made available about them, partly because brokerage firms and put and call dealer firms have been offering courses to the public for some years, and partly because this form of speculation has attracted the interest of the Chicago Board of Trade. Though the Board is primarily a center for trading in wheat, corn, soybeans, and such commodities, it recently began trading in puts and calls, going into a quite different field.

Briefly, a put is an option to sell 100 shares of a stock, generally a stock listed on the New York Stock Exchange, at a prearranged price within a certain time. A buyer of a put believes that the price of the stock will go down.

A call is just the opposite, namely an option to buy 100 shares of a stock for an agreed price within a fixed period. In this case, the buyer of a call expects the price of the stock to move up.

For the privilege of buying an option — either a put or a call — the buyer pays a premium, a fee in other words.

What are the advantages? Why, if you think that AT&T will rise in six months, would you buy a call rather than buying the 100 shares of stock? Leverage, for one thing.

For a small amount of money — the premium — the buyer of a put (or a call) has the right to sell (or to buy) as the case may be, a substantial amount of stock in terms of money.

On any given day the *Wall Street Journal* runs several advertisements from various put and call dealers. One of them recently offered a call on a stock priced at 57 to expire January 13, or in about five and a half months, at a premium of $137.50. At the time the price of that stock was about 53 a share.

Suppose that you thought that the price of the stock was cheap at 53 and would rise well above 57 by the end of the year or early in January. Yet, at the time you didn't want to sell more than $5,000 in stocks to pay for this purchase. So, you decide to buy the call. You risk only $137.50, which allotted among the 100 shares covered by the call amounts to $1.37½ a share.

If the price of the shares rises above 57 plus $1.37½ to cover the premium, you would just about break even, except for some brokerage commissions. For this you should allow another point, or about $1 a share. Thus your target price would be about $59.50 a share. Suppose that the stock, under the influence of good earnings, investor interest in it as a safe harbor, and a recovery in the market, rises to about 62 a share. You can take delivery of the 100 shares of stock, paying 57 each for them, or order your broker to give you the profits.

Then your profit would be about $2.50 a share, or $250. You would, in effect, double your money — your premium money, that is — in this investment.

If you were wrong about the stock the most you could lose

would be the premium cost of $137.50. You choose whether you want to exercise the option.

Naturally, buying puts and calls tends to be speculative, but it gives the advantage of leverage and a fixed, known, prepaid cost via the premium.

There is also another advantage that can take the use of puts, for example, out of the realm of speculation: the use of puts as a hedge against your portfolio holdings in a time of declining markets. (This tactic is discussed at length in Chapter 13.)

COMMODITY FUTURES. These offer still another way for a person to speculate. What is a commodity futures contract?

It is a little like buying (or selling) a claim on tomorrow in terms of a basic, useful product. Commodity futures cover essentials like wheat, corn, soybeans, cocoa, sugar, copper, silver, pork bellies (the raw material for breakfast bacon).

For years, commodity futures have existed in the shadow of brokers' doubts. Brokers feared their customers — especially unsophisticated ones — might lose money in commodities and hence their interest in putting their money in either stocks or commodities. No one likes to lose a customer as a result of a string of losses. It's bad business.

In 1966, a year when the stock market showed quite a snappy decline, trading in commodity futures set a new record of 10.4 million contracts, covering some $90 billion in commodities. It came at a time when stock market volume tended to sag and so the heavy commodities volume helped brokerage firms increase their commissions. No wonder so many firms at that point became increasingly interested in commodities, launching courses for their registered representatives and their customers.

It made money sense to be able to swing disappointed stock buyers into commodities. Furthermore, by 1966 the investing public had become much more sophisticated. The trend repeated itself in 1969–1971 in that trading volume in stocks dropped and volume in commodities increased, with the result that commodity trading in 1969 set a record. In 1970 and 1971 new records were set, and 1972 was another record year.

A principal lure of commodity futures trading is the leverage, not unlike the leverage in puts and calls. A person can speculate with a relatively small sum of money, making big profits if he happens to be right.

For example, a speculator who buys one contract of potatoes (50,000 pounds) need ante only about $200–$500, plus about $23 in commissions and $2 in clearing house fees. Some brokerage firms require a little more than this, depending on the price of the underlying commodity.

Other futures contracts are more expensive than potatoes, requiring 10 or 20 percent of the total value of the contract. Nonetheless, for a modest amount the speculator controls a large amount of the commodity, fraught though it is with doubts.

He can for example take delivery of the contract when it comes due, or he can sell it before the delivery date, thus getting out of his position.

Suppose, like many people, he thinks that the price of silver will rise sharply and he buys a futures contract in August of 1972 that calls for delivery in March of 1973. When the March delivery date comes around he could take delivery of the silver and store it in an approved depository (the Irving Trust Company is one) for a small fee each month. If he had speculated in platinum, he could fit the delivery in his pocket, because platinum is such an expensive metal, sold by the ounce, that the contract covers a relatively small number of ounces. Taking delivery of 50,000 pounds of potatoes, however, or 5,000 bushels of wheat is another matter. Hence most speculators sell out their positions before they take delivery.

Who are the speculators? A wide variety of individuals according to a study made a few years ago by the Commodity Exchange Authority. It found that they come from many areas of life, and included housewives, students, retired persons, lawyers, doctors, dentists, manufacturers and salesmen.

Perhaps the most striking category in the above list is "housewives," because many brokerage firms discriminate against women, refusing to permit them to open commodity accounts on the theory that they are more emotional than men and lack the necessary practical knowledge.

In New York I know an elderly housewife who trades daily from her wheelchair. In Chicago, I interviewed and wrote a story about a middle-aged woman who spent six hours a day following the market for egg, pork belly and live cattle futures — and her brokers told me she made a good living out of it. In Washington there is a general's wife who quite consistently makes money trading futures, mostly grains.

Enthusiasts of futures trading point out that there are fewer commodities to watch and analyze at any time than is true for stocks. Only about three dozen commodities are actively traded compared with those 1,941 stocks on the Big Board, and hundreds more on the American Stock Exchange, plus unlimited thousands over-the-counter. Furthermore only about a dozen commodities appear to be really active at any particular time.

Styles change fast in commodity trading, a factor that adds zest and opportunity. Speculators rush to put their money where the action is, and usually on the long side of the market. For example, for some years silver futures were largely neglected; then they suddenly came alive in 1967 when a silver shortage became evident. In the summer of 1972 wheat futures prices rose by about 70 cents a bushel, a huge increase which brought profits to some buyers.* The increase came following announcement of large wheat purchases by the Russians.

What makes a commodity futures market complex is that the two sides to a contract (the person who has bought and the one who has sold) consist not only of bulls and bears (optimists and pessimists) but also a group called hedgers. Hedgers generally are not apparent in the stock market.

In commodities hedgers are professionals in a trade who use commodity futures as price insurance. Without them there couldn't be effective commodity markets. In fact, futures markets arose mostly because of the need for such hedging as protection.

What is a hedger? It might be a meat-packer worried about

*In 1972, Russia became a surprise buyer of U.S. wheat, and wheat prices soared.

his future supplies of pork bellies, to be sliced into bacon. He can buy futures contracts now that call for future delivery of bellies. Then when delivery time comes he can take delivery on the contract, or he can buy his bellies in the open market and sell his contract. He has fixed his price at the moment he bought the contract. Suppose he buys bellies in September 1972 at 36 cents a pound for delivery in January 1973. Meanwhile, let us assume that the price rises to about 42 cents a pound in January. When that date arrives he can take delivery of them and pay the equivalent of 36 cents a pound (minus of course the margin he has put up to buy the contract), or he can sell the contract, and buy the bellies in the open market for 42. In this case the contract has also risen to about 42 cents a pound. Thus he makes a profit on the contract if he sells it, but must pay 42 cents for the bellies. He has protected himself because the six cents gained on the contract offsets the higher price in the open market. Or a businessman who imports copper might find himself with too much copper on hand, and he could sell a contract at current prices, if he liked the price.

In this way one can always protect both his money and his inventory position, at a cost of only the small commission involved in the buying and possibly selling of the contract. Thus professional hedgers take both the buy and sell sides of the futures markets, depending on their needs. But there must also be speculators, members of the public, willing to take the opposite side. For every buyer there must be a seller and vice versa.

Remember that it is unlike buying a stock or selling, because when you buy a stock you take delivery and are credited with the shares five days later, during which time you must pay the full price to your broker (or arrange for margin trading).

When you buy a futures contract (or sell one) you put up a small amount of money at the time and then you don't have to take delivery until some later date. If you sell a commodity contract, you also put up a small amount of money as kind of a margin payment and then you need not make delivery until the contract date arrives. At any time you get out of your position by doing the opposite. If you own a September delivery sugar contract you can sell it; if you have sold a contract for September delivery you can buy one. In each case you have evened out your position.

How should a novice proceed to learn about the futures market? She can ask her broker to give her some basic brochures on commodity trading and on specific commodities. Next she should obtain a good book, usually available at public libraries, on commodity trading.

Then, armed with basic knowledge, she next can ask her broker for some current analyses published by his firm on various commodities. Each day she can read the brief and sometimes useful commodity futures columns in newspapers like the *New York Times* and the *Wall Street Journal*.

Now she is ready to begin trading — on paper. She ought to pick some commodities in which 1) she has noticed good trading volume and 2) she has an interest. For example, a woman who winters in Florida might be more than a little interested and alert about frozen orange juice futures. If she is married to a man in the food business she might feel comfortable with world sugar,* potatoes, or pork bellies. A midwesterner with some knowledge of farming might like to try her hand at grains.

Once she has selected a commodity or two (but not more than that), the novice should chart its prices on paper and follow closely the news that apparently affects it. Most commodity traders use the fundamental and the technical approaches, so she might also have to study some charting techniques more intensively.

Fundamentals can swing a market sharply, such as the four years of disappointing cocoa crops that pushed prices high in the years 1966–1969. An oversupply of potatoes kept prices of that commodity low in 1969. Drought in India made that nation a large buyer of American wheat some years ago, leading to

---

*Domestic sugar futures are not actively traded. The government supports U.S. sugar prices generally well above world market price levels.

quite high prices. The silver shortage has influenced higher silver futures prices. Strikes of workers in copper-producing nations have tended to increase copper prices.

While the fundamentalist follows these changes in supply and demand, weather, political disturbances and competitive products, the chartist is busy analyzing the market by price changes and volume. Suppose that a political revolt breaks out in Nigeria, a big producer of cocoa, the fundamentalist would say, "Aha, cocoa might be in shorter supply. I'll buy a contract." The chartist ignores such news but watches prices increase on charts and when they penetrate certain levels the chartist says, "I'll buy a contract."

Most commodity traders combine both approaches, watching the news and watching the charts. A novice can gain experience by doing hypothetical buying (and selling) for a year or so on paper, before she risks actual money.

18 | The Magic of 72 and Other Helps

Chanel has number 5, but for the sweet smell of success investors can use number 72. It's a magic number that might be called a "handy double," not that it applies to horse racing or even bridge playing.

Number 72 works differently. Suppose you want to double your money in the stock market (or elsewhere) in five years and you want to know what rate of return is needed. Divide the number 72 by the five years, and the answer works out to 14.4, which is the percentage return needed yearly.

Or suppose you have an investment that appreciates in value each year and pays a small dividend. Together, they give you a 12 percent return. How long will it take to double your money if the dividends are reinvested and the stock continues to appreciate? Again, divide the 72 by the 12 percent, and you have an answer of 6 — the number of years required to double your money.

Obviously the number 72 has a real place in your investment thinking. It works fairly well even in cases where compound interest is involved. There are, of course, more accurate and complex mathematical tables to do the same job, but number 72 has the advantage of being mentally portable. Jot it down in your stock notebook as a handy method of calculating the expected return from comparable investments.

Suppose, for example, that your broker has recommended a

stock that he says is growing at the rate of 10 percent a year but it pays a mere 1 percent dividend and probably will not pay more. You will be getting roughly an 11 percent return.

Are you better off in a stock growing at an expected rate of only 6 percent a year but which pays about 5 percent a year in dividends?

Each adds up to about 11 percent return, which means that the investment at such a rate could be expected to double in a little more than 6 years. However, the high cash dividends on the stock in the second example are subject to income tax at regular rates. The stock in the first example — the stock which appreciates in value the most quickly — offers a greater amount of capital gain ultimately, subject to the lower taxation on long-term capital gains.

Return of Capital

When is a dividend not a dividend? One answer to that puzzler is when the payment represents a return of capital.

Sophisticated investors have long been taking note of the tax advantage involved in such investments, particularly at times when the stock market is in the doldrums, inflation continues to nip the dollar income in terms of value, and taxes are high.

Blue chip companies, conservative and yet offering some future growth plus dividends that are partly tax free, have an appeal to moderate and high income investors.

Many such possibilities can be found among public utility shares. A while back Standard & Poor's, the investment advisory service, recommended Consolidated Edison Company despite what it called the company's "mediocre" earnings. The reason was that a large portion of the 1971 dividend was nontaxable. Another suggestion was Orange & Rockland Utilities, serving a heavily populated suburban area of New York City, and another was Puget Sound Power & Light, which operates in a fast-growth area in the Pacific Northwest.

The reason for the tax-free status of certain dividends usually involves some complicated accounting procedures relating to accelerated amortization and depreciation charges. Utilities are the chief beneficiaries of this status from time to time because they spend huge sums continuously on capital equipment like turbines, generators, power lines, even dams for hydroelectric power.

Congress in some recent legislation eliminated or limited the possibilities of such tax-free distributions, which became effective late in 1972.

However, brokers perhaps can offer some recommendations. Other companies that have been able to return tax-free capital include railroads, real estate firms, and some industrial operations. Companies that have racked up large losses or are going through partial liquidation also offer the potential of tax-free return of capital.

For example, in 1969 a company called Mill Factors Corporation discovered huge losses suddenly in one of its divisions, large enough to exceed the stockholders' equity. Not realizing the company's condition, the directors had declared a 60 cent cash dividend on the common shares in 1968 and a 15 cent quarterly payment mailed out early in January 1969. But in fact, because of the heavy losses, that dividend and the payments of dividends made for quite a few years past represented return on capital. The point is that although the stockholders in reporting their dividends in such a case paid a regular income tax on them, they were really getting a return on capital and apparently need not have paid this tax.

Under IRS rules, such taxpayers could claim refunds for as many as three years back from the date they make their claim. Thus they should file for a refund within the statutory time limit, usually three years from the date of the filing of a tax return.

The point to remember about investments that yield a return of capital is twofold:

1. Return of capital is not taxable at regular rates, and thus offers, in a sense, tax-free income.

2. The amount received is applied to reduce the cost basis of the shares.

In cases where the stockholders receive a return of capital, the company usually takes the trouble to spell it out for the stockholder, either with a letter of explanation or a notice accompanying a dividend check. If you fail to understand a payment designated as return of capital, consult your broker, or write the company's secretary directly.

Arbitration

What many small investors do not realize is that there exists an inexpensive way of seeking redress if they think they have a reasonable complaint about their broker.

The method is called arbitration. When an investor becomes a customer of a brokerage firm he may sign a margin agreement — a form with quite a bit of technical language printed on it. In the small print of these agreements there is a statement that goes something like this: "Any controversy between the customer and the firm originating or relating to this contract or the breach thereof shall be settled by arbitration."

The New York Stock Exchange* has been using arbitration to settle securities disputes for more than a hundred fifty years. In 1967 it handled 134 arbitration cases. In 1968 the number ran to 120; in 1969 they totaled 152; in 1970, 183; and in 1971, 250. Ordinarily about 85 percent of the cases involve disputes between customers and their brokers; the rest concern fights between the brokerage houses and their employees. The rules of the New York Stock Exchange say that its member brokerage firms must submit to arbitration if a customer wants it, *even where no formal agreement to arbitrate has been signed.*

Arbitration is a formal procedure, recognized by the courts, in which a panel of disinterested experts reach a decision that is binding on both parties who have stated their cases before the panel.

*The American Stock Exchange also provides arbitration procedures.

The stock exchange provides a panel of arbitrators. However, if a customer of a brokerage firm is worried about possible bias of the experts he can insist that the case be handled instead by the American Arbitration Association. This is a nonprofit organization that handles thousands of cases a year in many fields, involving building-contract disputes, labor relations, customer complaints against dry cleaners (those shrunken dresses!), interpretation of business contracts, and the like. (In fact, a wife shouldn't sign — or permit her husband to sign — a building contract without insisting that the builder insert the usual arbitration clause to handle any difficulties or failures — such as water in the cellar, crooked windows, door frames, cracks in the ceiling.)

The Association's panel of arbitrators for a securities case might consist of such people as lawyers, retired bank officers and accountants. The procedure followed in arbitration is much more informal than that of a courtroom. In arbitration an investor or other complainant can present his case without a lawyer. This, of course, keeps costs down. Often she will run up against a lawyer representing the brokerage firm, however, so the complainant should have command of her facts and should be able to talk plainly and to the point.

Naturally, the arbitrators try to keep generalizations and the hurling of insults to a minimum, so leave your emotions home. If you think you might become emotional bring along a lawyer or an accountant who can help you keep calm.

The charge for the usual brief arbitration over a simple dispute might be no more than $25. It could run to $120 and more for each day the sessions continue.

Besides the relative cheapness of arbitration another advantage is speed. Most cases can be heard in about four months from the date the dispute is filed with the stock exchange. In one case where time was essential, the exchange was able to handle the arbitration in four days from filing to award. This contrasts with the months and even years it takes for a case to go to court. The delays can cause forgetfulness in witnesses, difficulty in obtaining evidence. Who knows, some of the contestants can die in the interim.

At the Big Board — and the American Stock Exchange follows similar procedures — a transcript is taken of the hearing. But if the customer wants one the cost might be $150 or more depending on the length of time consumed.

Generally, the finding by arbitrators comes quickly after the hearing and is presented as a decision, with no explanation of how it was reached. There is no appeal from the arbitrators' ruling except for a few very unusual reasons, rarely available, such as prejudice in the panel members or technical errors of fact in the award.

Recently, a woman customer of a brokerage firm who had filed a claim for $14,000 against a broker was disappointed by an arbitration award of only $1,500, so she went to court. But the court ruled that the award was final, mainly on the basis that she had gone into arbitration willingly. In other words she was trying not to play the game. She wanted to win in court if she couldn't get enough consolation from the arbitrators.

Sometimes this question arises: What if a customer, after having signed an arbitration agreement, wants to skip arbitration and go to court instead? Generally, the answer is that she cannot, unless the case involves a possible violation of securities law by the broker. In 1953 the Supreme Court upheld (in a case called *Wilko* v. *Swan*) the right of a customer to seek court redress because the broker had violated laws of the securities business.

Another source of help sometimes for an unhappy investor could be the Securities and Exchange Commission or the attorney general of the state in which the investor lives. Both could tell her whether any fraud has been involved or whether other laws have been abused by the broker.

However, keep the idea of arbitration in mind because it offers quick, presumably fair, and inexpensive redress. Furthermore, the fact that you file a complaint with the New York Stock Exchange or American Stock Exchange (and send a copy to the SEC, attorney general, etc.) might induce a brokerage firm to settle the dispute quietly, without even letting the matter go to arbitration.

Preemptive Rights

A preemptive right gives the stockholder a chance to buy a security in his company ahead of the public at large, and usually at a more favorable price.

The theory is that a stockholder by buying his prorated portion of the additional stock being offered can maintain his same percentage of ownership in the company. Thus, if a stockholder owns 1,000 shares of a company with 1,000,000 shares outstanding, he owns 1/10 of 1 percent of the company. If he received — and exercised — the right to buy one new share for every 100 shares owned, he would have a total of 1.010 shares.

The number of shares outstanding on the company's books would increase to 1,010,000 shares when the rights offering was completed. With his new shares the stockholder would still own the same 1/10 of 1 percent of the total. However, he would have had to spend money to keep his proportion. If higher earnings resulted from the inflow of the new capital, fine. On the other hand, not to exercise the rights would mean that the stockholder's relative slice of the company would be thinner.

When a stockholder opens the mail and finds a notice from a company that it plans to offer the opportunity to exercise rights to buy additional shares (often a computer card is enclosed for her to mark the decisions), she may not know what to do.

Is it worthwhile spending the extra money to buy the shares? Her broker can advise her on this point. He should also remind her that the rights themselves have value and should not be thrown away, even if she doesn't plan to buy the stock. There is a market for rights in most cases.

At first thought, stockholders tend to credit a company with benevolence when offered rights. In more cases than not benevolence has little to do with it, although few managements admit this.

A corporation needs to raise money from time to time for such reasons as to finance additional growth, enter new markets, launch new products, increase working capital or build new plants. It figures out the most advantageous way to raise the needed funds. The methods are many, such as direct loans from banks, insurance companies, the sale of bonds or preferred stocks, the issuance of convertible bonds or preferreds, and the sale of common stock.

Sometimes a direct sale to its own stockholders appears to be the best. After all, the stockholders can be easily and cheaply reached in this computerized age. Often an underwriting firm acts as a standby to buy up shares not purchased by stockholders.

From certain companies' viewpoints, and that of large stockholders too, the use of preemptive rights can help keep the stock from outsiders' hands by tending to maintain the status quo. Also since the offering price is usually well below the market price, perhaps 20 percent lower, it does create good will among stockholders.

Furthermore some states require that companies incorporated in them *must* provide stockholders with preemptive rights, and some corporate charters contain such provisions.

In the last twenty years many laws requiring preemptive rights have been changed, and so has the attitude of the Securities and Exchange Commission towards permitting companies more flexibility in raising money. There is a feeling that without preemptive rights companies might get higher prices for their new shares, or offer convertibles at lower interest cost or better conversion rates. For example, Eastman Kodak recently asked stockholders' approval for sales of securities abroad without preemptive rights.

Despite the trend, some prestigious companies traditionally offer rights, AT&T being the best known. It has raised hundreds of millions of dollars through rights offerings to stockholders covering both additional issues of common stock and convertible debentures.

HOW TO COMPUTE THE VALUE OF RIGHTS. A quick formula to figure roughly the value of rights follows:

$$V - \frac{C - S}{R + I}$$

V is the value of the right, the unknown which the stockholder wants to find.

C is the current market price of the stock.

S is the price the company has placed on the new stock, usually below the market price, to induce shareholders to subscribe.

R is the specific number of rights necessary to buy one new share. Generally, stockholders receive one right for each share they own.

1 is the mathematical "catalyst" that makes the formula work. Even a mathematician couldn't explain simply why it's essential:

Let's suppose that a stock now sells for $40 a share, and the company offers stockholders new shares at $30, on the basis of 9 rights for each new share. Here is the formula filled out:

$$V = \frac{\$40 - \$30}{9 + 1}$$

$$V = \frac{\$10}{10} \text{ or each right is worth } \$1$$

Usually the price doesn't work out quite so evenly. However, rights are quoted in the market — often on the exchanges — and your broker can get you a quotation. The price changes each day, but the formula will show you what you should receive for the rights. Don't ever throw rights into the wastebasket for they are worth money.

The company, sending the shareholder his rights, will explain how he can obtain the money for selling the rights if he doesn't want to exercise them. He can always sell them through his broker.

Warrants – but Not Rights

Brokers report that many investors are confused about the differences between rights and warrants.

Most every investor, sooner or later, receives a piece of paper which upon reading turns out to be a right — a right to buy extra shares in the company or to buy debentures (a debenture is a bond). Generally the right must be exercised within a specific period of time, and the company sending out the rights warns the stockholder that the rights have some value and should not be tossed aside.

Warrants are a little different, usually lasting for a period of years. They were issued in the beginning as a "sweetener." When a company sold an issue of debentures, for example, it also offered warrants to buy shares at a later date at a certain price.

For example, Avco Corporation early in 1969 sold more than $69,000,000 in 7½ percent debentures with warrants accompanying them. The warrants entitle the bearer to purchase common shares of the company at any time through November 30, 1978, at a price per share of $56. Avco needed the cash at the time to help finance a merger. While Avco common shares are traded on the New York Stock Exchange, the warrants are traded on the American Stock Exchange. Probably few of the warrants are now owned by the original buyers of the debentures.

Warrants receive no dividends, nor do the holders of them have any rights like stockholders' voting privileges at annual meetings. Furthermore, most warrants are issued in bearer form, which means they are not registered in anyone's name and hence can easily be stolen or mislaid. Furthermore, many investors apparently forget about them, letting the expiration dates pass, at which point they become valueless.

However, warrants have a certain speculative charm, especially in the case of volatile stocks or in a booming market.

The Tender Offer

The average stockholder must be aware of a popular maneuver called the tender offer. There's nothing altruistic about it, which means the investor should treat it with as much suspicion as if she were a mouse being played with by a cat.

A company or a group of outsiders with acquisition in mind approaches a stockholder with an offer better than the market price for her shares. Along with this, there usually comes a sweet-talking letter, perhaps even followed by a telephone call. The high price is intended to soften the investor. One study indicates that the price offered often runs about 20 percent above the market price for the shares, before the tender offer becomes public.

The stockholder should not jump to the conclusion that she is getting a bonus, or even a little more profit than she expected, for nothing. In fact, if she holds out she could do even better. After all, the outside group is making a bid for the company by means of a tender offer because it believes the deal can be profitable. So the wise investor should try to find out just why the outsiders think they want the shares.

This entails a little detective work. In the case of the typical raiders, it might involve a plan to liquidate the company at a profit, with the company's cash ending up in the raiders' hands. Or perhaps the outsiders plan to add the company to a conglomerate they are building — another dazzler in an add-a-diamond necklace.

Or perhaps the group has been lured by an incentive as simple as taking advantage of a tax-loss situation. For example, Haven

Industries recently acquired control of National Sugar, which had accumulated large losses. Still another reason, not usual, but it has happened: a father wants to obtain control of a company and place his son in the presidency.

The acquiring company might have a different and more logical goal, such as getting a foothold in a new industry. Corporations often find it is cheaper to enter a new field by buying an existing business than by beginning a product line.

Another twist for stockholders to consider comes when a company makes a tender offer for *its own* shares, for any of a variety of reasons.

The stock might be underpriced, and the company might consider it feasible to buy up the shares for its pension or profit-sharing funds.

The company might need stock to use for a merger it has planned.

The company might consider the stock much too low priced and hope to increase the price by indicating it has so much faith in the shares it wants to buy them.

Or the company might fear a takeover by outsiders and buy its own shares to cut down the risk of being outvoted at the next annual meeting, as well as to give the stock's price a boost.

There is always a solid reason behind a tender offer, and usually that reason is not volunteered by the group or company making the offer. Therefore the stockholder has to look elsewhere for the answer. Since her money is involved, she should regard the offer with cold cynicism.

What to do?

First, she can read through the company's latest annual report and interim statements for a clue as to why an outside group has become interested.

Secondly, she should contact her broker, who probably won't have an answer himself but he can obtain some sort of opinion from his research department. In such a case, a second opinion from another brokerage firm is also advisable.

Third, the shareholder can ask her bank what it knows. Big

banks not only have investment research departments but they handle trusts and have common funds for investment. If the company involved is well known some of its stock probably appears in the bank's portfolio — in the common trust funds, in personal trusts, in pension trusts that the bank handles. Sooner or later the bank will have to make a decision about what it plans to do with regard to the tender offer.

Fourth — and admittedly harder to do — the stockholder could contact one of the company's competitors. No one knows better than an aggressive rival what is happening in a company.

Through one of these sources, the investor should be able to find some reason for the outside group's interest. Undoubtedly it involves some hidden values. Under current accounting rules companies can report some assets at cost, rather than present market value. Often, too, there are valuable intangibles — mineral rights, patents, ideas — all of which might be unknown to the general public.

Remember Xerox and the process that made it so successful? And look at Minute Maid frozen orange juice. It is such hidden values that a typical stockholder might not realize unless he searches for them.

Stock Certificate Procedures

LOST CERTIFICATES. "Don't" is the best advice about losing stock certificates.

The still discussed classic example concerns an economics professor who thought he had inherited some railroad preferred stock from his father. No certificate could be found but the company kept mailing information to the deceased father's home and said he was a stockholder of record.

By the time the estate was settled, the preferred shares of the railroad, in the process of going through reorganization, became quite valuable. So the professor went through the rigamarole of taking out a surety bond and obtaining a new certificate from the railroad. Then he sold the stock for $8,000, divided the money with his sister and the estate was settled, or so he thought.

When the railroad finally reorganized, a broker suddenly presented a large block of shares, including the "lost" certificate. The surety company contacted the professor and forced him to pay back the $8,000. His father apparently had sold the shares, signing the certificate and thus transferring it to the broker. The professor had to mortgage his house to raise the $8,000.

Each corporation follows its own rules about replacing lost, strayed, or stolen stock certificates, but most are quite similar.

For example, after it hears from a stockholder that a certificate has been lost, Tri-Continental Corporation (the large closed-end investment company listed on the New York Stock Exchange) alerts its transfer agent to put a "stop transfer" notice on the account. Then there is a waiting period of about three months, during which the stockholder cannot sell his shares. Also, the stockholder must file an affidavit of loss that the company mails to him, and he must pay for a surety bond.

If he uses the company's blanket coverage, the surety bond premium is 3 percent of the value of the securities at the time of the assumption of liability. Thus, on shares valued at $5,000, the cost of the bonding would be $150. After this procedure, the new stock certificate is issued.

The American Telephone & Telegraph Company asks its stockholders to fill out a notarized "affidavit of loss" and then politely suggests that they wait six months. The wait doesn't have to be that long but a spokesman explained that "we find certificates turn up in most cases." The cost ($1.20 a share in the case of AT&T for the surety bonding) and the psychology of the long wait sometimes induce stockholders to search more thoroughly and turn up the errant certificates.

General Motors Corporation uses a similar technique — an affidavit and a surety bond costing about 3 percent of the shares' value.

What most shareholders do not realize is that the surety bond protects the company and its transfer agent, not the shareholder. If the shares show up, as in the case of the professor, the surety company can take civil action against the misguided shareholder. If a stolen certificate is processed, then the action might be against the culprit, possibly on charge of theft and forgery (if he can be found), because to be transferred a stock certificate generally has to be signed by the person to whom it is registered. In some cases, too, the brokerage firm that accepted the stolen certificate and passed it on for transfer could be held liable.

Clifford F. Scherer, senior vice-president of the Morgan Guaranty Trust Company, a bank that does a large amount of corporate stock transfer work, advised: "The stockholder had better be awfully sure that the certificate is really lost. He can't shrug off responsibility."

NAME CHANGES. Sometimes stockholders worry about a name change, following marriage, for example. However, a bank probably will continue to honor dividend checks under the woman's maiden name for a while until notification has taken effect. The quickest way to change a stock certificate to the woman's married name is for her to go to her local bank and ask it to guarantee her signatures — both single and married — on the back of the certificate.

The bank should certify that the woman is one and the same person. Then she can mail the certificate directly to the transfer agent. One transfer agent bank reports that it takes about a week once it receives such a certificate to issue another in the married name. However, if a stockholder goes through her broker the process can take much longer.

SIGNING YOUR CERTIFICATE. If stock is registered in your name you have to sign the back of the certificate when you sell it. At first glance the procedure looks confusing, mostly because of the type of printing used on stock certificates, and the legal language. It's much like endorsing a check.

The certificate reads "for value received . . . hereby sell and transfer unto . . . ." Don't sign your name there. Further down there is another blank space reading "do hereby irrevocably con-

SHARE PRICE	SHARES 5	10	20	25	30	50	75	100	200	300	500	1000
$37												
1/8	8.10	11.80	19.20	22.03	24.43	34.05	44.98	55.30	100.60	139.90	218.50	350.00
1/4	8.11	11.83	19.25	22.07	24.48	34.13	45.06	55.41	100.83	140.24	219.06	350.50
3/8	8.13	11.85	19.30	22.11	24.53	34.21	45.14	55.53	101.05	140.58	219.63	351.00
1/2	8.14	11.88	19.35	22.15	24.58	34.29	45.23	55.64	101.28	140.91	220.19	351.50
5/8	8.15	11.90	19.40	22.19	24.63	34.38	45.31	55.75	101.50	141.25	220.75	352.00
3/4	8.16	11.93	19.45	22.23	24.67	34.46	45.40	55.86	101.73	141.59	221.31	352.50
7/8	8.18	11.95	19.50	22.27	24.72	34.54	45.48	55.98	101.95	141.93	221.88	353.00
	8.19	11.98	19.55	22.31	24.77	34.62	45.57	56.09	102.18	142.26	222.44	353.50
$38												
1/8	8.20	12.00	19.60	22.35	24.82	34.70	45.65	56.20	102.40	142.60	223.00	354.00
1/4	8.21	12.03	19.65	22.39	24.87	34.78	45.73	56.31	102.63	142.94	223.56	354.50
3/8	8.23	12.05	19.70	22.43	24.92	34.86	45.82	56.43	102.85	143.28	224.13	355.00
1/2	8.24	12.08	19.75	22.47	24.97	34.94	45.90	56.54	103.08	143.61	224.69	355.50
5/8	8.25	12.10	19.80	22.51	25.02	35.03	45.99	56.65	103.30	143.95	225.25	356.00
3/4	8.26	12.13	19.85	22.55	25.06	35.11	46.07	56.76	103.53	144.29	225.81	356.50
7/8	8.28	12.15	19.90	22.59	25.11	35.19	46.16	56.88	103.75	144.63	226.38	357.00
	8.29	12.18	19.95	22.63	25.16	35.27	46.24	56.99	103.98	144.96	226.94	357.50
$39												
1/8	8.30	12.20	20.00	22.68	25.21	35.35	46.33	57.10	104.20	145.30	227.50	358.00
1/4	8.31	12.23	20.05	22.72	25.26	35.43	46.41	57.21	104.43	145.64	228.06	358.50
3/8	8.33	12.25	20.10	22.76	25.31	35.51	46.49	57.33	104.65	145.98	228.63	359.00
1/2	8.34	12.28	20.15	22.80	25.36	35.59	46.58	57.44	104.88	146.31	229.19	359.50
5/8	8.35	12.30	20.20	22.84	25.41	35.68	46.66	57.55	105.10	146.65	229.75	360.00
3/4	8.36	12.33	20.25	22.88	25.45	35.76	46.75	57.66	105.33	146.99	230.31	360.50
7/8	8.38	12.35	20.30	22.92	25.50	35.84	46.83	57.78	105.55	147.33	230.88	361.00
	8.39	12.38	20.35	22.96	25.55	35.92	46.92	57.89	105.78	147.66	231.44	361.50

SHARE PRICE	SHARES 5	10	20	25	30	50	75	100	200	300	500	1000
$40	8.40	12.40	20.40	23.00	25.60	36.00	47.00	58.00	106.00	148.00	232.00	362.00
1/8	8.41	12.43	20.43	23.04	25.65	36.08	47.08	58.11	106.23	148.34	232.38	362.50
1/4	8.43	12.45	20.47	23.08	25.70	36.16	47.17	58.23	106.45	148.68	232.75	363.00
3/8	8.44	12.48	20.50	23.12	25.75	36.24	47.25	58.34	106.68	149.01	233.13	363.50
1/2	8.45	12.50	20.53	23.16	25.80	36.33	47.34	58.45	106.90	149.35	233.50	364.00
5/8	8.46	12.53	20.56	23.20	25.84	36.41	47.42	58.56	107.13	149.69	233.88	364.50
3/4	8.48	12.55	20.60	23.24	25.89	36.49	47.51	58.68	107.35	150.03	234.25	365.00
7/8	8.49	12.58	20.63	23.28	25.94	36.57	47.59	58.79	107.58	150.36	234.63	365.50
$41	8.50	12.60	20.66	23.33	25.99	36.65	47.68	58.90	107.80	150.70	235.00	366.00
1/8	8.51	12.63	20.69	23.37	26.04	36.73	47.76	59.01	108.03	151.04	235.38	366.50
1/4	8.53	12.65	20.73	23.41	26.09	36.81	47.84	59.13	108.25	151.38	235.75	367.00
3/8	8.54	12.68	20.76	23.45	26.14	36.89	47.93	59.24	108.48	151.71	236.13	367.50
1/2	8.55	12.70	20.79	23.49	26.19	36.98	48.01	59.35	108.70	152.05	236.50	368.00
5/8	8.56	12.73	20.82	23.53	26.23	37.06	48.10	59.46	108.93	152.39	236.88	368.50
3/4	8.58	12.75	20.86	23.57	26.28	37.14	48.18	59.58	109.15	152.73	237.25	369.00
7/8	8.59	12.78	20.89	23.61	26.33	37.22	48.27	59.69	109.38	153.06	237.63	369.50
$42	8.60	12.80	20.92	23.65	26.38	37.30	48.35	59.80	109.60	153.40	238.00	370.00
1/8	8.61	12.83	20.95	23.69	26.43	37.38	48.43	59.91	109.83	153.74	238.38	370.50
1/4	8.63	12.85	20.99	23.73	26.48	37.46	48.52	60.03	110.05	154.08	238.75	371.00
3/8	8.64	12.88	21.02	23.77	26.53	37.54	48.60	60.14	110.28	154.41	239.13	371.50
1/2	8.65	12.90	21.05	23.81	26.58	37.63	48.69	60.25	110.50	154.75	239.50	372.00
5/8	8.66	12.93	21.08	23.85	26.62	37.71	48.77	60.36	110.73	155.09	239.88	372.50
3/4	8.68	12.95	21.12	23.89	26.67	37.79	48.86	60.48	110.95	155.43	240.25	373.00
7/8	8.69	12.98	21.15	23.93	26.72	37.87	48.94	60.59	111.18	155.76	240.63	373.50

Figure 16. New York Stock Exchange Commission rates at some typical share price levels.

stitute and appoint . . . " Here the stockholder should write in the name of her brokerage firm, although if the shares are delivered to the broker by hand, this line too can remain blank. The broker will use a stamper to inscribe the firm's name there. However, if the name of the broker isn't there, it could be "stolen" and negotiated.

Still further down is the simple, straightforward word "Dated" with space for insertion of the date, if you wish, but it isn't necessary.

Then comes the key line, apt to be a quite bare line, and this one requires your signature. Make sure that you sign it exactly as your name appears on the face of the certificate. Naturally, if the shares are jointly owned both owners must sign, just as they must sign a federal income tax return if they file jointly.

If the broker keeps your registered certificates and you order him by telephone to sell, he can send you authorizations to sign, in lieu of signing in person.

Commissions

Early in 1972, after several years of discussion, the New York Stock Exchange issued a new commission setup, which increased the former rates applicable some years ago but is generally lower than an interim schedule which included a surcharge.

Figure 16 shows two pages from a typical commission rate book that gives a quick idea of the charges. If you read them carefully you can see that the cost of buying shares is not very high. If you know the commission for a round lot, or 100 shares, then the commission on 200 shares would be twice the basic amount, etc. An odd lot applies to shares less than 100, and probably these are the commissions most small investors look at.

19 | Planning Your Portfolio

The young in heart and the bold in spirit can do well in the stock market, and so can the temporarily sorrowing widow. I don't intend to be lugubrious, but all married women should prepare themselves to be widows, no matter what their age or status in life. If they are not married they should prepare themselves for the loneliness of making their own decisions, in a world where opinions are a dime a dozen.

One day a man telephoned me at the *New York Times* with a puzzled urgency in his voice. He was only an acquaintance, virtually a stranger, calling me because I write a personal finance column. "My mother has just become a widow, and she has $100,000. How should she handle it?"

The question is ages old, one that recurs almost every day. Brokers, bank officers, lawyers and, even more often, sons hear it.

There are many answers, but one interesting approach is to set the question into some historical perspective. Back in the nineteen twenties and again in the thirties *Barron's,* the financial weekly published by Dow Jones, sponsored contests as to how a widow could invest such a sum.

The 1939 winning essay with its accompanying portfolio was submitted by Eugene M. Kaufmann, Jr., who showed the good investment man's interest in changing with the times. "Over many years," he wrote, "there has grown a tradition that the only safe medium for conserving principal and returning a safe income to widows are first mortgages on real estate, bonds secured by mortgages and government obligations." Such was the tradition that had gained popularity in the nineteen twenties, when mortgages returned 8 and 10 percent.

All that changed with the depression and the doldrums of the nineteen thirties. Mr. Kaufmann pointed out that during that period real estate and bonds suffered from government policies he called "prejudicial to creditors" — a polite way of saying it.

Also, the government assisted debtors by keeping interest rates low. Thus the high bond yields of the twenties gave way to 3 and 4 percent in the thirties, and a few years later when the Second World War began, interest rates fell even lower. Now rates are much higher again. (See the table of rates on pages 42–43.)

Looking at such factors, Mr. Kaufman wrote dolefully: "There is no means whereby we can estimate how long current chaotic political conditions will continue . . . a gradual attrition is the normal fate of most investment funds." The only way out, he suggested, was "a number of well-selected stocks so that the fund can grow. . . . I cannot escape the conclusion that the stock market offers quite as much safety at prevailing levels today as does the bond market," he wrote in 1939.

He suggested that the widow with $100,000 commit 50 percent of her money to common stocks "whose earnings seem capable of expansion," plus 15–20 percent in cash reserves for buying opportunities, and the remainder in short- and medium-term corporate bonds. His portfolio is shown in Table 16.

How have times changed since 1939?

The sum of $100,000 in 1939 is worth only about $45,000 in terms of today's purchasing power. So today's widow or working girl inheriting $100,000 has relatively less than the woman in 1939.

Interest rates today are high again, so that bonds are looked upon favorably for high yields and even appreciation if they are selling below par value.

Common Stocks

Number of Shares	Description	Market Value		Income
100	Am Gas & Elec	36 1/8	$ 3,612	$ 160
40	E I duPont	153	6,320	200
100	Gen Am Trans	48	4,800	225
100	Can Electric	34 5/8	3,462	100
50	Ingersoll-Rand	105	5,250	275
100	Int Nickel	48 1/4	4,825	200
100	Libbey-Owens-Ford	47 1/2	4,750	200
50	Owens-Illinois Gl	65	3,250	100
100	Pac Gas & El	33 1/4	3,325	200
50	J C Penney	88 1/2	4,425	212
50	Sears, Roebuck	75 1/8	3,756	150
100	Texas Corp	34 1/8	3,412	200
Total stocks			$51,187	$2,222
Current return				4.34%

Corporate Bonds

Quantity	Description	Market Value		Income
5	Western NY & Penn RR 4s, 1943	106 1/4	$5,312	$200
5	Louisv & Jeff Bridge 4s, 1945	108 1/2	5,425	200
5	Appalachian El Power Co 4 1/2s, 1948	106 1/4	5,312	225
5	Am IG Chemical 5 1/2s, 1949	102 5/8	5,131	275
5	Bethlehem Steel cv 3 1/2s	100 1/8	5,006	175
5	Ohio Valley Water 5s, 1954	108	5,400	250

Cash and Its Equivalent

	Market Value		Income
$10,000 U.S. savings bonds, due 9/1/1949	75%	$ 7,500	$ 210
$10,000 U.S. savings bonds, due 1/2/1950	75%	7,500	210
Fed Savings & Loan Assoc share account	100%	1,975	69
Total bonds and cash or equivalent		$48,562	$1,304
Current return			3.73 2/3

Table 16

The widow or retired working woman today, if she is over sixty years old, probably receives a sizable social security check, and possibly even her own or her husband's corporate pension, which might help compensate a little for the cost of living increases.

She pays higher taxes than in 1939.

Buying common stocks for growth has become much more prevalent and acceptable than in 1939.

Today's investment advisers believe even more firmly that a widow's portfolio should be handled aggressively, with the idea of appreciation through long-term capital gains rather than just reliance on income securities.

The reason is twofold — to fight inflation on its own terms and to save on taxes. Taxes on long-term capital gains, remember, can be one-half as high as taxes on dividends and other regular income.

I once asked Russell Morrison, president of Standard & Poor's, and a long-time believer in growth stocks, to suggest a portfolio for a widow with $100,000. He advised limiting the portfolio to four or five stocks in basic industries offering growth, plus keeping about $20,000 in short-term Treasury issues as a hedge fund for buying opportunities.

His suggestions: Ford Motor, for appreciation and income; Northern Natural Gas for slow appreciation and income; Union Carbide, a stock depressed in price but with good potential. "For play she might enjoy some shares of IBM," he added.

Table 17 shows the way such a portfolio might look.

The old-time investment adviser probably would say nothing about "play." It wasn't proper in those days to suggest that a woman might have some fun in the stock market! Playing might suggest that men thought she had brains enough to learn about the market, and most of them, sadly enough, did not give us the benefit of such a thought in those days.

More than ever today the stress is on appreciation, even for the widow. To invest even as much as $100,000 is no easy task because brokers and other advisers will come up with so many answers to the questions: What kind of stocks to select? What income to expect? What can be hoped in terms of appreciation? What about inflation rising at more than possibly 5 percent per year? When to sell?

Yet the sum of $100,000 is not large by today's inflationary standards, though it is about what a moderately prosperous businessman might leave a widow.

"As a widow myself it is a problem I can understand," says Mrs. Ione Sutton, a registered representative with Bacon Whipple & Co.

Security*	Rate of Return or Dividend	Return in Dollars
$20,000	6%	$1,200
400 shares of Ford	$2.60	1,040
400 shares Nor. Nat. Gas	$2.60	1,040
400 shares Un. Carbide	$2	800
50 shares IBM	$5.40	270
		$4,350

*When Morrison suggested these securities the price of the portfolio was a little below $100,000. Calculate its value currently.

Table 17

Based on a few assumptions about the typical widow, Mrs. Sutton's suggested portfolio is an interesting one. Her widow is old enough to qualify for about $1,800 social security income, owns a house on which the mortgage is paid but which requires about $1,000 a year for taxes and maintenance, and has $100,000 left to her by her husband.

She needs about $5,000 a year from her $100,000, if possible. "Such a woman," Mrs. Sutton explains, "wants security to cope with daily living and some hedge against inflation."

Mrs. Sutton's suggested portfolio (Table 18) combines a mutual fund (a steady, basic income), some bonds bought around par prices which might appreciate if interest rates decline (and they offer a high return now) and sound common stocks (with

			Cost		Annual Dividend, etc.	
Bonds						
10M	Guardian Mortgage Inv. 6 3/4/86	(90)	$	9,000	$	675
10M	Computer Science (convertible) 6/94	(60)		6,000		600
			$	15,000	$	1,275
Preferreds (convertibles)						
200	United Brands A-1.20	(16)	$	3,200	$	240
100	Studebaker Worthington B 5.00	(80)		8,000		500
100	Bristol Myers 2.00	(44)		4,400		200
			$	15,600	$	940
Utilities						
200	Brooklyn Union Gas	(24 1/2)	$	4,900	(1.72)	344
200	United Utilities	(18)		3,600	(.96)	192
200	Delmarva Power & Light	(17)		3,400	(1.12)	224
			$	11,900	$	760
Fund						
	Affiliated $75 Monthly Drawing		$	15,000	$	900
Commons (diversified and growth)						
100	Sears, Roebuck (retail)	(116)	$	11,600	$	140
100	Westinghouse Electric	(50)		5,000		94
100	Boise Cascade (bldg)	(15)		1,500	(+ stk)	25
100	American Can	(30)		3,000		220
100	Standard Oil N.J.	(71)		7,100		390
100	Chase Man Realty Trust	(55)		5,500	(variable)	420
100	Babcock & Wilcox (machinery)	(30)		3,000		55
			$	36,700	$	1,344
Cash (@ 5%)			$	5,800	$	290
Totals			$100,000		$	5,509

Table 18. Mrs. Sutton's Suggested Portfolio

good growth potential). On this portfolio the income would amount to about $5,500 a year.

A somewhat different approach was suggested by Charles Rolo, analyst, portfolio manager and ebullient writer on financial matters.*

For the widow with $100,000 he believes in more aggressiveness, meaning more stress on growth stocks. His idea is that the widow should take some of her income out of capital appreciation to supplement dividend income. This can also cut taxes because taxes on capital gains run at a lower rate — a point that cannot be emphasized too often.

"My conviction," says Mr. Rolo, "is that the best way to preserve capital is to manage it aggressively. When a client has insisted on high yields as a primary consideration, the account has turned in a disappointing performance. On the other hand, a number of clients have agreed to let me give them a monthly basic income they might require from the account and let me manage it primarily to achieve capital gains."

His mix consists of several quality issues ($45,000 worth) for high yield and moderate appreciation, plus $18,000 in bonds with high yields, and $24,000 in speculative issues in industries which stand to benefit from an end to the war in Vietnam and the new sociological approach to economics — building construction, medical care and education. The remainder is held in interest-bearing short-term investments, to provide ready cash for new purchases.

Mr. Rolo says, "It is my belief that under reasonably favorable overall conditions, a portfolio invested in this way can show an average appreciation of 10 to 18 percent annually. Obviously in bear market years, the portfolio would be likely to show a decline, but this could be made up in strong bull markets."

From these portfolios, suggested by some leading Wall Streeters, you can understand that the widow approaching the market

---

*Coeditor with George J. Nelson of *The Anatomy of Wall Street* (New York: Lippincott, 1968). I contributed a chapter, "How the Bears Operate," to that book.

conservatively and needing income should also invest with appreciation in mind because of taxes and inflation.

If the widow ought to kick up her heels financially this way, then the young career girl with a lifetime ahead or the more mature career woman looking towards retirement in ten years or so should perhaps place even more emphasis on growth. However, in such instances the working women should let their capital ride in the market, not taking a portion of the gains' cash. When stocks are sold for capital gains they should be promptly reinvested.

WOMEN WITH CHILDREN IN COLLEGE. Investing needs change with age sometimes or with altered financial needs, and therefore one woman's portfolio can be poison to another.

There comes a period in the life of many married couples — a midway period — when children are suddenly ready for college. It may come when the husband's income level has not yet reached its peak. Most budgets cannot stand the strain of sending several children to college, especially at the same time, without some borrowing. At times like this the husband might think in terms of taking out or increasing the mortgage on his house, borrowing on his life insurance policies or selling stock.

My advice is this. Don't add to the mortgage or take out a new one, because mortgages these days carry a high rate of interest and take many years to pay. Borrowing on your life insurance is a good idea because most life insurance policies stipulate that the money can be borrowed at about 5 percent interest, a low rate for these days when bank money costs 7 and 8 percent.

Don't consider selling your portfolio of stock, but you can winnow out some stocks in which you have good long-term capital gains. Put the same money into high income stocks, issues of sound companies temporarily low priced because of the business cycle or because demand for their products is temporarily low. For example, in 1969 when the steel industry was in the doldrums prices of shares in fine companies like Bethlehem Steel and U.S. Steel were low enough to pay a high return in cash

Shares	Security	Price	Cost	Ind. Div.	Ann. Inc.	Percent Yld.	P/E Ratio	5 Yr. P/E Hi-Low
200	American Can (AC)	$46	$ 9,200	$2.20	$440	4.8	10.0	18–11
200	American Tel. & Tel. (T)	53	10,600	2.40	480	4.5	13.3	23–13
300	Crocker-Citizens (OTC)	33	9,900	1.60	480	4.8	10.6	21–9
140	General Motors (GM)	73	10,220	4.05	567	5.5	12.7	17–11
270	International Paper (IP)	37	9,990	1.50	405	4.1	13.7	21–10
200	National Biscuit (BI)	51	10,200	2.20	440	4.3	15.7	24–13
600	Northeast Utilities (NU)	17	10,200	0.94	564	5.5	13.1	18–13
200	Sherwin-Williams (SHW)	50	10,000	2.00	400	4.0	14.9	21–9
300	Southern Pacific (SX)	33	9,900	1.80	540	5.5	8.3	13–7
150	Standard Oil of N.J. (J)	69	10,350	3.75	563	5.4	11.2	19–11
			$100,560		$4,879	4.9%		

Table 19

	Recent Price	1971–72 Price Range	Earnings per Share 1971	Earnings per Share 1972E	P/E 1972E	Div.	Yield
Eastman Kodak	$112	$112–72	$2.60	$3.10	36.3x	$1.34	1.2%
Evans Products	24	28–22	1.18	1.40	17.1	0.30	1.2
Max Factor	36	45–28	1.62	1.80	20.0	0.60	1.7
Florida Steel (Sept.)	36	36–18	2.68	4.00	9.0	1.00	2.8
Goodyear Tire	31	35–27	2.34	2.60	11.8	0.88	2.8
P. R. Mallory	56	57–38	2.93	3.00	16.0	1.80	3.2
RCA	43	43–26	1.69	2.50	17.2	1.00	2.3
Sheller Globe	33	33–16	1.73	2.00	16.5	0.80	2.4
Standard Oil of New Jersey	75	82–67	6.76	7.00	10.7	3.90	5.2
Zenith	49	55–36	1.70	2.50	19.6	1.40	2.9

E = Estimated   x = ?

Table 20. A Suggested Portfolio

For those undertaking an investment program at the present time and, as well, to provide an example of the kind of diversification we have in mind, we have prepared a suggested portfolio. Note that it consists of ten stocks, a number we regard as a maximum for accounts up to $1 million in value. For portfolios in the $10,000 to $20,000 range, fewer issues can be used, but we would not suggest using less than five. We have often stated that no one can be 100 percent accurate in predicting the direction or shape of the stock market. Diversification is necessary to avoid overexposure to one segment of the market or to the fortunes of just one or two companies.

dividends. Construction industry shares also appeared to be a good buy. The list of undervalued stocks is a long one and your broker can help you with suggestions. Then, once your child is out of college and the financial load is off, you can reinvest your money into fast growth stocks.

If more money is needed than the loans on life insurance policies and the return from stocks, then take the shares to your bank and borrow on the stocks. Collateral loans require lower rates of interest than most other types of installment borrowing. And psychologically this is a good idea because it is so hard to save up capital for investment. So, don't cash in your chips; keep them and borrow on them. Debts, of course, have to be paid but people can gear themselves to pay off debts on time while it is hard to set aside funds for building up investment capital.

Table 19 is a typical portfolio of high yield securities formulated late in 1969. Don't take these as good examples for 1973 or later because investments change and your broker can offer you another, better list. But just for fun, check the prices and dividends these same stocks pay in 1973, and you will see how durable a portfolio like this can be — even after weathering a bad downturn like that of 1969–1970.

In the spring of 1972 Burnham & Company came out with a suggested portfolio (Table 20) for aggressively oriented investors who also like good quality. Like so many brokerage firms Burnham puts out a market letter, offering views about the economy and specific suggestions about stocks. Ask your broker to put you on the mailing list for some of your firm's publications, or pick up copies from the brokers' offices.

Tables 21 and 22 give some suggested portfolios for growth stocks for a widow. They are from a 1972 issue of *The Outlook* published by Standard & Poor's, the investment advisory company.

Many of the names you will know, like Eastman Kodak, but some are unfamiliar such as Evans Products (building materials, homes); P. R. Mallory (electrical and electronic components);

Florida Steel (specialty items, structural steel); Sheller Globe (auto parts, office equipment, mechanical and rubber goods).

THE OLDER, RETIRED COUPLE. The older couple needing high income probably will concentrate on such stocks as listed in Table 20, with shares that offer a good income potential and some possible gains. The market of 1969, with bond interest rates high and prices of many bonds well below their par value to reflect 7 percent yields, was a good time, perhaps the best in history, to accumulate high return investments that also promise excellent capital gains.

Ironically, inflation that has hurt so many older couples has been good to them in this particular way. The government in its fight on inflation has permitted bond yields to rise to historic high levels. It is a situation that probably won't continue forever, but some economists do predict that interest rates will not return for many years to the low levels of 4 percent which prevailed back in the early nineteen sixties.

THE PRUDENT MAN RULE. Many women have to deal in their lifetime with an entity called "the prudent man" — a man like a lawyer or bank officer plus an idea. The phrase unfortunately conjures a grandfather image — straitlaced, conservative, unbending, which somehow doesn't fit into a woman's life in these days of emancipated thinking. Yet the concept has much to do with investment planning still and also with the attitude of many men in your life.

For centuries women were dependent on men — grandfathers, fathers, husbands, who were supposed to earn enough to leave their women sufficient money. Even today the average man dies earlier than the average woman. Look at a typical list of premiums for insurance policies and you will see that a woman of thirty buying a policy would pay the same premium as a man of about twenty-six. In other words there is a four year or more difference in their calculated life-span. No organizations analyze life-spans more closely than the actuaries of insurance companies.

Since most women inherit money sometime in their lives,

Established Growth

	Earnings Per Share ($)			Indicated Div.	1970-72 Price Range	Recent Price	P/E Ratio	Yield %		Latest 5-Year Growth Rates		No. of Earn. Gains '67-'71	Interim Earn. Trend	Price Action vs. Mkt.	
1970	1971	E1972								Sales	Earn.			5-26-70 to 4-28-71	Since 4-28-71
3.83	4.03	4.50	0.60	177 1/2–78 5/8	170	37.8	0.4	Burroughs Corp.	15%	18%	5	+8%	0.87	1.20
1.51	1.82	2.25	0.43	119 1/8–37 1/4	118	53.0	0.4	Johnson & Johnson	20	20	5	+21	1.44	1.39
1.86	2.56	3.15	0.52	119 1/4–33 1/4	115	36.5	0.5	Kresge (S.S.)	22	24	5	+31	1.40	1.41
4.22	4.75	5.40	1.46	193 1/4–51 3/4	191	35.4	0.8	Schlumberger	15	14	5	+16	1.34	1.60
3.01	3.56	4.00	1.55	116 3/8–51	110	27.5	1.4	Sears, Roebuck	8	8	5	+19	1.16	1.17
1.28	2.30	3.10	0.40	119 1/2–18 1/8	86	27.7	0.5	Syntex	13	–2	4	+60	1.78	1.39
1.65	1.99	2.20	1.04	128 –37	128	58.2	0.8	Tampax, Inc.	13	13	5	+15	1.25	1.76

More Speculative Growth

	Earnings Per Share ($)			Mill. Shs. Outst.	1970-72 Price Range	Recent Price	P/E Ratio	Yield %		Latest 5-Year Growth Rates		No. of Earn. Gains '66-'70	Interim Earn. Trend	Price Action vs. Mkt.	
1970	1971	E1972								Sales	Earn.			5-26-70 to 4-28-71	Since 4-28-71
1.01	1.20	1.40	5.8	36-7/8–16-1/4	26	17.9	–	Intl. Chem. & Nucl.	96	22	5	+14	1.04	0.90
0.68	0.87	1.05	5.2	53 –11-3/8	49	46.7	0.4	Std. Brands Paint	17	18	5	+19	1.82	1.50
0.77	0.93	0.95	5.0	60-3/4–18-5/8	56	58.9	–	Wang Laboratories	59	57	5	+3	1.42	1.14
1.90	2.11	2.50	17.0	47-5/8–20-1/8	46	18.4	0.5	Warner Comm.	42	15	5	+13	1.16	1.17

Table 21. Stocks with Promising Growth Prospects

These stocks promise to enjoy well above average growth rates in earnings per share for the foreseeable future. Stocks in the second category carry a higher degree of risk, but by the same token offer greater reward potential. Income is not a consideration here. Earnings are for calendar years or for fiscal years ending as indicated after names. Unless otherwise noted, they are based on common and common-share equivalents, excluding nonrecurring items and including restatements. E-Estimated. P-Preliminary. d-Deficit. Indicated Dividends include actual or possible extras. Price/Earnings Ratios are based on the latest shown estimated or actual earnings.

Earnings per Share ($)			Indicated Div.	1970-72 Price Range	Recent Price	P/E Ratio	Yield %		5-Year Growth Rate	No. of Ann. Incr. 1962-71	5-Year Avg. Payout	Latest Increase
1970	1971	E1972										
3.99	3.99	4.20	2.60	53 7/8-40 3/8	43	10.2	6.0	Amer. Tel. & Tel.	5%	6	61%	1-2-70
	2.53	4.15		62 3/8-24	55	13.3	7.5	Chase Man. Mtg.				1-27-72
3.02	3.06	3.20	2.28	42 3/4-28	33	10.3	6.9	Cleve. Elec. Ill.	8	10	68	2-15-72
2.41	2.81	2.90	1.70	38 -24 5/8	30	10.3	5.7	Idaho Power Co.	4	9	68	8-20-71
1.99	2.26	2.40	1.36	31 1/4-23	30	12.5	4.5	Lone Star Gas	3	4	71	9-7-71
3.98	4.85	5.50	2.08	52 -21 3/4	48	8.7	4.3	Southern Pacific	3	9	43	6-21-71
5.91	6.77	7.00	3.90	82 3/8-49 7/8	71	10.1	5.5	Standard Oil (N.J.)	5	9	64	9-10-71

Table 22. Liberal Income, with Inflation Protection

If high yield alone were the goal, it would be simple to devise a list of high-quality bonds yielding 7% or more. But the individual who must rely to a major extent on his investments for income must take into account the prospect of continuing inflation. Accordingly, this group presents a list of quality high-yielding stocks which in our opinion offer the prospect of dividend growth at least sufficient to compensate for inflation over a period of time.

either a little such as $10,000 or a lot like $1,000,000, they have inherited the grandfather complex, or the prudent man rule. More often than not, a woman will find that she has little to say about the investment of the money she has inherited, at least if her husband is typical and has not been pressured by her to give her more latitude. When she investigates, she will find that the bank officer or lawyer handling her money, often in the form of a trust, will speak to her of the prudent man rule, which goes this way, as defined by the courts: "The exercise of sound judgment and care under the circumstances currently prevailing, which men of prudence, discretion and intelligence would exercise, not in regard to speculation, but in regard to investment, considering income as well as safety of principal."

This legal definition of prudence is a logical outgrowth of the idea that such funds for a widow and children should be safely invested. A trustee violating such an approach might find himself open to censure by a court, and even to being surcharged if the investments went awry.

In the past twenty years even conservative lawyers who draw wills and trust agreements for the men in our lives have begun to realize the importance of providing for investment in growth-type securities to help keep pace with inflation. Even so, the typical trust today probably invests at a 60 to 40 ratio — sixty percent in bonds, forty percent in common stocks.

The woman faced with this situation and wanting more growth in her portfolio should 1) be sure that she reads and understands the trust agreement — the document signed by her husband, father, etc., stipulating how the money should be invested; 2) use her pleasant smile and voice in an effort to convince a conservative trustee to take a few more chances in the portfolio by investing in somewhat livelier stocks — IBM, for example.

Trustees, especially bank officers, like to keep their customers happy if they can do so within the limits imposed by the terms of the trust agreement. Often they will consult with a widow or daughter to find out whether she needs high income or whether she wants appreciation from reasonably sound growth stocks.

Probably many women will find that their trusts have been set up in such a way that they alone cannot decide what stocks to buy, but their opinion can be expressed. Here a little psychology can help induce the trust officer to put the woman's opinion into action.

For the woman stuck with a trust that makes no provision for investment in growth stocks and that is strictly interpreted as money to be invested in superconservative issues, there is an out.

I have one friend who found herself in this situation — a trust invested superconservatively, mostly in bonds, handled by a man who showed no interest in her opinions. So, out of the money she earns she invests each year in go-go growth stocks, thus getting her capital appreciation and fun this way, as well as moving out of stocks fast when she thinks turns in the market are coming. This reminds me of the teen-ager who can't drink or smoke at home in front of her parents, so she drinks a little extra and puffs madly at parties outside.

In spite of her unhappiness and sense of frustration at the way her trust is handled and its lack of growth, she has the best of two investment approaches — a sound trust invested in conservative bonds and a few stocks and fast appreciation in her sideline investments.

General Advice on Portfolio Planning

If you can, handle your own investments. Don't put all your money into one or two stocks. Remember the adage about all those eggs in one basket. The exception to this would be the new investor just starting out with 1) small sums of money invested monthly in one stock to build up the number of shares towards a round lot or 2) with a small sum for investment all at once — $1,000, $2,000 or maybe $5,000 — in which case she might be well advised to split the sum between just two stocks.

If your money is limited don't buy two or three shares of a dozen stocks, thus scattering your shots and paying relatively high commissions. In fact, even with a portfolio of $1,000,000, a half-a-dozen stocks or so are enough since they do need some TLC — tender loving care. Buy round lots if possible to cut commissions.

Keep an opportunity fund of cash, perhaps 10 percent of the money available, for any special "buys" that come along. This money can be invested in government securities (if interest rates look desirable) or kept in the savings bank.

Put at least 20 percent of your portfolio in good stocks, which I like to call "pivotal" shares — shares around which you build your portfolio. These are the shares of good, conservative growth-type companies with some appreciation expected. Generally they will be the shares you live with for some years.

Set yourself specific goals for your stocks, to be acted upon without emotion. Jot these goals in your ever-handy notebook when you buy a particular stock, noting the price at which you expect to sell it. Then sell when it has achieved your aim and invest the money elsewhere. Greed for a little extra profit in a rising market has tripped up many new investors. You don't want to play with stocks like paper dolls — because there is no profit in those crisp-looking certificates until you sell.

Do use stop orders to help achieve your aims. Downside orders will help protect you in a fast-falling market; the upside stop orders will ensure unemotional exercise of your plan to sell the stock when it reaches your target point.

Don't overlook bonds as an investment possibility for appreciation if they sell below par value and carry high yields. Also don't forget about convertibles, because 1) they can give you a conservative investment with possible conversion into common stocks at a favorable price if the company fares well, and 2) they can be used as very acceptable collateral for loans.

From time to time measure the performance of the stocks in your portfolio against the averages — the Dow Jones and the widely used Standard & Poor average of 500, as well as any of the growth stock averages. Do your stocks as a group measure well in comparison?

Don't discuss your investing — success or failures — with other people. For some psychological reason it's bad luck. Even good friends become either envious or bored by talk of your "killings" in the market. Discussion of your failures can lead them to derision and you to some self-doubts.

Read continually — newspapers with financial pages, brokerage firm market letters, bank economic letters. Such reading widens your knowledge, piques your curiosity and stimulates your imagination.

Maintain careful records of your transactions, for tax purposes, for your own edification, and also for your heirs.

Learn how to keep simple charts as described in Chapter 14. They give you a better view of your shares' performance.

If possible join an investment club both for fun and profits. It gives you a chance to exchange ideas and pit your investment knowledge against mutual funds and professional investors.

A growth rate should be formulated in your mind, perhaps 10 percent a year in earnings for the pivotal stocks in your portfolio — the solid, big old growers — and perhaps 15 percent or more for the go-go types.

It's possible that in the next four or five years growth rates of some companies classed as go-go types will slow down. Certainly many dropped sharply in price in the 1969–1970 decline. This market break probably resulted from some overspeculation plus the belief that the government's attempts to control inflation through high interest rates and discouragement of capital spending might hurt corporate earnings.

Here are some typical growth rates in price, taking into consideration stock splits for a variety of growth-type shares over a period of ten years:

	1958	1968	1972 HIGH
Xerox	1	109	160
Polaroid	5	133	150
Eastman Kodak	16	86	140
Control Data	2	163	79

What price growth is a question that will always baffle thoughtful stockholders. To some people IBM has always seemed too high priced; to others small investments in it from time to time have brought fancy profits. One woman I know put $1,000 in IBM back in about 1946 and today, through splits, her money has grown to $60,000. To determine what price you will pay for growth you will have to get help from your broker — or rather the analyst who backs him up.

Don't forget that as night follows day speculative booms eventually collapse, so try to avoid buying a go-go stock at a peak in the market. Perhaps by now you can be more forgiving of analysts when they make mistakes in recommendations and fail to call an exact turn in a market.

Do try to buy a go-go stock at a low point in its price during the year. As you know in a single year the price of the same stock can vary widely. At some time during the year the market, as measured by the stock market averages like the Dow, will be battered down by economic or political events. This can give you an opportunity to buy a growth stock you want.

Don't forget the underprivileged or undervalued stocks. These are shares that have had their day in the market for some reason, usually a cyclical downturn in their industry. It often happens in basic stocks like steels, construction, oil, public utilities.

For example, Texas Gulf Sulphur is a solid blue chip company with good earnings. For some time it was so rich that it could afford to pay out about 75 percent of its earnings each year in dividends, because it literally sat atop a huge dome of sulphur which it mined (sulphur is mined by the so-called Frasch process of forcing hot water into the earth and piping up the molten sulphur). Then TGS ran into competition and price cutting from Mexican sulphur and from a smaller but higher cost producer in this country called Freeport Sulphur. Investors lost interest in TGS, except for a group of faithfuls who thought that sooner or later the company's skilled management would make a find or diversify. One morning they woke up to find that TGS had struck it "rich" in Canada. The stock price soared, from the equivalent of about $7 in 1964 to $53 in 1967. A sudden growth stock, yes! Today it has a shortened name, Texas Gulf Company, and a lower price, around 20 in 1972.

For some years the paper-producing industry went through a period when new plant facilities had been expanded so much that demand lagged, but that period ended about the end of 1966. Demand for paper, wood and such products has soared. An example is Boise Cascade Corporation, which could have been picked up for 16 a share back in 1966 and moved as high as 72 in 1968; in 1972 it lingered around 9–10. Thus some investors profited from the turnaround in the industry's fortunes.

In Summary

Like having your cake and eating it too, there are three digestible ways to approach this idea of growth and more growth to combat inflation and alleviate high taxation.

Number one approach is through investment in sound companies participating in natural growth factors such as rising population (food makers), more usage (cars), and high living standards (cosmetics).

Number two approach is through the go-go stocks, generally smaller companies which are expanding into new technological fields. These would include computers (IBM); office equipment (Xerox); medical technology (Merck & Company, Beckman Instruments); oceanography (General Dynamics); nuclear energy (General Electric); learning aids (Bell & Howell); pollution control (Culligan, Inc.). Also, waste removal is a new growth industry. These are called by some Wall Streeters "emerging industries," although you will recognize some of the names as already definitely emerged. Naturally there are many more names in each of these categories, and just because they are mentioned specifically here does not mean this is the right time to buy them. But like nicknames for people, the names of companies can stimulate your thinking. Ask your broker to send you the firm's latest brochures or list of go-go growth industries and the principal companies in them. Some of the big brokerage firms like Merrill Lynch publish elaborate brochures on them.

Number three approach is found in the undervalued, overlooked blue chips that have had a play and might make a comeback. The savings and loan stocks made such a return a few years ago. The steel stocks, now unwanted and unloved by many investors, perhaps will recover someday.

20 | Don't Be a Hetty Green

The last chapter remains — to tell you that the world's best woman investor and the worst possible penny-pinching, husband-destroying female used Number Three Approach, mentioned in the previous chapter.

Her name is Hetty Green, and she parlayed $1,000,000 into $100,000,000 in a relatively short period during her unpleasant life. One observer described her as being so mean that when she got her hands on a dollar bill she squeezed so hard the eagle screamed.

Hetty, in one of her rare terse, tight-lipped, unsmiling moments of comment, said: "I buy a good stock when prices are low and no one wants it and hold it until they do. I never speculate. There is a price on everything I have. When that price is offered I sell. I never buy anything just to hold it."

I am willing to believe that she never did, though she bought into some underprivileged (not enough equipment, rights of way, etc.) railroads and proceeded to make them successful or desirable to the railroad empire builders. She was so smart that it became a game for years in Wall Street to try to outwit Hetty Green. Since she lived in a freebooting period when there was no Securities and Exchange Commission to act as umpire, she had to be shrewd to outguess the opposition. Few, if any, businessmen got the best of her.

To her credit, she operated in an era when women in business were scorned. About the only respectable career available for a woman with intelligence was being a schoolteacher. All the more power to Hetty's success, testifying to the lessons she had learned as a child from her father who ran a successful trading business (import-export) in Massachusetts. In the early part of the nineteenth century the family fortune had been founded in the whaling business — a shipping business that included that famous old whaler, the *Charles W. Morgan.**

It is easier for a smart woman to make money in the stock market when she has a sizable sum and doesn't have to start from scratch and invest small amounts periodically.

Hetty Green did start with a substantial sum, but she had to fight bitter legal battles to get her hands on the money, and much of that fortune was left in trust, which meant in those days it was handled very conservatively and unimaginatively by the trustees. The wealthy heiress has other problems that we save-and-invest small stockholders don't have. She attracts sycophants like a queen bee around which the lesser bees swarm, all interested in honey. Too much advice can confuse and destroy a woman's confidence. Hetty Green soon learned to trust no one except herself.

If you want to learn more about her go to the public library. Since she lived from 1835 to 1916, her specific investments do not seem pertinent to us today, but her theory of picking undervalued situations and waiting for them to recover is sound. In fact, I think in the future we might find that the go-go growth stocks, by which so many investors were "burned" in 1962 and in 1969, lose much of their following as investors become more cautious and sophisticated. It is logical that then they will see the value in turning to Hetty's type of undervalued, cyclically or otherwise depressed stocks. Her approach represents a combination of a more sophisticated and yet less speculative investment method.

Please, if you copy Hetty's investment theory, don't model

---

*Last of the big whaling vessels, it now is berthed at Mystic Seaport, Mystic, Connecticut.

your life after hers, not even for $100,000,000. She didn't enjoy the money, just the grubby fight for it. She wore one black dress so green with age that newspapers often commented upon it in the articles they wrote. Today, it seems, journalists tend to be much politer about what women wear. She hated publicity, and moved so unobtrusively through the streets that few reporters could catch her. She seldom went to parties, though for a while she was married to a gregarious and successful businessman. When he lost his money in the stock market, she let him fail and then gave him a tiny pension, ousting him from her home. With her son and daughter she lived in grubby apartments in cities like Brooklyn and Hoboken.

Her son limped all his life because she would not pay for a proper operation to save his leg. Her daughter in later years commented bitterly, when asked in court where she had lived at a certain time: "With my mother, if you call that living." For years Hetty apparently walked with pain from a hernia. She supported the offending part of her innards by a little platform of wood worn under her dress. A New York surgeon knew the story because she had invited him to examine the hernia, but when he quoted her a price for the operation she angrily said it was too much and stalked from his office.

Making money is at once a challenge for a woman and a source of security, but this combination should bring more joy than it apparently did to Hetty.

Successful investing ideas exist everywhere, anywhere around you, if like Hetty you develop an approach and do some searching. As you sharpen your investment talents as she did for so many years, consider some of these ideas.

STOCKS OF COMPANIES IN YOUR NEIGHBORHOOD. Like most housewives you probably pay by check some basic household bills to local electric light, gas, water (unless municipally owned) and telephone companies. What do you know about them? Do you live in a growing area where their services are in demand? Are they well run? They might be a good source of investment.

There probably are some local industries in your neighborhood, perhaps even some go-go growth types, such as exist along Route 128 outside Boston, such as dot the suburbs of New York and some California cities. Don't overlook your local department store where you buy clothes and home furnishings. It can be part of a big chain or it might still be an independent company, perhaps dominated by a local family.

There is also your local bank. It can be a branch of a much bigger bank within the state or owned by shareholders locally. Some banks operate statewide such as in California, where a few big banks have many branches throughout the state; other banking chains are limited to operations in a few counties or smaller areas. In Chicago the Illinois law still restricts banks to operations within cities. Banks can be a fine-growing investment these days because of the move to the suburbs and industrialization of smaller cities.

Who better can prowl quietly around an area and learn about local business than a housewife with some time on her hands, good local contacts, and the inoffensive curiosity of an innocent woman? It can be done discreetly by leading questions, by observation, by checking through investment manuals, by asking a local broker.

Many fortunes have been made in local businesses — and many growth opportunities have been overlooked by investors because they were so close to local business they lost perspective. Often the family that has been the founder of a local business — such as a power company or a bank — are prominent people in the town or city. If they have done well, there may also be a chance for you in this age of fast expansion.

If you do buy a stock of a local company, it might be preferable to keep it unregistered, that is in its "street name" (the name of your brokerage firm), just to prevent local people from knowing you own the shares. Or to be even more clever, if you make a sizable investment just have a few of your shares — say 10 — registered in your name and then you can attend the annual meeting, receive the material the company sends out. In this way you keep the extent of your interest hidden.

THE PRODUCTS YOU USE. Still another source of investment ideas, where feminine buying expertise and intuition can help, lies in the stocks of companies whose products you use. Is the construction business increasing in your area? Then it may be about to boom all over the country. It could be a good time to invest in construction stock. You can ask builders or architects you know what products they use, what products have a future.

Who is a better judge of food brands in a supermarket than a housewife who each week struggles to keep within her food budget? Has Campbell Soup come out with a new line of foods or new types of soup that you and your friends like? Has one of the packaging companies put out a really more effective baking/boiling plastic bag? Is one supermarket chain capturing most of the business in your community? There must be a reason.

General Foods a few years ago put out a line of gourmet foods, but it flopped because housewives didn't buy in enough quantity, something that shrewd shoppers probably noted. Now some other companies have entered the gourmet food business, such as Holly Sugar. Can they succeed? If so, it might be an opportunity for investment in such a field. Certainly Birdseye, the pioneer frozen food line, made a great success, so much so that Mr. Birdseye, its developer, sold out to a big company, retiring with a fortune.

One of the most dramatic successes in recent years involves Crest toothpaste, which, because it contained fluoride to help retard tooth decay, won approval some years ago from the American Dental Association. The other toothpaste makers, especially Colgate, were caught in the embarrassing situation of not having a competitive product ready. Despite Colgate's irate protests and legal challenges, Crest became the biggest volume seller. Why? Women with families want to improve their children's teeth (or at least stave off decay more effectively) and save on dentists' bills. Any mother whose child eats candy and drinks soft drinks these days has to worry about teeth.

THE CRUSADERS AND OTHER LIFE IMPROVERS. Watch Ralph

Nader in action, the crusader who campaigned successfully to make cars safer. Believe me, seat belts and other safety devices probably wouldn't be in cars today if Nader hadn't launched his campaign against tremendous odds some years ago. Remember how General Motors assigned detectives to try to discredit Nader through some flaw in his personal life — and could find nothing. Then we watched the spectacle of the head of mighty General Motors confessing to Congress that this had been done and apologizing.

Unfortunately, part of the blame can be placed on leading advertising men because they in some cases advised auto makers not to stress safety since that would make people think that cars were unsafe. This is the kind of attitude of total irresponsibility that sometimes is apparent in advertising.

Today, thanks to Ralph Nader, General Motors, Ford and all car makers, domestic and foreign, periodically recall cars — sometimes hundreds of thousands at a time — for repairs of unsafe parts. Do you think that Congress would have set up safety standards for cars (and an administrative staff to handle them) if Nader had not campaigned so loudly, and if the death toll from car accidents had not mounted to such appalling totals?

What industries did Nader help indirectly? The seat belt makers, for example; makers of safety locks, especially now that car thefts have been on the increase; emission control devices, which soon will be mandatory in many states; makers of padded panels; makers of collapsible-on-contact highway signs and guards to keep cars from head-on collisions. Chains of service stations have grown up to take care of car repairs following analysis with computerlike devices that can detect a variety of engine troubles.

So watch the crusaders, of which there are always a few at any given moment. If the crusade became effective, it could often lead to new industries for life-improving devices.

Don't be upset if you miss opportunities. I have made some serious boners in investing, not so much in what I bought but in what I didn't buy. The one I most regret missing involves Minute Maid orange juice. Back in the nineteen forties I worked as a copyeditor on the *Wall Street Journal*, one of the few women in such a job on a New York paper. One day a male reporter came back from a company press conference bearing several cans of Minute Maid frozen orange juice, by then unfrozen from resting in his trench coat pocket. As the only woman around the city room of the newspaper at the moment, he invited me to test drink the orange juice for an opinion before he wrote the story. We stood around the water cooler, and he mixed me some juice in a paper cup. I tested it and said, "Well, it's better than canned orange juice, but it will never replace the fresh."

How wrong I was! How I underestimated the American housewife's liking for the convenience of frozen juice. In those days, I could have bought some shares cheaply, with the glamour of Bing Crosby as an added asset because he was one of the company backers. I should have known that he would make a wise investment, just because I knew he was a shrewd businessman. Today frozen orange juice is big business.

Unfortunately, I "missed" another good investment, too. Years ago I went to Allen & Company, an investment-banking firm, to interview Herbert and Charles Allen about one of their business ventures. While there, I was told of their interest in a company headquartered in Latin America called Syntex, maker of birth control items. "Buy some of the shares," I was advised. My problem as a financial writer has been a psychological one — a cynicism that most financial writers develop. Almost every businessman we interview enthuses over his company. I remember vividly the president of a leading oil company telling me that "Our gasoline is better, Miss Fowler." This came after a statement by me that, after all, oil comes out of the ground, is refined into gasoline and the brand name doesn't make much difference. I still believe this.

This explains my cynicism about Syntex and my failure to buy some shares at the time. Such disbelief, when it is ingrained as mine was, should be tempered with logic.

Syntax,* to make my humiliation worse, rose from about $1 a share in 1958 to a peak of $124 a share in 1966, adjusted for stock splits. I could have outdone Hetty Green on that one!

Experiences like these happen to many investors, probably all of them sooner or later. It's sobering, like a cold shower, and shuddering, too. Yet an investor can learn from it, developing an instinct for separating shining opportunities from shooting stars.

LOOKING FURTHER AHEAD. If you are forty-five years old or younger, you are a lucky investor because opportunities abound in the future. The chances are that you will have a definite stake in the year 2,000 because you will still be alive.

Today's middle-agers probably grew up on comic-strip characters like Buck Rogers, on the Tom Swift series, on Jules Verne's ventures into tomorrow and perhaps on Aldous Huxley's *Brave New World*. Somehow, today, with Americans walking on the moon, and a scientist named Piccard and others venturing under the sea to promote the science called oceanography, those earlier flights of scientific fancy seem all too real.

In a book called *The Year 2000*,† its authors speculate on the future with more seriousness and more pertinency than most literary commentators. Working in their "think tank," called Hudson Institute, the authors wrote the book out of a study they did from the American Academy of Arts and Sciences, the Carnegie Corporation and the Corning Glass Works Foundation.

What will A.D. 2000 bring to the average American, in terms of his way of life and his financial planning?

Family income will be much higher by then. So high in fact that a new gentleman class may emerge — people who work little or not at all because they have enough money for leisure.

---

*The company operates in Panama. Competition has hurt its prospects somewhat in recent years, along with high developmental costs, and its shares ranged in price from 53 to 79 in 1968 but in early 1972 it was as high as 120. Thus, because of its interest in birth control, skin biology, problems of aging, etc., it once more became a good speculation.

†By Herman Kahn and Anthony J. Wiener (New York: Macmillan, 1967).

Often I hear some of my young businessmen friends say, "If I work ten more years and make 15 percent compounded on my investments I can retire."

It is the kind of aristocratic concept that Europeans have been able to understand in past years, because many of them grew up on the theory nice people shouldn't work but live on their income from investments. It is also a kind of thinking that generations of American businessmen indulged in not at all, preferring to work vigorously for money until they reached age sixty or sixty-five or died before, a kind of Puritan belief in the sanctity of work and money growth. Most businessmen still like to think or talk of themselves as hard workers, with some even saying they cannot take vacations.

Perhaps when today's "hippie" generation grows up it will relish ideas for little work and much leisure expounded so logically in *The Year 2000*.

The authors project a range of per capita income (disposable income after taxes) of $4,900 to $8,947. This range would be for the typical middle-class, middle-management family of four. This group consists of well-paid white collar workers, technicians, and some high-paid blue collar construction workers, and others. Thus the family would have an income after taxes of four times this per capita amount, ranging from $19,600 to $35,780. Of course, inflation would take a toll.

The work week, which even nowadays is getting shorter, will become so short by the year 2000 that people will work no more than four days a week and less than eight hours a day. With legal holidays and long vacations, this could result in an annual working period of 147 days and 218 days off.

Filling this leisure time may become a serious problem, as well as an opportunity for investment. Children will be encouraged to develop a wider variety of talents not connected with their possible careers, such as sports, music, art. In fact, the pressure could be so great that going to museums, theaters, and other places of entertainment might have to be rationed. Think of the tight 3-by-6-foot spaces available now for individual bathers at some public beaches!

Women, both those with children and those without, will continue to play an increasing role in the labor force. "We estimate there will be an increase in the female participation rate partly because it seems likely there will be an increase in the attractiveness and availability of part-time and intermittent work," the authors suggest. Even now several employment agencies for part-time workers have formed corporations and sold the stock publicly.

The average American family will have more of its relatives alive, which may or may not be a problem. In your area even now you can watch the proliferation of nursing homes to care for the elderly or disabled.

With artificial kidneys, heart devices and other substitutes for vital organs, people may increase their life spans to a hundred and fifty years, especially in view of the wide use of diet foods, the stress on proper nutrition (protein, for example) and exercise, plus other health measures like immunization against most diseases. Presumably, with high incomes oldsters will not become a burden to most families.

Perhaps one change that Americans may find hard to grasp is entirely new forms of transportation, a trip down an air street to see a neighbor may be on top of an individual platform (the Army is testing such devices for infantrymen now); a trip to Europe by rocket might take only half an hour, with the Taj Mahal a little longer trip for quiet contemplation. This compares with long-distance trips of two or three hours promised by supersonic commercial plane builders in a few years.

The housewife will run a push-button home, thanks to computers. She won't need much cash because the local supermarket and other stores will be computerized to accept a credit card. Banks will be equipped to pay her bills almost instantly. She probably will dress her family in paper clothes that can be thrown out after a little use.

Many Americans will live in Boswash, Chipitts, or SanSan, three giant megalopitan areas that may well be envied by other nations for their high standard of living. Boswash will extend from Boston to Washington and will remain the financial and governmental center of the country. Chipitts will encompass the Great Lakes area in the neighborhood of Chicago and Pittsburgh. SanSan is the fast-growing region stretching from San Diego to San Francisco, California. These areas will hold 80 million, 40 million and 20 million respectively out of the total projected population of 300 million people.

Land prices almost everywhere will be high as the population expands, and more Americans than now will live vertically — in high-rise apartments, even in rural areas.

With all the changes, by the year 2000 there will be many problems to be solved, not raised so much by the better standard of living but by the individual's relationship to the terrifyingly huge, faceless bureaucracy called the U.S. government.

As you have read this perhaps you have been able to visualize the opportunities for investment that the future holds. They merit continued reading and thinking about as they slowly evolve, because change does tend to come slowly or with little sudden jerks.

This book began with a chapter on inflation and it must end the same way, because progress will take a toll in the dollars we know today.

There are some stories to point up the impact of inflation worth remembering, such as the one the late Dr. Marcus Nadler used to tell his classes in international banking at New York University's Graduate School of Business Administration. To emphasize the terrifying impact of inflation in post World War II Germany, he told his students this one:

It seems that a German businessman who died before the First World War left his fortune divided among his two sons, with the admonition of a careful German father that they invest carefully and keep their capital. One son dutifully put his money into German government bonds and also worked in the family business. The other son — the prodigal — preferred the lively existence of wine, women and song with some travel as a chaser.

Then came the war and the ensuing inflation. The family business was bankrupt. The German money — the mark — was devalued so badly that it required a wheelbarrow filled with paper money to buy a loaf of bread and a container of milk. When workers received their pay they rushed out the same hour to buy bread and milk, knowing that by the next day the paper money would purchase less food.

The conservative son found that his bonds were valueless. However, the prodigal son soon made a startling discovery. He could sell the large collection of empty champagne bottles filling his cellar, for good prices because postwar Germany needed glass.

The moral of this prodigal son tale is that fixed income securities do not enable an investor to keep up with inflation these days, unless of course they have some built-in appreciation possibilities such as bonds selling well below face value in 1969 and yielding high rates of interest.

A modern version of the prodigal son story was issued by Harris Upham & Company, a leading brokerage firm whose ace investment analyst, Ralph Rotnem, recently retired, has long written with an imaginative flair.

The story is good enough to print verbatim.

HOW TO INVEST FOR GREATEST PROFITS OR THE LESSON OF THE SEVEN BROTHERS DURING THE PAST TWELVE YEARS

On December 31st of 1959 a father gave each of his seven sons $10,000 and asked them to invest as they saw fit during the next twelve years. On January 1st 1972, he called them together to compare results. Their methods of investing and the present values of the original $10,000 funds were as follows:

Current Values of Original Funds (each) $10,000*

FIRST SON Extremely conservative—decided not to take a chance on the stock market and invested his money in high grade corporate bonds which he continued to hold throughout the twelve year period. Very unimaginative. $7,030

SECOND SON Also conservative but he decided that stocks would do better than bonds in the twelve year period so he put all of his money in the stocks included in the Dow Jones industrial average. But he was both lazy and unimaginative and just stayed with his original purchases for the twelve year period. $13,100

THIRD SON Also invested in the Dow Jones industrial stocks but decided to take advantage of the major bull and bear trends and to be invested only when bull markets were in progress. He bought five times and sold four times during the next twelve years and did the impossible by always catching the major tops for selling and the major bottoms for buying. $51,465

FOURTH SON Invested only in the five groups that he thought would advance the most in the next twelve years. He too did the impossible and chose the correct ones — soft drinks, up 763 percent, cosmetics, up 517 percent, air conditioning, up 496 percent, coals up 491 percent and truckers, up 473 percent. $64,810

FIFTH SON He guessed that there would be fads and fancies during the twelve year period so he would try to be in whichever group was most popular. When a favored group peaked out he would shift the proceeds into the next favorite. He was in vending stocks

---

*These figures do not include commissions, taxes, dividends or interest payments.

(up 98 percent) from January 1960 to April 1961, in golds (up 30 percent) to June 1962 when most stocks declined, in airlines to June 1966 (up 570 percent), in savings and loans to December 1968 (up 200 percent), in cosmetics to December 1969 (up 30.6 percent) and in mobile homes to December 1971 (up 117 percent). An impossible but excellent record. $1,466,248

SIXTH SON He invested only in the group that went up the most in each year. $4,749,730

YEAR	GROUP	PERCENTAGE OF GAIN	YEAR	GROUP	PERCENTAGE OF GAIN
1960	Canned Foods	48.4	1966	Radio & TV Broad.	26.6
1961	Life Ins.	76.6	1967	Bread & Cake Bakers	107.8
1962	Integ. Intl Oils	13.2	1968	Savings & Loans	86.0
1963	Airlines	99.4	1969	Cosmetics	30.6
1964	Sulphur	73.8	1970	Coals	53.3
1965	Radio & TV Mfrs.	132.3	1971	Restaurants	103.0

SEVENTH SON He bought only the stocks listed on the New York Stock Exchange that went up the most each year. $29,750,168,400

YEAR	STOCK	PERCENTAGE OF GAIN	YEAR	STOCK	PERCENTAGE OF GAIN
1960	Chock Full O'Nuts	135.6	1966	Howmet Corp.	139.8
1961	Korvette	287.0	1967	Republic Corp.	1290.0
1962	Natl. Airlines	76.8	1968	Duplan Corp.	297.1
1963	Monon Railroad	227.4	1969	Japan Fund	111.1
1964	Boston & Maine	200.0	1970	Overnight Transp.	122.7
1965	Fairchild Camera	447.3	1971	Winnebago Ind.	462.3

$29.7 billion! That's the power of compounding growth stocks.

Good luck! When you make your first million dollars, write me a letter, except if it's after the year 2000 I may not be available, unless you have developed extrasensory perception — another growing field.

Bibliography

In recent years publishers have been turning out investment books the way women turn out apple pies. Unfortunately, many of them have been too crusty to digest or the filling has been too mushy to have much taste. In other words, many investment books are too sophisticated, while others talk down to women. However, there are a few basic books that are worth reading:

Edwards, Robert D., and Magee, John. *Technical Analysis of Stock Trends*. Springfield, Mass.: John Magee, 1966.
For investors interested in learning about technical aspects of market movements, this is the basic book.

Galbraith, John K. *The Great Crash, 1929*. Boston: Houghton Mifflin Co., 1955.
History always adds perspective to our thinking, and a person who has read this book should learn enough to sell out before the top of a bull market so that he will have cash to buy when the bear market comes inevitably.

Leffler, George L. *The Stock Market*. New York: Ronald Press, 1963.
Dr. Leffler is dead but he left behind one of the most informative, well-written basic books on investments.

Loeb, Gerald. *The Battle for Investment Survival.* New York: Simon & Schuster, 1965.
This book is for investors who know the basics and are ready for more. Its author is a well-known, now semiretired Wall Streeter.

Mackay, Charles. *Extraordinary Popular Delusions and the Madness of Crowds.* New York: L.C. Page, 1932.
This chestnut was published many years ago but can be found in almost any public library. A few of its chapters about the crazy speculation of our ancestors are worth reading.

Samuelson, Paul A. *Economics: An Introductory Analysis.* New York: McGraw-Hill, 1967.
This weighty tome is a modern classic on the subject.